D1257168

THE
FLORISTRY
HANDBOOK

THE FLORISTRY HANDBOOK

HAROLD PIERCY

New Century Publishers, Inc.

Printing Code

14   15   16   17   18

ISBN 0-8329-0373-6

Printed in Great Britain

CONTENTS

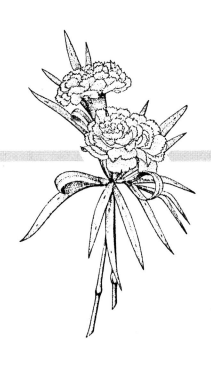

ACKNOWLEDGEMENTS

During the last two years many people have been involved with this book in one way or another, and I would like to offer my grateful thanks to them. It has not been an easy task and at times we have run into some difficulties, but thanks to everybody being so understanding we have produced a book which I hope will be of help to everyone wanting to know more about the details involved in flower arranging and floristry.

My special thanks go to Rosemary Minter who has helped me with the arranging and making-up for all the photography, and to Sue Barrett who has put my very rough notes into readable form. Without these two people there could not have been a book.

Mike Lake-McMillan's photography is excellent, and David Henderson has portrayed our ideas beautifully with his drawings. Both must have wondered what they were letting themselves in for when we first started working together but I believe we have been a happy team throughout and Rosemary and I certainly enjoyed working with them. To Ann Borrett I offer my thanks — she worked on the first draft which spurred me on.

I am indebted to Winkfield Place and Chris Holland Studio for hospitality for all the team who produced the book and to Fred Wilkinson who found interesting materials from the garden at Winkfield. Grateful thanks are also due to all those at Constance Spry and in the office at Winkfield.

To Cranbourne Church, Berkshire and All Hallows by the Tower, London, I say a big thank you for allowing us to set up the right backgrounds for our church flowers.

Geraldine Christy has worked wonders in setting out all the contents with some order and has advised me so willingly on the text.

Finally, my thanks go to Jo Hemmings, Melanie Crook and their colleagues who have taken over all the typed papers, drawings and transparencies and made a book from them.

FIGURES AND TABLES

NOTE ON STYLE

For ease of reading, all flower and foliage names – whether generic or otherwise – have been printed in roman type: for example, Carnation, Holly Berries, Cineraria maritime. The names used are the popular ones for the flowers concerned, rather than the strictly correct botanical names.

FIGURES

TABLES

COLOUR PLATES

Between pages 76 and 77

Plate 1: Examples of the equipment a florist will need when arranging flowers. In the centre is a turntable, which is helpful if you have difficulty in getting a good round shape to your arrangement.

The vases range from simple plastic bowls to the expensive gold-rimmed china, seen on the right. You will notice that many of the containers have a footed base – when raised off the table, flowers appear to take on a more important role. On the far left is a copy of an original tazza-shaped vase which is so useful and easy to arrange. In front is the 2in (5cm) wire netting, oasis tape, silver reel wire and pin holders. A basket always gives a simple effect – a good-shaped one stands just behind the oasis block.

Plate 2: A facing arrangement in an 8in (20cm) plastic bowl. Very suitable for shop sales – a small number of flowers are arranged to give a good effect.

This group has been made up from three medium-sized Chrysanthemums, five 'Mercedes' Roses, one bunch of outdoor pompom Chrysanthemums, three stems of Alstroemeria and nine stems of spray Carnations. The foliages used were variegated Box, Paeony leaves turning red and, at the centre, three Megasea leaves.

Plate 3: An all-round arrangement in pinks and grey in a tazza-shaped container. It is made up quite economically of five 'Bridal Pink' Roses, three Nerine, seven stems of spray Carnations broken down, two stems of all-year-round Chrysanthemums broken down into many stems, three stems of garden Roses with buds and a mixture of grey-green foliages including Cineraria maritima, Anthemis and Senecio.

Plate 4: This oval table centre in cream and yellow colouring has been arranged in the shallow oblong container with rounded ends, illustrated bottom

right in Plate 1. It contains six 'Harvest Moon' Carnations and three stems of pale yellow spray Carnations. 'Roselandia' is the cream Rose – always popular, but not a Rose to last once it is fully open. Yellow Freesia, Rudbeckia, Marigold and green Nicotiana make up the other flowers, with variegated Gold Ivy ('Buttercup') as the foliage.

Plate 5: This Sussex trug basket has a metal lining, giving an excellent wide area in which to let your flower stems flow. The overall 'L' shape is suitable for use on a mantleshelf, above which is a picture or mirror.

Here seed heads and berries have been used, with three stems of Gladioli, Alstroemeria, red Anemones picked out from mixed bunches, a head of red Hydrangea, small outdoor spray Chrysanthemums, spray Carnations and 'Love Lies Bleeding'.

Plate 6: A table centre of the perfect florists' flower: mixed Freesia always please with their beautiful colours and delicate perfume. Eight bunches have been arranged in two candlecups with tiny-leaved wild Ivy trails for foliage.

The vase is from Spain and is made of pewter-coloured pottery. The colour of the candles should be chosen to pick up one of the main colourings of the room.

Plate 7: There can be nothing nicer than a group of green and white flowers: they give an air of coolness to the room. This group has been arranged in a simple basket with a plastic lining. It would be suitable as a gift for many occasions – a new baby, a birthday or as a decoration at a summer party.

It contains six stems of 'Carte Blanche' Roses, three garden 'Iceberg' Roses with buds, seven stems of Freesia, five Chincherinchee and three stems from your 'private grower' selection such as Nicotiana, Snowberries, two variegated Iris leaves,

Laurustinus and one stem of Astrantia 'Margery Fish'. To the left of the open central Rose are a couple of small Angelica flower heads.

Plate 8: A gold Holly tree made from long fronds of glittered plastic Holly bound onto false stems which, in turn, make up the trunk of the tree. Set in a base of quick-drying cement, it makes an ideal table centre. The Holly is bent and twisted to give it interesting lines, rather than just straight flat plastic fronds. Three robins and a few lace metallic bells give the finishing touch.

Plate 9: This brass candlestick has been fitted with a candlecup, which holds oasis sec into which the candle has been stuck. Pieces of artificial materials are arranged in the oasis, with all stems flowing from the centre point – as when working with fresh materials. Fresh Larch and Pine cones and 'silk' Christmas Roses complete the arrangement.

For the wreath, a circle of wire is bound with crepe paper, onto which small pieces of plastic fern and flowers are bound, keeping the width approximately the same all the way round. Always keep the pieces flat on the frame.

Plate 10: This is a very attractive wall drop, ideal for Christmas time, which will hang on any flat surface. It is made up of artificial flowers – red crinkle paper petals with Scots Pine centres – and real 'Abies' Cones which have been sprayed with glitter, which hang from the centre with two different ribbons (velvet and metallic) in loops and trails. A few fronds of plastic Fern make up the foliage. The metal stem mounts are all bound together at one point, and it hangs from a loop at the back.

Plate 11: This door knocker is made mostly from plastic materials, plus a little 'silk' and natural Cones for additional texture and shape. They are all mounted on wire legs and bound onto a single wire frame which has been covered with crepe paper: this does help the wire mounts to grip onto the frame and stay firm. Keep the frame flat on the table and lay your pieces on the frame as you twist the mounts. Keep to a pattern of the mixed materials, and watch your width as you wire round the frame.

Plate 12: Party pieces. The three items on the left are sprays of mixed materials to go on parcels as extra special gift wrappings. Top centre is a posy of mixed Christmas pieces, held within a posy frill, which could be given to a lady at a party. They also look most attractive as place settings on the party table. On the right is a serviette ring made from the centre of a ribbon reel. This has been covered in velvet ribbon and a small spray attached.

All these items may be made from the oddments left over when making larger Christmas decorations.

Plate 13: A large green and white group standing on a well-selected pedestal has been chosen for this church interior. A flat plastic bowl was used, containing a block of oasis plus wire netting. Three extension tubes have been used to get height at the top of the group. The flowers are made up of sprays of 'Refour' and 'Tokyo' Chrysanthemums, Longiflorum Lilies and white Gladioli. The mixed foliage is of Portuguese Laurel, Garrya elliptica, Artichoke leaves and variegated Ivy.

Note the way each flower shows up and is lifted on its long stem, flowing from the centre of the group.

Plate 14: There is nothing more perfect than a vase of Longiflorum Lilies on the altar. So often you will see Lilies worked into the embroidery on the altar frontal – so they always seem correct to me and show up well.

The Lilies shown here were arranged in a vase belonging to the church. Just one bunch of short Lilies with twelve flower heads was used and, since the foliage was perfect, nothing more was added. The flowers were simply stood in the vase, in the bottom of which a small amount of netting had been placed.

Another Lily which is often seen in church work is L. candidum, but this is only available in June/July.

Plate 15: A pew end in pink and white colouring, with silver-grey foliage and a pink bow. It has been made up in an oasis saucer, held in place with string and 'gaffer tape' (available from photographic suppliers). This tape is excellent and means no wires or nails are needed.

The flowers used were Rue, Santolina and Viburnum tinus, with side shoots of white and pink spray Carnations, all year round 'Refour' Chrysanthemums, three Nerine, Snowberry and pink Freesia. A pink striped ribbon gives a good finish to the flowers.

Plate 16: Set on a side table here, but ideal for a long buffet table in a marquee, this old meat cover (inverted and set in a wrought iron stand) makes an ideal silver buffet vase. It contains Holly-leaved Osmanthus, Privet Berries, a purple Cabbage, Eucalyptus and silver-grey Cineraria. The Rose is 'Leframe' with pink Nerine, purple spray Chrysanthemum and blooms, shocking pink Carnations and pink spray Carnations.

Plate 17: This cake top has been made as a loose posy and stood in a silver trumpet vase. It contains white and cream Hyacinth, Lily of the Valley, small Helleborus foetidus flowers and Ivy leaves – all wired up for lightness. (The cake was beautifully made and decorated by Anne Grubb, a Director of The Cordon Bleu Cookery School and of Winkfield Place.)

Plate 18: This magnificent font cover by Grinling Gibbons has just a few white flowers around the base of the figures. The main flowers, all in mixed spring colourings, have been added to the base of the font so as not to detract from the importance at the top.

    The flowers used in the top were Hyacinth, Snowdrops, Jasmin, green Hellebore, Ivy and baby Cyclamen leaves. The base was made up of Alder, Pussy Willow, Hazel, Daffodils, 'Monarch' Narcissi, Tulip, Snowdrops, Polyanthus, Iris, Primroses and Petasites set in oasis amongst rock and moss.

Plate 19: This narrow-necked 'Spode' base, standing in its own little saucer, lends itself to wire-stemmed materials. All these pieces are either 'picks' or mounted on single legs and stuck in to a small piece of oasis sec. The Maindenhair Fern is lightly glittered, and picks up the colour of the metallic Daisies. The 'crystal' star shapes reflect any light from the Daisy petals.

Plate 20: This curved handspray is one of today's most popular bouquets. It can be made of just one flower, but more often is of mixed materials. We have used variegated Ivy leaves with white Freesia, Singapore Orchids, white spray Carnations, with Roses as the main flower for the centre. When using mixed flowers, try to have four or five different shapes and sizes.

Plate 21: This back spray of artificial materials is not easy to make, because it is difficult to get graded sizes in some of the materials which, in many cases, are provided by the bride. To be correct, the ends of the head-dress should be narrow, working up to fullness at the centre. This can be done when grading fresh flowers and foliages, but so often the 'silk' pieces cannot be cut down. The framework of this head-dress is somewhat like a horseshoe in shape, with the open ends turning up and outwards.

Plate 22: A tiara made solely from Chincherinchee flowers. It took 38 flowers and buds to complete, and was made in five separate upright standing pieces of three sizes, to get the shape. These were bound onto the frame and the row of flowers at head level was worked in as one worked from the centre spray. In this piece of floral jewellery white gutta percha has been used, but a silvery effect can be obtained by taping the wires with silver paper.

Plate 23: A crescent bouquet in cream and yellow colouring: very popular for bridesmaids. Yellow roses give weight to the centre; Euonymus leaf sprays make the main foliage trails; with a lemon-scented Geranium leaf over the handle. Yellow Freesia and spray Carnations add two other different flower shapes.

Plate 24: A spray for a prayer book is sometimes chosen by the bride instead of the usual bouquet. This one is made of white/cream Singapore Orchids and small Euonymus leaves. It has been stitched onto a white ribbon with a fine gold edge, thus complementing the gold lettering on the prayer book.

Plate 25: I dislike the term 'cremation basket', but I know that it is often used today. This real basket, rather than a plastic one, of mixed flowers has a wide flat base so that it stands well and firmly on the ground. It could easily be used as a normal home decoration, which is what I like about it.

    It contains a mixture of flowers including 'Roselandia' Roses, Iris, Freesia, Anemones, Alstroemeria and a stem of Chrysanthemum, broken down to give many short-stemmed flowers.

Plate 26: A posy pad arranged in an oasis saucer. This design was first introduced by Constance Spry over 50 years ago, when all mixed spring flowers such as Hellebore, roman Hyacinth and Violets were used in little groups, and wired on a flat pad of moss. Today they are still extremely useful as a funeral tribute but tend to contain rather large flowers – and are used throughout the year. This posy, made in the autumn, contains Anemones, three Roses, spray Chrysanthemums, spray Carnations, five pink Freesia and a head of red Hydrangea together with silver-grey foliage.

Plate 27: This is a naturally tied bunch, which can be used as a funeral tribute or given as a gift of flowers at a presentation. Nothing is wired; it is just the natural flowers and foliage bound in one place, and all the stems can then stand in water if one does not wish to untie the bunch. Although it appears simple, these bunches are not easy to make and need practice until you can get them right.

This green and white collection contains white Freesia, Roses, Chincherinchee, white spray Carnations and mixed foliage. Finish off the binding and, for a presentation, make a good bow to cover this. For funeral work, wrap over the stringing with plaited raffia or other binding in a neutral colour.

With delicate-stemmed flowers, such as Lily of the Valley, it may be a good idea to bind with gutta percha rather than string. This would be used for small bouquets presented on Royal occasions.

Plate 28: This autumnal-coloured spray has been arranged on an oasis tray rather than on a mossed board or wired frame. Quick to do, and long-lasting because everything can be kept in water, it makes an excellent base for a floral tribute and can be easily dismantled afterwards, if the flowers are not to remain at the graveside. It is heavy to handle and needs lifting up properly, so you must see that the flowers at the top and bottom are securely fixed. I prefer to use less than a block of oasis, and onto this I secure a little wire netting which is clipped over the plastic tray. It gives a strong but lighter base on which to work.

The stems should be wired and mounted to give strength and support, but often short stems are just tucked into the oasis. It is most effectively done as a bunch of flowers with a return end of stems, rather than in this case with one of flowers.

Plate 29: Flowers for a party are often best set up well out of the way, and here they have been placed in a trough on a carved wooden mantleshelf. This simply-arranged yellow group is made up of Eleagnus foliage, Cornus and mixed Ivy trails; yellow 'Golden Times' Roses, yellow spray Carnations, Alstroemeria and single yellow Chrysanthemums.

Plate 30: On this occasion, the customer supplied this alabaster tazza vase to fill with cream and green flowers and foliages. It is nice to use good containers when working in the customer's home, but one would not want the responsibility of having them in the shop.

This group contains Winter Sweet, Alder, Straw Hyacinth, cream Freesia, Lachenalia, green Hellebore, Daphne and Arum italicum.

Plate 31: A wreath of five clusters of different flowers and foliages. These are very beautiful and more pleasing than the mixed wreath so often seen.

Choose different foliages and flowers to suit each group. The wreath can be all in one colour or mixed. A wreath for Christmas time can be done in the same way, or just using foliages, for example Ivy, Holly (green and variegated), Eucalyptus, Box, Yew or Rosemary.

Plate 32: A real Constance Spry arrangement of 'Constance Spry' Roses in a pewter measure, given to the author by Mrs Spry and arranged by Evelyn Russell – a great friend of the Spry family who also taught me in my early days. (Photograph by David Davis; kindly loaned by Evelyn Russell.)

INTRODUCTION

I have been asked many times to write a handbook for students that will clearly outline the principles of the work necessary to know if one is to become a proficient florist. It has been quite impossible to cover everything in this book, but I hope that the knowledge gained from reading and studying it will be of use when entering the florist's trade.

The book has not been easy to compile — in fact it has proved to be quite a big job. Much of the work it contains can be tackled in various ways. May I suggest that you follow the methods we have used in the School for many years — we have found that most of our students have been able to obtain good results from using them.

The late Constance Spry had very strong views on certain aspects of the trade and in reading through this book you will find how these views have rubbed off on her School staff. You will, I hope, notice that there are no set rules, but guidelines are suggested; this was Constance Spry's way of teaching. Everyone is an individual and no two people want to achieve exactly the same effect. It is important to get the best from your flowers, however, and to do this you will need common sense — something which this book cannot teach you, but may help to develop and encourage.

PART ONE

FLOWER ARRANGING AND DECORATING

1. FLOWERS AND FOLIAGES

The way in which you treat your flowers and foliages will make a very big difference to their lasting qualities. The quicker they can be in water after being cut, the less chance the stems have of drying out and the flowers wilting.

This is a very important point to remember. It always pays, for example, when collecting small amounts of flowers and foliage to make into a bouquet, to place these pieces straight into a polythene bag to keep them airtight — a small piece of damp tissue in the base will help keep a moist atmosphere. Never cut flowers and leave them on the path or border to be collected later; always pick and place them immediately into a bucket of water when gathering for an arrangement and treat the individual stems as required when back in the house. It is still true to say that flowers are better gathered in the early morning or late evening when they are full of moisture, but I know that this does not, nor can it, apply to the commercial growers.

Ideas change and often revert to the old methods and there are many views on how flowers should travel. Finances come into it, especially with materials coming from abroad, and there are many factors to be considered. I can remember so clearly the great fun we had unpacking the gifts of flowers and foliages that arrived for the Coronation decorations in 1953. The way that they were packed was unbelievable — sewn into boxes with linen covers, rolled in rattan mats, hidden in reams of newspaper in bamboo baskets, and many other forms of packaging. When we eventually extricated the poor flowers, many had been so long out of water that they had completely wilted and never recovered to their normal beauty, but we learnt a lot from this and have progressed greatly today — or have we?

There was nothing to beat the old boxes of roses or carnations — the flowers were laid carefully in a neatly lined box with heads on pillows, perfectly graded, and in no way crushed, for everyone to see what they were buying. Today tight rolls of cellophane or greaseproof paper with hundreds of flowers per box arrive in the market. The flowers have little chance of not being marked. In the case of roses the leaves are damaged by the thorns rolled on to them making them look as if they have been shot at! It is often difficult to find a perfect leaf let alone a set for making a rose spray. Nowadays many consignments of flowers also travel with their stems in a container of water. Provided the notes on the box sides are read and understood all is well!

To my mind flowers are often picked a little too early and never develop to their full beauty but, of course, when only just showing colour they are so much easier to pack and in theory should last longer in the purchaser's home. Some are wonderful at 'growing' in water, e.g. Iris, Tulip and Gladioli. Others, such as Chrysanthemums and some Rose varieties, remain small if too backward and are less pleasing.

Equipment For Flower Arranging

A fresh supply of commercially treated water is necessary. Do not use water from the rain butt or garden pond because this will be teeming with bacteria, which under room temperatures breed rapidly and soon make the water dirty. Warm, and in some cases boiling, water will be needed for special treatment.

You will need scissors and secateurs which are well maintained and make a clean cut. Keep the cutters oiled and never wrench the material when trying to cut through it. Secateurs with the blade kept uppermost and a clean basal plate make the best cut. For really thick branches use long-handled secateurs to make a good cut. A sharp penknife will be helpful when removing the outside bark at the base of the stem.

A wooden mallet or hammer should be used to split woody stems — a tree trunk at the correct height will be ideal as a block on which to hammer. Hold the stems firmly and just split the bottom inch (2.5cm) of stem to help with water absorption. Do not rest on a table while hammering because you will find the stems tend to spring back and the flowers are bruised as a result.

A range of clean buckets of all sizes are needed to allow a good 'long' drink, even to the extent of a plastic dustbin for really tall material for use in large groups. Metal buckets are heavier and less likely to topple over but difficult to obtain, so plastic ones are mostly used in floristry today.

Flower heads such as individual Cymbidium Orchids are best laid on a pierced layer of greaseproof paper over a shallow container. The freshly cut stem will rest in the water yet the flower is kept dry so will not become spoiled.

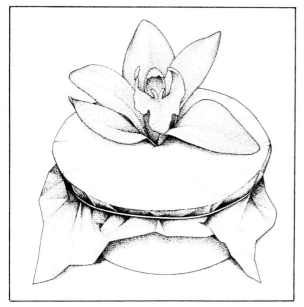

Figure 1.1: Preparation of single Cymbidium Orchid, prior to making up

Stiff brown or wetwrap paper will be necessary to roll up bunches of limp flowers to help keep stems straight while they are having a drink. Tissue paper and newspaper is no use because when it becomes damp it goes limp and, in fact, weighs down the limp flower heads making them worse.

Chemicals

The use of chemicals is an extra cost and should not be necessary. Start clean and keep clean and all should be well. An old penny or an aspirin used to be a favourite trick in grandmother's day and it was not so silly as we may think. A trace of copper was given off by the penny and this acted on the bacteria which was present in the water. No thought was given to leaves below the water or a really clean container so the water soon became tainted, but the poison from an aspirin worked wonders!

The addition of a few spots of sterilising solution or bleach will stop the water smelling so quickly when using flowers and foliage of the cabbage family — in fact, I often place a decorative cabbage in a small plastic bag containing treated water and then place this into the vase. By keeping it separate the water in the vase stays fresh much longer.

Starch, sugar and other plant foods may help a little in some cases. Alcohol certainly revives flowers, but money spent on this is better used in other ways! Have a drink and believe that they have revived!

Proprietary agents, such as Chrysal, Florever and Aaduralp, which contain plant food and steriliser, are no doubt useful and we always add one of these to the water at the Chelsea Flower Show, but I would not think of using them with delicate containers in the home. These products contain chemicals which seem to be both plant foods and disinfectants, but might well damage a good china or silver container — in fact, the manufacturers advise against their use with metal containers.

Aspirin will also prolong the life of a flower. It reduces the rate at which the leaves lose moisture to the air. Water containing very low aspirin concentrations closes the pores in leaves and limits their moisture loss.

Lemonade can also revive flowers — the ordinary fizzy drink will help to bring flowers up if they are rather limp. This is due to the sugar, carbon dioxide and other additives which seem to react on the cells and movement of moisture through the plant tissue.

All flowers are best placed in a cool damp and dark area while having their first drink. The advantage of the even temperature of a cellar is a point worth considering when buying a flower shop if there is not to be a coldstore in the building. Stone or concrete floors are ideal because they hold the damp whereas wooden flooring does not.

Points to remember

Always make a slanting cut at the base of the stem.

Woody stems do not take up moisture as quickly as soft stems so should have a longer period in deep water before being used, especially if they have been dry-packed and have travelled far.

Always use tap water and clean buckets. Remove all damaged and unnecessary foliage before giving the flowers their initial long drink. Remove all foliage which will be below the water line. Limp material will pick up quicker in warm water. Never put too many flowers in a bucket; as they take up the water the stems expand, and if they are overcrowded you may have trouble getting them free from the bucket.

Care And Handling Of Flowers And Foliages

Flowers and foliages for the florist come from varying sources. Those purchased from the market come from either the large commercial growers or from overseas and are sent regularly to the main wholesale markets. In both cases today, much of the required material has been packed tightly in a dry state and in a very backward condition. Material in this state needs special treatment before it can be used. Flowers and foliages also come from small private growers, often delivered straight to the shop premises, and you may also use flowers from your own garden or, occasionally, local hedgerow.

Irrespective of the source of supply, each flower or piece of foliage should be properly treated before it is used in make-up work or in an arrangement. All materials should have the base of the stem cut at an angle and should have a drink before use. The necessary treatment is easily grouped as follows.

Hard woody stems
All tree and shrub foliages and blossom, and flowers such as Chrysanthemums, Stock and Wallflower, come into this group. They should have the base of the stem hammered to split the wood fibres, or have the bottom half-inch or inch (1.25–2.5cm) cut up with

scissors or a knife. The outside bark can also be removed for an inch or two (2.5–5cm) down to the white 'cambium' layer when the stem is very thick. Branches of blossom, such as Philadelphus or garden Lilac, should have all their leaves removed carefully, so that the moisture absorbed by the stem can reach the flowers at the tip of the branches. Arrange non-flowering shoots of the same material with the flowering shoots to retain the natural look. If the foliage is very tired, place well under lukewarm water for a few hours to revive. The stems of the Dutch or 'forced' Lilac should be cut and hammered and the stem tips then placed in boiling water for 30 seconds. Fill up to the flower head with warm water for a few hours. The leaves have been rubbed off as the stems grow to produce the flower bud in the forcing houses so they are no problem. If the stem will carry blossom and some leaves, it is good to leave it as natural looking as you can.

Stems which bleed
Some interesting materials are to be found in this group. The Euphorbia or Spurge family with E. pulcherrima (Poinsettia is a Christmas favourite) and also the Poppy. All Poppies must be gathered really early, just as the bud scales are bursting and showing a trace of colour.

The cut surface must be sealed straightaway by placing in a flame or in a shallow tray of boiling water for up to 30 seconds. When using the boiling water

Figure 1.2: A woody-stemmed flower — Garrya. The tip of the stem should be hammered.

Figure 1.3: A stem which bleeds on cutting — Euphorbia. The cut stem must be sealed by placing the tip in a flame

method, only the tip must be under water and protection must be given to the foliage and flower against damage from the steam.

In the case of Euphorbia, any leaves which have been removed should have the resulting scar sealed straightaway; this can be done with the flame of a candle or a taper.

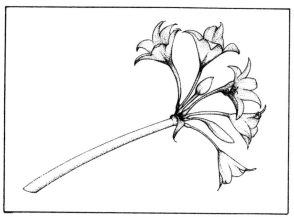

Figure 1.4: A soft-stemmed flower — Crinum Lily

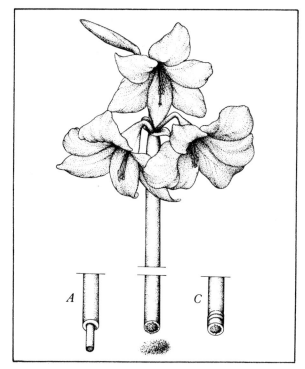

Figure 1.5: A hollow-stemmed flower — Amaryllis
A. *A piece of cane has been placed inside the stem*
B. *The base of the stem has been plugged with wool*
C. *The base has been tied or secured with raffia or a rubber band*

Soft succulent stems

Hyacinths, Arum Lily, Vallota, Echevaria and Eucomis fall into this group. These stems just require to be cut at an angle and placed straightaway in deep water.

Plants with hollow stems

This group includes Lupins, Delphiniums, large Dahlias and Hollyhocks. These flowers are useful in large decorations and can be made to last a little longer by inverting and filling the hollow stem with water, plugging them with a little cellulose wool and then standing them straightaway in a deep bucket. The more the hollow stem dries out the more difficult it is for moisture to cling to the hairs on the inside wall of the stem.

Amaryllis is a plant with a hollow stem that needs special treatment. Before filling with water it is a good idea to place a piece of cane up inside the stem carefully, without fracturing the stem tissue, going right up to the flower head. Fill up with water, plug as before and then tie the base of the stalk or secure it with a rubber band. This holds the stick firmly and prevents the tissues splitting and curling at the base.

The following flowers are of particular importance to the florist, so a few notes on their special needs are given below.

CAMELLIAS AND GARDENIAS. Both these flowers are available in small quantities during the flowering season and are very fragile. Camellias come in two forms. They are available as long branching sprays of dark green foliage with the occasional bud which will open under ideal conditions. The foliage lasts well. They are also available as flowers, which are grown under glass and in areas protected from frost. They arrive in the market lying on cotton wool in boxes. The flowers are borne on very short stems and are sometimes cut with one or two leaves. They are best left in the boxes covered with damp wool or paper, and placed in the coldstore. Before wiring, they can be floated in shallow water in a tray.

Gardenias come to the market in boxes, mostly as pot plants today and are rare as cut flowers. They are cut with stems of about 3in (7.5cm) and laid on cellulose wool. They have glossy dark green leaves. Again they keep best in cool damp conditions. Before use, they should be floated in shallow water to have a good drink. They are a perfect white when fresh, going through cream to pale brown as they age.

CARNATIONS.   All Pinks and Carnations tend to have stems with thick joints. Some varieties, especially those from Spain and South Africa, tend to be woody. The stem should have all the grass removed from the base and then a slanting cut made between the leaf joints and not at a joint. Hammer or split up the bottom half-inch (1.25cm) of the stem. Some Carnations grown outside and abroad in sunny climates must have two to three days in deep water before they are fit to use. Since these flowers have such woody stems and are often packed in a dry state, they take a while to come to life, so are not suitable straight from market. Keep any of the bottom foliage 'grass' to use in making sprays.

GARDEN LILAC.   First remove all non-flowering shoots, and place the stems in deep water after lightly hammering. Now look at the denuded branches with the flower heads and shape up, removing unwanted wood. Hammer the stems and if very thick remove bark from the bottom inch (2.5cm) of stem. Place in deep water for a long drink — if the flowers are limp, hot water may be used for these bare branches.

To make your Lilac last, first arrange the flower stems in flowing lines and place the short stems of foliage in between the branches.

GENTIANS.   Gentians are usually available in the market at two periods of the year. G. acaulis, the large-trumpet variety on very short stems, comes in the spring. G. sino-ornata, the longer wiry-stemmed variety with a smaller trumpet comes in the early autumn. Both are a heavenly blue colour and look super in small table decorations or added last thing to make-up work, but they should not go in the dark coldstore — once they close up they seldom open again. Remember also that blue flowers do not show up in artificial night light.

GERBERA.   This flower has become far more popular in the last few years and is available in many colours. It is now grown as a commercial crop in England. Once it is fully charged with water it lasts well. Packed in special boxes, the flowers are slotted into a card lining which is lifted out to stand over the bucket while the flowers have a drink. I prefer to cut each stem and treat the tips with boiling water for 30 seconds, then place in warm water up to the flower head for four to six hours.

GLADIOLI.   Cut the stems and remove the bottom leaves. You can take out just the tip of the stem to encourage the movement of moisture up to all the flowers. The flowers should develop from the base.

HELLEBORE.   This group of plants is very important to the flower arranger. They flower from early December through to April, with seed heads into July on some, and include the Lentern Rose, Christmas Rose and a number of green flowering forms, e.g. H. viridis, H. foetidus. They vary in their lasting qualities and some forms are difficult. They should be treated quickly after cutting from the plant, the tip of the stem going into boiling water for up to 30 seconds, then up to the neck of the flower in warm water to have a drink. Some people recommend pricking the stem with a needle just under the flower; some suggest scoring down the complete stem with a razor blade before putting in water. I have found both methods work well sometimes, but so much depends on the state of the flower from the market. They are better when taken straight from the garden.

HYDRANGEA.   These flowers should be on stems which are not more than two years old. If not required straightaway they are best left in their box, sprayed over with water and kept cool. The day before use, place the flower heads under water for three to four hours, then bruise the tips of the stems and stand them in a bucket of water until required. In arrangements, spray over regularly to prevent wilting. Some varieties are better than others for lasting. The latter part of the year produces longer lasting flowers since they have not been forced. In large groups it is a good idea to leave the flowers growing on the pot plant and place the whole thing in a vase. (This applies also to Begonia Rex.) If growing as a pot plant and the flowers wilt, place the whole plant pot in a bucket of water, allow all the bubbles to rise, then lift the pot out to drain, spray the foliage and flowers with a heavy mist of water, cover with polythene or damp paper, and stand in a cool place; the plant should soon revive.

LILIES.   This name covers a wide selection of florist's flowers which are increasing in popularity. Some are not true Lilies. They are available in different varieties throughout the year. All need careful handling. For make-up work, and where the flowers will be near delicate fabric, it is necessary to remove the pollen-bearing anthers as the flower opens. This should be done carefully by lifting off the anther from the stamen (rather like a ball and socket joint) before the anther splits and the pollen is shed. Never attempt to open the flower, it will bruise very easily.

The stems should be split and the base leaves removed. At some times of the year, just the single flower heads on short stalks come into the market. These should be carefully cut and laid on paper over a bowl of water as for Cymbidium Orchids. The flowers themselves should not get wet. One or two stems of Lily will do great things for a large group.

LILY OF THE VALLEY. There are two forms of Lily of the Valley on sale in the market.

Forced Valley: this is available throughout the year in small quantities. It arrives in the market with its roots attached. Usually the roots are rolled in newspaper, with coloured paper on the outside. The foliage is a lime green colour and the stems and flowers are very delicate. Remove the flowers from the paper, cut off the roots and place the flowers carefully in an upright container; the base of the stems can be cut and if very limp just crush at the tips and place them in warm water. The leaves are very beautiful and should be used (you cannot afford not to!).

Frame and Outdoor Valley: available during normal flowering seasons May–July. This has very dark leaves and the stems may be quite woody. Bruise the tips and give them a good drink before using. These should be cut when just the bottom bells (flowers) are out. The bells are closer together on Garden Valley and the scent is much stronger. The dark leaves of the Garden Valley tend to look very heavy and only a few should be used in an all Valley bouquet.

MIMOSA. Do not expect Mimosa to last long. The whole beauty of the flower is when it is fluffy and this is the stage of full pollen, the penultimate stage in the life cycle of the flower. Some varieties last longer than others. Keep Mimosa in a polythene bag in the cool until needed. Arrange it on its own in a large group and keep it in a room which is as cool as possible. Hot dry conditions, typical of a sitting room, encourage the pollen to dry up straightaway. Arranging in hot water will help a little, as the steam provides a moist atmosphere round the flowers. The addition of chemicals makes very little difference to the lasting qualities. Once finished, remove the flowers and just use the foliage which can look very pretty.

ORCHIDS. Orchids arrive in the market from many sources today. There are many species and varieties, but they can be divided into two types for treatment purposes. Those with a single stem, e.g. Cypripedium or Slipper Orchid, should be cut at an angle, split up $\frac{1}{2}$in (1.25cm) and placed in warm water round the edge of the container. Those with many flowers on the stem can be treated as Cypripediums or each flower taken off the stem and placed in a paper tray over water. Orchids should never be sprayed with water.

The main Orchids available today are the 'Singapore' type. These have flooded the market of late and brought the value of the Orchid as something very rare and exotic down to that of an everyday flower. Long lasting, these orchids have many uses. They can be used as complete stems in decorating and bouquets or pipped down (see Chapter 10) for corsages. Many good colours are now available. They come in packs of five and ten stems, each in a phial of water. Sometimes they are known as 'Spider Orchids', but this is a bad name from a selling point of view, and can be very off-putting to certain customers.

ROSES. Most roses on sale in the market today come in a rolled pack. Such a pack has its good points but does so often mean that the foliage is damaged. Roses should be cut at an angle and the base of the stem split. All thorns should be carefully removed and the base leaves removed. (These should be kept for make-up work.) The flowers should then be tightly wrapped again in rolls of stiff paper and given a good drink. Any roses which are very limp should be given hot water treatment before wrapping up for their long drink. The water in this case should be as hot as the hand can bear, and the stem (about 4in, or 10cm, in length) is put into this water for 15–20 minutes. The length of the Rose stem will vary with the variety. Very long Baccara could have 12in (30cm) of stem in hot water.

STEPHANOTIS. The flowers of this climbing plant are excellent in bouquets and corsages. Highly scented, they last quite well and are used as 'pips' in make-up work, or sometimes in clusters in expensive table decorations. They can be bought as pot plants or as flower heads in plastic bags. Usually available when the Hyacinth is out of season, they are similar in shape but are only pure white and much larger. Keep the flowers in a sealed bag in the cool. Place each flower stem under water for four to six hours after cutting from the cluster, before using, to give flowers a good drink.

SWEET PEAS. These are difficult flowers for the florist. They are never long lasting, but make beautiful table decorations. They should never be made up and sprayed and placed in the coldstore because they will damp off very quickly. If required in make-up work, this should be done on the day of the function.

TULIPS. These flowers are popular for decorating and if treated properly take up some very attractive shapes when in arrangements. They should be cut when taken from their boxes and any trace of the white tip removed. Roll up the bunches tightly in stiff paper so that the heads are well supported and the stems keep straight while having a good drink. Once fully charged with water, they will take up the elegant shapes and when arranged should not flop over, causing trouble.

VIOLETS.   These also benefit from very moist conditions. Keep them damp and boxed down when not on display. For shop display float them in a shallow container, and spray the flower heads regularly. Violets look best arranged on their own or in groups, close together. Keep them down in the bowl where they can remain cool and moist. The Violet is a less common flower than formerly; at one time it was a great crop featuring in the Cries of Old London. It is a labour-intensive crop to grow, and does not bring a return to the grower to justify growing large crops. Regretfully, the Parma Violet has now gone. The variety 'Princess of Wales' has the scent and longer stem. 'Herrick' is the hard non-scented darker short-stemmed variety.

2. SUPPLIES OF MATERIALS

It is a mistake to buy poor quality materials and expect them to last and make a spectacular arrangement. One or two good quality stems treated properly will give very much better results and will be no more expensive in the long run. You only get what you pay for as with everything else.

Today, very many flowers come from abroad and in some cases from the other side of the world. These will be backward when picked and in most cases packed dry. This prevents bruising and heating up when they are packed closely together in transit. They will be in first-class condition and all perfectly graded.

Their cost of production will be low and they will have been grown in ideal conditions. The biggest cost to the grower will be the transportation charges, and this is why they try to get so many stems into each box. On arrival in this country, they will appear somewhat crushed and soft but with proper treatment will soon recover. The Middle East and South America have now become areas of very high production and the pattern is always changing.

When I was a student we longed for the short-stemmed bunches of white and pale pink Stock from Malta, the Spanish field-grown Carnations that were so woody that two to three days in water was necessary before they ever came up to the shop floor for sale, and the joy of the pad baskets full of pale pink and white Roman Hyacinths coming in just after Christmas is a sight that I shall never forget. Alas, those days have gone, but other crops and growing areas take their place. I believe that now we have such problems with high costs in the production of flowers in Britain that we shall always be having to support our flower industry with crops from abroad. It has changed the pattern of the flower trade and the true seasonal flower period has gone, giving way to such flowers as Chrysanthemums all the year round. Growing methods change and what in some cases used to take up to nine months from the rooted cutting stage to picking the blooms now takes only 12 to 14 weeks — four crops a year from the same piece of land is

sense from the economic point of view, but how much nicer when flowers were in their true season. Mrs Spry used to talk of the sparseness of winter and tried to echo in her flower arrangements the outdoor scene. I can remember her demonstrating with enthusiasm in the very early spring and saying, 'The strength and austerity of a leafless branch used properly with a few flowers, especially those which belong to the season, can give as much pleasure as the gayest of summer bunches'. Many people today seem to think that unless there is plenty of colour and a lot of flowers present they have not got their money's worth.

Just after Christmas we now have a wide range of 'summer flowers' — for example, Marigolds, Cornflowers and Poppies from Israel — so, to many, the little bunch of Snowdrops is too insignificant, but what nicer arrangement can one have than a posy bowl of these with the beautifully marked ivy leaves to be found at this time of the year?

I always say to my students that there are five sources of supply in Britain, and the 'overseas' flowers are the first. The second is the English glasshouse crop and nobody can grow flowers better than the English grower, but today he does have difficulties. High costs of production have reduced these supplies and only the crops giving good economic returns are to be found now in the market. Labour-intensive crops and shy-flowering varieties have given way to rather more disease-resistant crops, and we have unfortunately had to introduce ideas from other countries which to me is very sad.

Dyed flowers, in most cases, are the last straw and to my mind always look artificial, but a white strong-growing and free-flowering Carnation lays itself open to the grower who accepts dyed flowers as a modern practice and is prepared to grow just one variety, and colour it to suit the needs of the market. Gone are those wonderful shy-flowering varieties we had in the 1950s such as the pale green 'Shamrock' and that wonderful variety 'Porcelain' with a colour that perfectly fitted its name. Why must we always want something that is not available? We don't really need blue Carnations, yet they are always being asked for by the public.

Probably the light factor is the biggest problem for the glasshouse grower during the winter months, and it cannot be denied that the Carnations from abroad at this time of the year have better and stronger stems.

British Chrysanthemums, Roses, Freesia and Gerbera grown under glass are superb and provided that they are graded properly make very good buys.

The third section on my list — the field crops — are again important. In Britain they spread over the whole year from the south-western part of England right up into Scotland, and the range of temperature and different conditions prevailing in the British Isles give a seasonal difference of almost three months between flowering times.

British bulbs provide a wonderful group of flowers and are available in so many varieties today. Anemones, Scabious, Pyrethrums, Sweet Williams, Gladioli and Annuals are a few outdoor crops that come to mind that find a ready market, if well grown.

The other two sections are small and should remain so, but are extremely useful to the florist trade. The 'private growers' are people who still run large gardens with a wide range of materials, and who are having difficulties in keeping going with the expenses of today. Many are prepared to sell small quantities of interesting materials that, let me say straightaway, would not market as a commercial crop. These are the flowers and foliages on which Mrs Spry built up her reputation and which make all the difference to an interesting arrangement. A visit once a week to the garden will bring forth perhaps pieces pruned in the normal garden practice, which otherwise may have been burnt, together with seed heads and blossoms which are so different from the commercial supplies. Many oddments of foliage can be turned into something really wonderful.

And last, I want you to think of the seed heads and grasses of the hedgerow. They are not free because they take time to collect and time is money in the trade, but they will add interest and lightness to some of the heavier type material which is marketed today.

What I do not want to encourage, however, is large numbers of people raiding the countryside for the bits and pieces that I have just mentioned. Always cut with great care, and ask before you start cutting at someone's hedge.

There is an area that I used to visit en route home nearly every weekend, and on the walls grew superb Ivy trails. Some of the large ones were ideal for big decorating, and the small trails for head-dresses, etc. I contacted the owner who was delighted to help me and said that it was only cut back and burnt each year, so in some way I felt I was helping both parties.

I did not realise that nearby was a big mental home, and that it might cause concern to see someone jumping from here and there cutting pieces of green and brown foliages. (All this to be put in a large black plastic bag.) It is said that the locals had to be told of this strange activity that would take place at weekends, and that the person was harmless and not out on parole! All is well and I am now accepted in the area, but sad to say a lot of the land and my Ivy has made way for a new building site.

The Flower Market

This, in my case, is the New Covent Garden but all markets are run more or less on the same lines today, so my comments to you will apply all round.

I believe that one should be organised before arriving at the market, and have a list prepared of materials which are needed to cover orders and for shop display. Make a note of any future big job so that you can talk to your salesmen about it and warn them of your needs. Compile a list of the sundries that are getting low — don't wait until you have run out and then be waiting for fresh supplies and, of course, have an open mind and eye for any new season flower so that you are the first to have it.

Treat the salesman as a friend — he is there to help you and will, I am sure, be fair if you treat him likewise. The person who goes into the market always grumbling about prices and quality is not going to be a favourite! Be helpful and guide him with your needs and he can pass these on to the growers.

There are no fixed prices and these will vary according to supply and demand, but if you are noted for always knocking down the price, they will increase it when they see you coming. In other words, by lowering it for you it may still mean that you pay the same!

It is important to get to know some of the market packs and growers because things do vary a great deal, and some of the special and more interesting things have to be found and then encouraged. The old idea that good materials sell themselves is very true. It is only the second quality that stands around and has to be pushed to make a sale. Once a salesman gets to know you, he will be only too pleased to hold back materials for you, and much of the good stuff coming into the market is 'sold' before it arrives.

With trade today ideas have had to change, but it

still pays to have a small standing order on a regular basis and then to buy the extras when they are needed. I would suggest that you have accounts with a few of the main wholesalers, and then pay cash for the other items that you find from time to time. Do not forget to keep good records of everything that you purchase and any payslips because all this has to be accounted for at the end of the day.

Telephoning the order through, once you are known, will be all right, but it does pay to visit the market all the time to see for yourself what the position is with regard to supplies, to talk generally to the salesmen, and to make your presence known by showing an interest. Keep an eye open for supplies in other flower shops, and keep mental notes of deliveries coming in from other areas.

An attitude of 'give and take' will certainly help and generally being known to be a firm but pleasant individual will prove useful. Buying is not something you can really learn from a book — you have got to jump in at the deep end and try for yourself.

My first buying experience was when, having led the protected life of a floristry student, I started out in the big world myself. It was in the Midlands and I remember so well that I thought anything 'big and bright did for Brum' after the subtle colourings and jewellery-like floristry of Constance Spry. Let me be fair straightaway and say that this is not the case today and there are some lovely flower shops to be seen in the Midlands, and very good floristry work is carried out throughout the country.

The Buyer had fallen foul of a bus resulting in leg injuries so without warning I was put to the test. My boss, who was well known for his flower work and, may I say, bad temper too, came to me and said, 'You will be in the market at 5.30 a.m. tomorrow' — so the challenge was on! Once again, I believed in saying, although it was only too obvious to the salesmen, that they had a real novice in their midst. I explained that I had not been involved with buying before, but wanted to learn and to please put me right — knowing full well that if it was not so, I may well have had the wooden boxes (in those days) thrown back at me when I returned to the shop and some salesman would have been blasted down the phone by my boss. It gradually worked, and slow but steady progress was made.

I tell my students that when they start they should go and see the heads of a few firms and explain the position. Get set up on the right footing and all should be well — after all, the more the salesman can sell, the happier he should be.

Availability of materials

Changes take place all the time and availability of materials can be a problem especially when estimating for a function which may take place some six months later.

I believe a very important word in the florist's vocabulary is 'if'. Never promise anything, but say, 'Certainly you can have whatever it is, if available', and then should the materials not be available you are able to substitute, provided you let the customer know. Always try to play safe and any doubts should be warned by a telephone call saying, 'We are trying to get your . . . but they are off crop or hard to come by at present'. Forewarned is forearmed and it does help soften the blow. If not warned beforehand, however beautiful the result, it will not be right and then there is trouble.

It is sad to say that the range of interesting flowers available today in the markets is less than in the eighteenth century. Richard Weston, writing in *Tracts on Practical Agriculture and Gardening*, 1773, lists flowers which are no longer with us, but it is true to say that we have many more colours and sizes in fewer types of flower available. Another loss is the scent factor which has given way in plant breeding for greater size, productivity and other vital factors in this commercial world.

Another point comes to mind and that is the re-occurence of plant popularity. The Aspidistra has now become popular again, but for how long? Let us hope that some of the plants mentioned in Loudon's *Survey* in 1827 such as Auricula, Myrtle, Mignonette and Moss Roses may have a chance to return.

How To Select Your Flowers

Look at the presentation and packing. Are the flowers firmly held or can the ends of the petals be bruised up against the box end? It may not show up straightaway but bruising develops as the flowers open. Fresh bright looking materials, not too open, are the best to go for, and not the limp wilted flowers and foliages.

ANEMONES. These should have good clean straight stems. Flower heads should not be too tight and certainly not blown. You need a full range of colour in mixed bunches with freedom from mildew and muddy calyx.

BLOSSOM. Look for well-shaped branches with good clusters of blossom in bud stage, but showing colour. They should not be too heavy in leaf, Viburnum, for example, because most of this will have to be stripped off.

CARNATIONS.   Petals should not be curled or rolled. The flowers should not be too open. Check for straight stems, especially in winter months. Flowers tend to go square in thundery weather. The stigma and style should not be showing in the centre and the calyx should not be split.

CHRYSANTHEMUMS.   With single varieties there should be a nice hard green centre with only a trace of pollen round the outside of the centre disc. Foliage should be strong and healthy, the stems firm and not damaged from cross pieces in packing. In sprays, watch for a good length to each flower stem. Short stems make heavy heads which cannot be split up in small vases. With all year round (AYR) Chrysanthemums the stems in January/February in Britain seem to be at their weakest, and if flower heads are heavy they will snap over very easily.

DAFFODILS.   These should have a nice crisp feeling, with a greenish tinge to the petals. They should rattle when shaken. No pollen should be present and they should not be papery in appearance.

DAHLIA.   Dahlias do not pack well, and I would say buy direct from private growers if you can. They bruise so easily when packed for market. They are better if picked and put into warm water straightaway and carried in buckets. Pompom, small cacti and decorative classes are the best. If buying in the market, look at the back of flowers for damping and bruised (cracked) petals.

FREESIA.   These should have good straight stems and not be too coarse. Only the bottom flower should really be out. The length of stem and colour fixes the price. Buy for make-up and small posy bowls, or larger decorations and wedding work.

GARDEN LILAC.   Look first at the shape of the bunch, and condition of the foliage.

GLADIOLI.   See that the bottom bloom is perfect and the correct colour.

LILAC.   The Dutch comes in plastic sleeves with a sachet of Chrysal attached. Follow the instructions. The top of the flowers should be slightly green, not too crushed and certainly not dropping.

LILIES.   Many different types are now available. All open well in water. Look for good clean stems and foliage. The flowers should be just showing colour, but no pollen should have been shed. Watch for broken flower stems.

ORCHIDS.   Many more are available today in the market. Small stems come in wraps — five or ten stems per bunch, and these are in moisture holders at the base — either in a tube or damp wool. Larger stems are packed in shredded wax paper or cellulose wool, each stem holding its own water supply. Watch for bruising, missing lips and spotting of petals.

PAEONY.   These are normally sold in bunches. The flower heads should be well formed and showing colour, but not fully open. These flowers should be kept in the coldstore.

POPPY.   The stems should be burnt at the tips. Only a split in the calyx should show the colour of the flower.

PYRETHRUM.   Look for good clean foliage and a fully round flower with a hard green centre disc. Only a small amount of pollen should be round the edge of the green centre.

ROSES.   Look at the foliage and ends of flower petals for bruised lips. No petals should have been removed. Buds should be crisp and not too tight. If too backward the roses will not develop properly.

SCABIOUS.   Look for good round flowers with a nice hard centre and no pollen showing. Stems and foliage should be clean.

STOCK.   The stems should be strong, but not too thick, and with clean foliage. The bottom flowers should be open but not papery. They should be crisp to the touch.

SWEET PEAS.   The bottom flowers should be open. Stems should be strong and straight. Look for good colours. They should feel crisp, not soft and papery. Pale colours normally sell the best.

TULIPS.   Look for good straight stems of fair length. Foliage needs to be clean and free from spots (tulip fire). The buds should be greenish. The flowers develop well in water. Take great care with buying wrapped tulips.

Any troubles should be reported straightaway to the salesman. He will warn the grower, and it is hoped that a price adjustment can be made. Play fair and you will be treated fairly.

Keep your eyes and ears open when in the market. It can be great fun and worth the early start. Do try any new varieties that you may be offered. It is only by doing so that you keep up to date with the trends. If you do not have a go yourself, you cannot speak for or against a certain flower, and you will be sure to be asked by a customer about them.

Something that has worried me for many years is the transport of materials from the market to the business premises. How many times have I seen tender material (because of the way it has been grown, maybe) being blown about on the back of an open truck. These plants will suffer from this treatment, and no wonder the poor customer has bad luck with her pot plant, and it does not last very long. In the London streets I pass boxes of pot plants set up on the pavement with a price tag above them. Many may well be containing plant material which can stand the cold draughts, but a number have often come from a heated greenhouse. These have been grown quickly so that they flower early and are on the soft side, so are far more likely to be damaged. What a pity, and how sad to think that all that careful handling in the nursery can be wasted in one day. I would always recommend that, when buying flowering plants out of season, you go into the shop and see that your purchase is wrapped before coming out with it.

The same applies to cut flowers — really it is far better to go into the shop and perhaps pay a little more for flowers which have been prepared and are standing in water, rather than buy from the boxes standing up on end at the front of the shop. Many will have partially dried out, and you will have to get this moisture back into the plant tissue if the flowers are going to last. I must say that the barrow-boys do tend to pack their flowers lightly on the barrows and to keep damping them down which does help, but, again, many of their supplies are of lower quality. Either the flowers themselves are inferior, or they have been bought on a quick-sale basis as they had been hanging-on in the market due to lack of buyers in the early morning. There is nothing one can do to make flowers last longer. Buy the best, look after them properly, and you should not be disappointed. Remember that some flowers have only a short life span; others last a long time. Try, when mixing, to keep all short-lived flowers together, so that your arrangement will not soon be marred by dead flowers among the fresh.

Growing Your Own Flowers

It is always a problem to know what to grow in the garden, and there are various ways of approaching it. First, check on the type of soil, then forget materials which are known to be not suitable — there are so many that you can grow happily, so why try something really difficult, costly in materials, and take up a lot of your time unnecessarily.

Now that you have got that sorted out, it will pay you to really clear the ground that you are hoping to use — dig it well (double dig, maybe) and attend to any feeding with farmyard manure or old compost. Out come all the perennial weeds and rubbish at this time, because you will never have the chance again. My own little garden suffered in this way — it had been a rubbish dump at the back of a scrapyard for many years, and naturally I wanted to get going straightaway. If only I had spent the first year in building a proper wall around it and preparing the soil properly, I would be free of so many problems today.

Personal taste will play a big part in what you grow, but I would certainly go for foliages because you are always able to buy flowers in the market, but interesting small foliages so often are not available. The grey/greens and silver grey colours are so useful in make-up work. Interesting shapes to the leaves and a wide range of greens will help you a great deal. If your area of land is large enough why not have a special part near the house. Then have nursery beds or cutting areas further away, because to get good colour and shaped material it does pay (where the plant will stand it) to cut back hard so that you get new growth all the time, and this method may be too severe if the garden is used as a true garden and you will spoil the habit of the plant. In other words, you must get your priorities right, and think for what purpose do you want that particular plant?

When planning the garden you should work on the same principles as when doing a flower decoration, so the positioning of each plant is important. Keep the different shaped foliages and colours next to one another so that each shows up well. Remember the size to which your plants will grow (even with the pruning to which they will be subjected), and leave plenty of room when planting. You can always fill up with annuals until the plants have grown. Do try and play fair with your plants — those that grow well and keep producing elegant little shoots must not be over-picked at the expense of others that are, perhaps, further away from the house and not too easy to reach on a wet night in the dark! How easy it is just to pop out to the nearest plant and keep cutting at it.

These are some of the trees, shrubs and plants I would suggest that you grow because they are the most useful:

Acer
Alchemilla
Alnus glutinosa
Aralia
Arbutus unedo
Artemisia
Arum italicum
Acuba japonica
Berberis
Bergenia
Betula
Bocconia cordata
Buxus
Camellia
Carpinus betulus
Cedrus
Cineraria maritima
Cornus mas
Ccrylopsis pauciflora
Corylus avellana
Cynara scolymus
Cytisus
Elaeagnus
Escallonia
Eucalyptus
Euonymus
Euphorbia — epithymoides and E. wulfenii
Fagus
Foeniculum vulgare
Geranium
Hedera
Hosta
Ilex aquifolium
Lamium
Larix
Ligustrum ovalifolium 'Aureo Marginata'
Lonicera
Mahonia
Onopordon
Osmanthus
Paeonia
Phalaris arundinacea
Phormium tenax
Pieris
Polygonatum
Prunus
Pulmonaria
Pyracantha

Rhododendron
Ribes sanguineum
Rosmarinus
Ruta
Salix
Salvia
Santolina
Senecio laxifolius
Smilacina
Sorbus aria 'Lutescens'
Spiraea
Stachys lanata
Symphoricarpos
Typha
Verbascum
Virburnum lantana
Vitis

3.FLOWER ARRANGING

A great change has taken place over the years in the art of flower arranging, and any old vase arranged in any way stuck about here and there is no longer acceptable. Flowers have to suit their background, be the correct size for the given area, and they must be arranged in something suitable. Arranging flowers can be likened to an artist painting a picture, but instead of using a canvas, oils and brushes, you are creating a picture with your flowers, vase and a suitable background.

Mrs Spry always told her students that there were no rules, but a few guidelines that they could follow when arranging flowers. She said, 'Never forget that in arranging flowers you have an opportunity to express your own sense of what is beautiful, and you should feel free and uninhibited in doing so.' I would like to quote further from her writing because it paints such a clear picture of the whole subject.

'People sometimes ask if there is any one method or procedure better than another. I don't really think there is — different arrangers have different methods. Some of them are inclined to state first the height and width, and then to fill in an outline, and finally to fill in the centre.

Others like to start on a special point of interest and then to work round it. Of course, a great deal depends on the flowers you are using and certain types of arrangement seem to require or have this special point of interest, but it is not essential. The first consideration in choosing an arrangement is suitability.

There are places which may call for grandeur and elaboration, but more often it is simplicity and 'artlessness' which pleases. You do not hang gingham curtains in a gilded salon, nor brocade in a country cottage. Let suitability be your vouch word. Studied effects, apart from in exceptional circumstances, are generally less pleasing than artless ones. It is quite possible to retain agreeable lines and good outlines without over-working and

over-styling the flowers. Never mangle your flower material to make it conform to some geometric shape. Avoid overcrowding and when in doubt, leave out.

Every time I read these words I can picture Mrs Spry writing at her desk, and I think back to the happy days I spent working with her and her team at Winkfield Place. She really did love simplicity and got just as much pleasure from a stem of Alder with its cones and catkins arranged with a base of moss and a few of the first Snowdrops, as she would have done from a big bowl of Auratum Lilies. I shall always remember these words and cannot think of anything more helpful than to pass them on to you for consideration.

Containers For Flowers

Today there are so many to choose from that it is difficult to know where to start (see Plate 1). All that I would suggest is that you start collecting useful shapes and types and look after them properly. Always put them away clean and ready for use next time.

The first important thing to be taken into consideration when selecting a vase is that the flowers and foliage must be arranged in sufficient water for their needs. So often a beautiful flower design wilts within a short space of time because the container does not hold enough water for the amount of material used.

The actual shape and cost of a vase is immaterial, as long as it is suitable for the flowers. Glass is more suitable in summer, and pottery and china for other seasons of the year. A vase with a stem or plinth base is generally an added advantage, giving additional grace to the finished arrangement. On the other hand, a simple cooking dish can easily be used, especially for a table piece or for a mantelpiece or shelf.

Whether the container is made from pottery, glass, plastic, basketwork or metal, it should be simple in design. Some can be home made. Fibreglass is excellent for copying lead urns, etc., but the bases must be weighted to get them properly balanced. Try to suit the container to the flowers and the decor of the room in which they are to stand. The arrangement should add to the overall effect, and not stand out or detract from the general picture. Always try to pick up one of the colours in the room in the choice of colours of the flowers.

Very ornate containers can look beautiful and, at times, can be used, but for everyday use keep to self-coloured vases and simple classic shapes — white, green, grey, black and bronze are the usual colours. Over-elaboration, either in shape or colour of the vase, can detract from the general effect at which you are aiming.

Keep in mind the whole picture you are making. For example, suppose you have Marguerites, Garden Poppies and grasses. They can be arranged in something as simple as a tin-lined basket providing it is a nice shape and really suitable. On the other hand, if you have Arum Lilies then you would not be satisfied with a basket at all — you would need a heavier type of vase such as a bronze or marble urn.

Vases seem to change with the fashions, and those that were thrown out in grandmother's day are at a premium now. Cut-glass rose bowls and silver trumpet vases are out at present, but keep them. They may well return to vogue in a few years' time. A really pretty epergne will fetch big money today.

Marble and alabaster

Both these are excellent, marble being a lot heavier and the less fragile of the two. Alabaster is more varied in colour, and must always have a water container or lining inside. Keep clean by wiping with olive oil. Water will roughen the surface, and eventually it will crack and disintegrate. Heat also makes it go opaque after a time.

The old vases of these materials are such wonderful shapes. Imitation vases made from a composition can be quite effective, but they are always so light and subject to over-balancing unless very carefully arranged.

Soapstone vases are seen occasionally. Often they are very ornate, but they can make very pretty containers for just a few specimen flowers rather than an arrangement.

Glass

The beauty of glass to my mind is when it is seen with the light coming through it, and very seldom have I seen clear glass used effectively as a flower vase. The

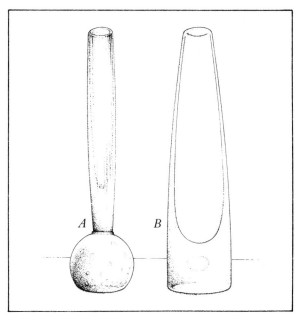

Figure 3.1: Specimen vases
A. A bad design — unstable   B. A good design

specimen vase, on which I have very strong views, can be excellent, but the shape has to be correct and not one which overturns all the time. Vases of antique glass and milk glass can still be found from time to time, often in the shape of very pretty baskets. Some glass in very modern design can be quite beautiful, but are totally impractical for flower arranging.

If you do use glass, however, clean it well each time after use because in this way you can stop watermarks appearing and the glass becoming stained. Ordinary Paris goblets make excellent vases for small bedside arrangements. They are as cheap as any container, and can be used afterwards. It is best to obtain them through bar fitting suppliers; 6–8 oz. (150–225g) size is the most useful. A small piece of oasis in the bottom, with a little netting over the top held with oasis tape, will be all that is needed as a good base for the stems. Small foliages — Freesia, Carol Roses or Border Carnations — make ideal flowers for this type of container.

To travel with the flowers already arranged, have a board with slots in the side fitted on to another plain board, with just enough area between the two boards to let the base of the glass into the slot. Plug with paper to hold firmly.

China and pottery

In this class there is available a very wide range both in colours and shapes, and a great range of price. The shape is the most important point to consider, and the ability of the vase to stand well is essential. Remember many vases on sale will be purchased filled with flowers, so they must stand well in transit.

Modern Cherub-type vases are much in demand, and care must be taken by the florist to see that only those with good features are purchased. Next time you go to a fancy goods fair take note of the cheaper range of ugly faces! The number of times I have heard people looking at the range in the shop and the remarks made such as, 'Oh have this one, he's got a pretty face'! Plain colours are still important so that the true colour comes from the arrangement. White vases can be painted with matt paint — black and a little aluminium make an excellent pewter.

For special effects I have picked out the foliage and garlanding on the side of a vase in delicate colourings, so that cheap Italian ware looks like a piece of Sèvres (from a distance!). All this takes time, but it does serve a purpose, and can be done for a reasonable price.

Cheap pottery may not hold water — always check before selling, to avoid trouble.

Other containers

Metal containers are excellent for flowers and some certainly seem to help the flowers last — probably from the trace elements given off to the water, and their reaction on any bacteria which may be present. Bronze, copper and brass are excellent colourings for autumnal groups. Pewter and silver look well with the mauves, silver/grey, petunias, cerise and pink colourings. Antiques are expensive, but worth collecting.

Wooden containers, either polished or in natural wood, make good background colour for the brown, orange and yellow colourings. A natural wooden garden trug filled with mixed summer flowers can be very attractive and well suited to the decorations in the garden room or interior of an old cottage.

Today, there are baskets of every size and shape, and a very extensive price range. If they are too cheap you cannot expect them to last, so it is false economy to purchase them. The day when baskets came from market with a good tin lining is long past. Choose those of a pleasing shape, and find linings to suit them. Some come with thin plastic linings, but these very soon puncture with wire netting, and the resulting flood can be disastrous. Play safe and get a clear pie dish or similar to fit inside, and it should then last a very long time.

Aids To Flower Arranging

Now we come to the mechanics of flower arrangement. There are many people who feel they know just the effect they want to achieve with their flowers, but are defeated because they do not quite understand the technique of making the flowers remain in exactly the positions they wish.

Netting and pin holders

There are many useful aids, but the most useful is wire netting. This must be a big enough mesh so that when it is *crumpled* up the apertures are big enough to take the stems. There must be several layers for the stems to pass through exactly where they are wanted. If your stems are big and tall the diameter of the netting must be sufficient to allow the stems to pass through four or five layers, so that you can get a secure hold; 2in (50mm) mesh is about right. Take care that the netting does not slip in the vase, or you will have trouble because as soon as you have the flowers arranged they shift, so the first thing is to get your netting fixed so that it will not move. If the netting cannot be seen from outside the vase, always have one layer right down on the base of the vase to stop the stems slipping.

One way is to pull out three or four ears, as it were, of the netting and bend these over the rim of the vase. This is easy with a tall vase, and for most bowls, but sometimes you have a bowl that has an awkward shape; in such a case it will help you to make your triangle of netting into a dome shape or a pyramid, so that part of it rises above the rim. Then, if you take a piece of string or raffia and tie right over vase and wire — just as you tie up a parcel — you will find your wire will stay in place. When the flowers are arranged you can cut away the string, or it may not show at all, so can remain. If you use a clear glass vase and you need netting, crumple up a small piece and fix it by the ears over the rim. An overhanging leaf or flower will hide it, and it will not be seen in the base.

For certain uses there are pin holders, which originated in Japan. They are very useful for thick-stemmed flowers, particularly for arranging these in shallow bowls when you want to see a good expanse of stem. People do not always remember how beautiful the stems of some flowers are. Tulips, for example, have stems of architectural beauty. If you have very heavy flowers you can sometimes use a combination of wire netting and pin holders which gives them tremendous strength and support. One rule for all plant holders — they must be hidden from view.

I must say that in some instances, especially with shallow containers, I do like to use a pin holder under a little wire netting. It also helps to weight down the vase a little, and help with the balance.

Oasis

Available as Oasis, Oasis Springtime and Oasis Sec,

there is no doubt that this material in both its wet and dry form has proved most useful to the florist, and makes the transporting of material much safer. The biggest mistake I find that people make with oasis is not to leave a large reservoir for water. They fill the container full of the soaked material, which quickly dries out, and forget to fill the container again. In fact, with a full container of oasis it is nearly impossible to get water into the vase.

A small piece of oasis in the centre of the vase is all that is needed, then a layer of wire netting on top fixed with oasis tape, leaving at least half the vase area for water. (Half the cost of material equals twice as long lasting time for the flowers.) I would never buy rounds of oasis because this is an expensive way of using it. Bricks are ideal, and can be cut into as many pieces as required.

Remember that once oasis has been soaked, it should not then be allowed to dry out again. It is best kept in a polythene bag where it can remain damp.

It has also given the amateur confidence because flowers placed in the vase remain firm from the word go, whereas with wire netting the first few tend to move around. However, oasis does not suit everyone, and spoils those with the light, delicate, flowing touch, making flowers look rather stiff and tucked in. My advice to all students is learn to arrange in wire netting first.

The brick-like constructions you see in some church festivals and flower shows are quite outrageous. The cost of the oasis is prohibitive, and flowers were never meant to be displayed in this unnatural way. They look fine in the beginning, but think of the person who will have to maintain the groups for the next few days. In most cases it is impossible to water the structure, and any flowers past their best with short stems cannot be removed easily without bringing in steps to reach them!

Glass marbles, chunks of rough crystal, glass and wet sand can all be used to hold flowers in position if needed. The important point is to keep the water table up.

Glass domes and small mesh wire cages for the centre of rose bowls are best forgotten because it is so seldom that they can be used.

Remember to line your silver or valuable china vases with brown paper before placing the netting inside, to prevent scratching before filling. You can use plastic wire netting which will not scratch, but I prefer the paper lining — the plastic netting is so bulky and difficult to shape to the vase without it springing out all the time.

A few points to remember when arranging flowers

It is important to bear in mind the proportion of the height of the flowers to the vase. This is difficult to describe and there are no rules. I would suggest you get a piece of bamboo with a marker on it and set it up as the height of the arrangement. Look at it from a little way back. See if it looks right, it may go higher or it may have to be lower — once set, keep within this imaginary point. So much will depend on the material you are using and where the container is standing. It is important to arrange the flowers in the position in which they will be displayed, or at a similar height elsewhere — different working levels make a very different picture later on. Light, feathery foliage can go a little higher than large leaved, heavy foliage, and both will look right in the same container.

The width should be set next. Remember the shape you are aiming for, and that a good outline pleases the eye and, again, that a clumsy one distracts.

It is a good guide for beginners to try to work within the confines of an imaginary triangle, but do not turn your flowers into geometric shapes, and never mangle plant material to make it conform to conventional lines.

Generally table flowers should be kept low, and though this is practical it need not be a must. In fact, the use of candles and posies high on a table is most attractive, and makes a little material go a long way. Many of the really special banquets have a combination of both types of flower arrangements — perhaps the top table flowers being kept low and those down the line set up high along the centre.

Table flowers look best on polished tables where lovely reflections add to the beauty. The most difficult of all backgrounds is the ordinary white tablecloth. For parties, both inside and out, the use of coloured hessian is fine, choosing one to suit the occasion. Mrs Spry used a brown one for Daffodils in the spring, a wine-coloured one for Cornflowers, and a navy blue one roughly embroidered with sprays of white daisies, which was ideal for baskets of Marguerites and grasses. All can be finished with a white cotton fringe.

It is sad to see flowers wilting because you have failed to fill up the vase. More flowers die through this neglect than by any other way. Take care to fill your vases up to the top after you have arranged them for the first time, and after that fill them up each day. Use tepid water and even quite hot water if they look at all limp. Take care to see that there is no leaf or stem to act as a syphon; it is amazing the amount of water that can be syphoned off down the mid-rib of a broad leaf.

4. BASIC FLOWER DESIGNS

A Facing Arrangement

A facing arrangement can look quite full of flowers (see Plate 2), but on the whole it is a saving on material as flowers and foliages are not necessary at the back of the vase — except for a few short pieces to cover up the mechanics.

Start with a baking tin or upright urn-shaped vase adequately filled with wire netting, which has been properly secured. If the netting is not firm, you will not be successful, so always get this right first. I always remember my Cookery School lessons, and one in particular on cake making. Your fruit cake will not be a good shape, we were told, unless you spend time lining the tin properly — it is the same with wire netting!

Place your back piece of foliage in first, two-thirds to three-quarters of the way back in the vase. Get the height right — a very rough guide to start can be one and a half times higher than the height or width of the vase, whichever is the greater. Then place two more pieces of foliage, one to the right and one to the left of this centre piece — both should be a little shorter than the first, the second one a little longer than the third. Now set the width, which will be about three-quarters of the height. Place this material in the sides of the vase threading the stems at an angle in under the netting across the back of the vase towards an imaginary line in the centre of the vase. This gives the overall size and outline of the design.

Do not cross stems as you work — all should flow towards a centre point and lie beside one another as fingers of the hand. At this stage add a few large leaves to the centre of the arrangement.

When starting to place the flowers it is important to try and use your palest or lightest weight flowers at the top, working down to stronger colours to give weight and finish to the base. If three tones of flowers are used, take the second colour from side to side making

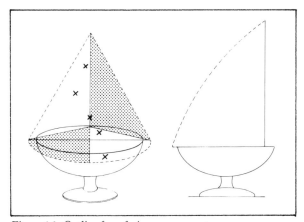

Figure 4.1: Outline for a facing arrangement

the correct balance. Then start the third colour from the opposite side and carry through to the other side.

The flowers for filling through the middle of the arrangement should be a little shorter. At the same time, they are brought forward to fill the base of the vase. Finish with a few stems of foliage from the centre front, working inwards to give a finished middle. To achieve a graceful and relaxed outline, material must be worked through the netting and *across* the water, as opposed to the placing of the flowers and foliage straight *down* into the water. This will avoid the 'surprised look' one often sees when flowers are all standing upright.

The back of the vase should be tidied up with a little foliage to hide the mechanics.

Example of a facing arrangement
Approximate measurements:

Side width: three-quarters the height of the main flowers
Front width: half the height of the main flowers

In this arrangement all materials should appear to radiate from the base of the first and tallest piece of foliage. No stems should cross at the centre. The side and front outline curve softly over the container. The foliage and accompanying flowers should be grouped from one side of the arrangement through the centre to the opposite front edge, i.e. flowers and foliage from the top right, through the centre to bottom left and vice versa. The main flowers should be kept close to the centre of the arrangement.

Suggested materials:

a few stems of Portuguese Laurel and Hemlock
1 bunch or 10 stems of Daffodils
1 bunch or 10 stems of 'Verger' Narcissus
1 bunch or 10 stems of 'Soleil d'Or' Narcissus
1 bunch or 10 stems of 'Ice Follies' Narcissus
5 stems of yellow Tulips

Group together the Hemlock, Daffodils and 'Verger'. Then group together the Portuguese Laurel, 'Ice Follies' and 'Soleil d'Or'. The five Tulips should then curve softly through the centre.

Ensure that your grouping merges gently, avoiding a 'blocked' effect. Do not overcrowd your arrangement. Leave room for the butterflies!

An All-round Design

An all-round flower arrangement (see Plate 3) is suitable in a large size for the centre of a hall table, which has to be seen from all sides, but it can also be scaled to any size for use as a dining-table centre, or for a sofa table, etc. A fairly deep bowl is suggested, adequately filled with wire netting, and this is a case when a pin holder in the centre base of the bowl is very helpful. The previous rule acts as a guide for size; thus a piece of foliage one and a half times higher than the vase should be placed in the centre. Then place pieces of foliage of about half to two-thirds of the centre height round the edge of the bowl in a wheel from the centre. This then gives the circumference of the all-round shape. Continue to work the flowers down from the centre, cutting each flower a little shorter than the last, and coming in from the outside edge *through* the water with blocks of colour again balanced from side to side as in the facing arrangement. To obtain a good shape, keep turning the vase around as you work.

Example of an all-round arrangement of Anemones, Eucalyptus and Santolina
Try this arrangement, using Anemones, Eucalyptus and Santolina.

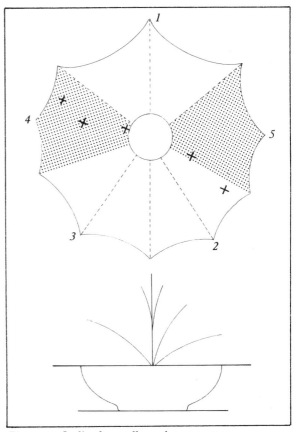

Figure 4.2: Outline for an all-round arrangement

Arrange five pieces of foliage, all about equal length evenly around the edge of the container. In the illustration points 1, 2 and 3 should be of one foliage and points 4 and 5 of another.

Strengthen the outline by placing slightly shorter pieces of foliage in between.

Do not cross the foliage stems over the centre of the container. If you are working with a larger container you might prefer to work to seven points.

Grade out your Anemones for colour and size. Keep the open 'heavy' blooms towards the centre on short stems. Buds appear 'lighter' and should be on long stems. Group your colours bringing these up through the arrangement in flowing lines.

Mantel Vase

A trough is needed for a mantelpiece design, with a pin holder at one end and wire netting spread through it. The flowers and foliage are then arranged in an 'L' shape from either end. A first piece of foliage is placed at one end as high as is required with a shorter piece at each side in the same way as for the facing arrangement, then a long piece of foliage about one and a half times longer than the original piece is put through the netting coming forward over the front, and the flowers are then banked down in groups of colour. On the other hand, if the mantel needs a central motif, the work is much the same as in the original facing group. Remember that a mantel vase will often stand in front of a picture or mirror, and that it should be in proportion and not hide either from view.

Table Centre

As with the mantel vase, the container should be a low trough or bowl, again with a pin holder or piece of oasis in the centre to take the upright flowers. The length can be determined by using trails of ivy at either end. The centre flowers should not be more than approximately 10in (25cm) high to enable a comfortable view over the arrangement. As before, the colours should be carried through from side to side with any special flowers, such as Roses, Carnations, etc., placed outward on either side so that guests on both sides of the table have a pleasant view. (See Plate 4.)

Baskets

Baskets have a special attraction with autumn colours, and look exceptionally pretty with the addition of fruit to tone with the flower colouring. A lidded basket is attractive with an 'L' shaped design similar to the one already explained for the mantelpiece. This enables a section of the lid to be seen when the basket is filled. A round hamper basket, on the other hand, has the lid slightly pulled down and is arranged simply with the flowers resting in it, but not appearing to be flattened under the lid. If a basket with a handle is being used, care should be taken to ensure that part of the handle can be seen when the arrangement is finished. (See Plate 5.)

Candlecups

Candlecups were first used by Mrs Spry when she was decorating for a luncheon party given for Queen Elizabeth II in the week of her Coronation.

There was little room for flowers on the table and certain pieces of silver and gold had to be present, so it was decided to use flowers in the candelabra instead of candles. To hold these Mrs Spry had little glass dishes made that fitted into the candle holders. These were excellent, but fragile, and did not last long, so to counteract the breakage problem, she had them made in a light metal and then painted them to suit the colour of the candlestick. These are now used throughout the world and made by numerous manufacturers — another brilliant idea which Mrs Spry so readily passed on to everyone in her generous way without getting any credit for it.

We use them with candles in the centre for evening functions, and they are very easy and inexpensive to do. They require light and airy handling, and should not be overcrowded with flowers. Try and obtain trailing pieces to come down well over the edge of the candlecup. (See Plate 6.)

Party Flowers

These must be studied very carefully in relation to the occasion, situation and, if indoors, general room colouring.

It is useful to remember, when doing party flowers, that one or two good-sized groups at or above eye level are much more exciting to look at than smaller bowls put about the place, which become quite lost once numbers of people begin to fill the room.

The general colouring of the decor must be taken into account. If the room is dark and sombre in effect, pale cream and peach into flame is a good colour combination. Try to keep the effect light and, if possible, use light, airy foliage which outlines the arrangement in the same way as for the facing arrangement. If extra tubes are put into the container to make the flowers (sometimes on the short side for a large group) appear longer, care must be taken to keep these filled with water. Baskets filled with flowers and hung from the walls with decorative ribbons give a gay party look. They can also be used with good effect if arranging flowers in a marquee, as the temporary floors on these occasions are often not safe for standing arrangements of flowers. Remember to give the flowers to be used for parties a good deep drink in water for as long as possible before arranging them.

Let us now discuss other aspects of the florist's work, but before we do let us recap with the following brief notes. If you remember these 15 points, you should not go far wrong:

1 For a 'facing' arrangement start three-quarters back in the vase.
2 Remember to consider the height and the width of the arrangement in proportion to the container, and the position in which the vase will stand.
3 Different types of foliages and flowers will make for different sizes within the given vase.
4 Make use of interesting curved stems for the sides and coming over the front of the vase.
5 Place foliage and flowers over the rim of the vase to break the hard line.
6 Remember, the whole effect is to be a pretty group of arranged flowers, not just a collection of materials standing upright within a container — this is what we term as a 'surprised look'.
7 Keep some flowers well down into the centre of the vase to add weight.
8 Group different colours and flowers carefully — avoid spotting them about in the vase.
9 All stems should flow from a centre point, and must not cross.
10 See that each stem is under water — it can be in an upright or horizontal plane, as long as it is covered by water.
11 Have flowers of different lengths next to each other — this applies to all arrangements.
12 If working with pointed and round-shaped flowers, have the point at the top and work down through the vase.
13 See that you do not get your colours in a straight line through the arrangement — this can cut it in half from a distance.
14 Arrange natural-looking vases, and avoid geometrical designs.
15 Hot, dry air quickly dries up flowers and hastens their death. Flowers of a tender nature can easily be killed by sudden changes in temperature and draughts. It is better to keep flowers at a fairly even low temperature.

Colour Schemes And Lighting

Colour is a very personal thing, and whereas some people are clever when combining colours, others have little colour sense.

There are rules about the use of colour, but these are rules which I feel can be broken, and I would be far happier to see one's own personality coming through in the arrangement rather than being bound to opposites of the colour wheel. For example, some people love mixed reds, and there are occasions when these look fine, but others find them overpowering. As a guide, I would say that to do a really good mixed red arrangement you need to go into as many different ones as you can find at the time. Personally, I hate blue and orange together, but these complementary colours are correct and I am sure that a person who likes this combination could use the colours to good advantage.

A great deal has been written on colour and the use of the colour wheel, and you should read this subject up for yourselves. I recommend the chapter on 'Colour Awareness' in Eric Roberts' book *Flower Arrangement* in the Teach Yourself series.

For my part, I would suggest that you carefully study the room in which the flowers are to be placed. Pick up the colour of one of the main items in the room (for example, curtains, carpet or an item of soft furnishing), and work to this with shades, tints and tones. The use of greens will always soften a group, the addition of white will highlight it.

Light plays a big part and flowers differ as they open, changing colour slightly. Texture also comes over in different shades. Colour awareness cannot really be taught — it is something which we possess in differing degrees. Colours look better used in sweeps rather than blocks in your arrangement, and visually they carry different weights. Remember that dark colours tend to appear heavy and should be down towards the centre of the group.

If in doubt fall back on greens and white, or something to tone in with the setting (see Plate 7). Some flowers look well against the light — silken-petalled Poppies and French Willow Herb look good with the light shining through their translucent petals. Others can look quite wrong in this position, and confused if set against a window. They would be best with light shining on them, not through them.

Never light the flowers from below, such as standing on a lighted plinth. It only warms up the water, encourages the breeding of any bacteria and illuminates the tangle of stems if using a glass vase.

If you want to create a strong note of colour, perhaps to echo the tones of some point in the background, such as curtains, increase the strength of colour by using less green. This does not mean that you should strip the flowers of their foliage, however, but you might want to reduce this in order to gain the full richness from the colour chosen. You may often see inferior blooms on show with just one or two leaves under the flower. A customer who knows about growing will be very wary of purchasing plant material denuded of its foliage. Good clean foliage is a sign of good growing, and suggests that the plant is healthy.

White and pale-bloomed flowers will create a highlight in a room and there are highlights within the group itself. To realise this you have only to study the flower paintings of the masters of the eighteenth or early nineteenth centuries. You will see how they use a pale flower to create a highlight.

Blue flowers sometimes look grey in artificial light, and in the dim light of a church. They must be used with care as they can become obliterated. Gentians — those wonderful blue flowers so well known in Switzerland, and available for short periods in Britain in spring and autumn — can look superb on a shallow dish with silver-grey leaves and chunks of ice (glass) for a lunch party, but in artificial light for a dinner party they can be lost.

There is a very important point to remember about mixed colours or about mixed bunches of flowers which, by the way, always look pretty in simple containers. If you arrange the flowers in light sweeps of one colour, you appear to achieve a more pleasing effect than if you dot your colour about. In every mixed bunch the eye is relieved if you can introduce a restful feel. This may be done by including one or two bold and shapely leaves or even a flower of a very definite form, and these are best introduced towards the base of the arrangement.

It is possible to combine flowers in a way which would not be pleasing in other media. Take red, for example — you can take flowers and leaves of almost every known shade of red, scarlet, vermillion, etc. right up to orange, and then put them together with courage (I may tell you it is fatal to weaken half way); it will create a brilliant effect of richness. It was Mrs Spry who really brought mixed red groups into the limelight, and these can be really striking if you want to make a bold splash of colour.

Another colour scheme for which Constance Spry was famous was the mixed green arrangement, using not only green colours but various shapes as well, which are so important when doing any kind of arrangement. Colour is one thing, shape is another, and to really succeed with your flowers you must combine the two.

Flowers look their best against a plain background, a surface uninterrupted by design. If you find you have to work against a very detailed background contrive something to alter this. For instance, use the Eastern idea of hanging up a plain piece of fabric with a wide hem at the top and bottom. A thin rod to go through top and bottom will make it hang well.

A mirror is an excellent background. Do remember that you should not have too many flowers because they will be multiplied in the mirror; also the back of the vase must be tidy because this can be easily seen.

Today silk flowers are very popular and may well stay in vogue for some time. Only the best should be used, and then arrange them as naturally as possible. Get the stems shaped up before attempting to use them — movement is so important. Colouring is also important, so try to keep to those that the real flowers carry. There is not a true blue rose, for instance, so do not use one.

Remember always to use buds, half-open flowers and open flowers to get a natural-looking effect. Remember also 'suitability', 'simplicity in everything you do' and 'if in doubt, leave out' — all sayings of Constance Spry which cannot but help you with your flowers. They are points that cannot be over-emphasised.

5. DRIED FLOWERS, SEED HEADS AND FOLIAGES

These are most useful in the late autumn and winter, but do need to be looked after properly. Once they become old they tend to get brittle, and many flowers and small stems seem to snap off. When not being used, keep them boxed down in tissue paper, and watch out for mice if storing away in a shed. They must be kept dry, otherwise they tend to become mouldy.

I was interested to see 'drieds' on display in San Francisco market when I was there a few years ago. They were hanging from the ceiling, heads down, and just out of reach, but very much in view for shape and colour. In this way they could not be handled; they kept clean; and it was easy to see the whole range without unpacking box after box.

Drieds are arranged in exactly the same way as fresh flowers, but you do not have to worry about filling up the vase! Use oasis sec, and add a little wire netting round it. You may find that the vase is very light and liable to fall over. I often put some stones or dry sand in the bottom of the container to weight it down. Certain flowers will have to be put on false stems, and leaves will be mounted on wires and guttared to make false stems. Otherwise, there is no real difference in the way that you should use them. Keep your colours grouped, with proportion and shapes in the same way. Just because the flowers do not need to be in water does not mean that you can go in for contrived shapes. A lot of the daisy-type flowers call for simplicity.

There are some flowers that are not actually real, but made up from real flower materials, and these can be quite effective. Keep to natural colours — those that are dyed are usually such awful colours.

I have an old student, whom I visited in Kenya, making these dried flowers, and they were quite amazing. A small factory, in fact, was doing nothing else, and the flowers were going to many parts of the world. The dried materials were collected from the bush and wild areas, then they were brought home, sorted, graded, treated and cleaned, before being bound or glued into 'new species'.

Much of the foliage we obtain has been treated by standing in a solution of glycerine and water. This does change the colour of the leaves, but allows them to become softer and less brittle. Beech, Lime, Hornbeam, Eucalyptus, Laurel and Box are very good subjects for this treatment. Do see that they do not take in too much of the solution and become sticky, because then they really do pick up the dust.

Bleached materials can also be effective for certain groups. This is done by drying after a little glycerine treatment first. Hang up in bright sunlight for a few weeks — a glasshouse is an ideal place in which to hang the stems. Good supplies are not widely available in Britain, and it pays to find one of the private growers and buy your materials direct. In this way you can buy smaller amounts of a wider range, and they will have been handled well.

One of the most informative books on the subject of drying flowers is *Dried Flowers — The Art of Preserving and Arranging* by Nina de Yarborough Bateson.

Dried flowers are useful in the workroom. A touch of Statice or a head of Hydrangea tucked in deep down may give just the right colour when it cannot be obtained from the fresh stock in the shop or workroom.

During the summer months when trade may be slack, but at the same time one has to have something on show in the shop, it will pay the florist to split the market box straightaway and dry or preserve half — this cuts the loss due to waste and offers something for sale later on. It is amazing the number of people who ask for dried material, so provided you keep it well, you will be sure to move it later in the year.

What never ceases to amaze me is the request for dried in the middle of spring when one is just longing to fill the shop or your home with the fresh flowers in all their bright colours, and in comes an old soul wanting dried Honesty or Achillea heads. I like, if possible, to have a good display of many dried flowers, seed heads and grasses in late autumn, then to clear up before the true Christmas stock comes in, and after Christmas the early spring blooms, but always to have some dried handy!

First and foremost, only try and dry or preserve the best quality material. Any old bits and pieces will be a waste of time and material, so the golden rule is to select only the best in ideal condition. Flowers for drying if too far advanced, for example, will drop many of their petals before properly dry.

Air Drying

Air drying gives a natural look to the finished product. The flowers should be picked dry and in most cases hung upside down in a reasonably warm room with good air circulation. If it is too warm the petals dry too quickly and will shrivel. The room should not be in direct sunlight because the colours fade very quickly.

Hang the flowers in small bunches with the excess foliage removed. They should be in a clean air zone, not somewhere where they are likely to get dusty. Arrange the ties with slip knots so that as the stems shrink, the ties can be tightened. The time the flowers take to dry will depend so much on the material and its moisture content at picking time. It is usually two to three weeks. Keep cutting all the time you have materials available.

A number of stems can be dried standing in a vase and some can be dried laid in a box — see Table 5.1.

Table 5.1: Air Drying

Name of plant	Hang down	Method Stand upright	Lay flat
Acanthus, bear's breeches	X	X	
Achillea	X	X	
Alchemilla mollis	X		
Allium	X	X	
Astilbe	X		
Barley	X	X	X
Bells of Ireland	X	X*	
Buddleia	X	X*	
Chinese lanterns	X		
Clarkia	X		
Delphinium	X		
Globe Artichoke	X	X	
Gnaphalium	X		
Goldenrod	X	X	
Grasses	X		X
Gypsophila	X		
Heaths and heathers	X	X*	
Helichrysum	X		
Honesty	X		
Hop	X	X*	
Hydrangea	X	X*	
Larkspur	X		
Lavender	X		
Love-lies-bleeding	X		
Marjoram	X		
Oats	X	X	X
Rhodanthe	X		
Rue	X	X	X
Salvia	X	X*	
Santolina	X	X*	
Sea holly	X		
Sea lavender	X		
Spiraea	X	X	
Statice sinuata	X		
Statice suworowii	X		
Sweet William		X*	
Tansy	X		
Wheat	X	X	X
Zinnia		X*	

*Stand cut stems in 1in (2.5cm) of water and leave to evaporate.

Drying In Desiccants

This can be a simple process with just dry silver sand or using chemicals like borax and silica gel. It is the way to dry perfect single flowers which should be mounted on false stems when dry.

You will need plastic boxes or biscuit tins with lids or strong wooden boxes. Cover the base with a half-inch (1.25cm) layer of desiccant and arrange the flower heads flat on this surface — the petals must not touch each other. Cover carefully with a fine layer of the drying substance. You may then place another row of flower heads which in turn are again covered. Any cup-shaped or trumpet flower such as Gentian must be fully charged with the drying agent.

The flowers will take between 7 and 14 days to really dry. Remove them carefully, brushing any dust from the petals with an artist's paint brush. Store between tissue paper in strong boxes in a dry place. The desiccant used may be dried in an oven and used time and time again.

Table 5.2: Drying in Desiccants

Name of plant	Notes
Broom	short sprays
Buttercup	dry buds as well
Carnation	cut before fully open
Cobaea	cut when fully open but fresh
Cornflower	try all colours
Daisy	wire the stems
Forsythia	short sprays
Gentian	single heads
Hyacinth	wire the stems
Larkspur	small side shoots
Lily of the Valley	colour deepens to cream
Marigold	wire the stems
Pansy	wire the stems
Pinks	miniature varieties good, too
Polyanthus	push wire right through flowers
Poppy (double varieties)	reds and pinks both become dark cerise
Rose and rosebuds	cut blooms before fully open
Rudbeckia	small flower types are best
Scabious	try both mauve and white
Stock (single varieties)	scented varieties retain scent
Sweet Pea	discard some flowers for best results
Violet	cut strongest stems
Wallflower	dark reds go nearly black
Zinnia	'Persian carpet' variety prettiest

Preserving In Glycerine

This is easy to do, but glycerine is expensive unless you need enough to go into the commercial grade and buy by the 5 gallon (25 litre) container. Anti-freeze does give good results, but some have a colorant in them which may come through to the flower tissue.

We always use a fifty-fifty mix of glycerine and hot water, although some people use $1\frac{3}{4}$ pints (1 litre) of glycerine to $3\frac{1}{2}$ pints (2 litres) of water. Do make sure it is well mixed.

About 2in (5cm) of liquid is all that is needed in the container. Only treat well shaped stems and branches and remove any unwanted leaves before treating. Bruise, hammer or scrape the bark to get moisture into the stem straightaway. The normal time for treating is between 7 and 28 days.

The foliages will change colour somewhat and they do develop a softer texture. Any berries treated will benefit from a spray of lacquer to give them extra 'lustre'. You can dye flowers and foliages in cold water dyes, but I think it is preferable to use natural colours only.

Once the stems have 'taken', clean the base with a cloth and any large leaves which may be dusty, then store in a dry clean place — they can be boxed down between paper and kept in a dry place.

Table 5.3: Preserving in Glycerine

Name of plant	Part of plant	Approx. no. of days
Bay	sprays of leaves	14
Beech	large sprays of leaves	4–7
Bells of Ireland	stems of bracts	14–21
Berberis	long stems	14–21
Blackberry	leaves and fruit	14–21
Cupressus	leaves and small cones	21–28
Dock	seedhead spikes	12–14
Euphorbia	whole heads	8–12
Hellebore	flower heads	18–21
Holly	leaves and berries	18–21
Hop	green bracts	9–12
Ivy	leaves and berries	10–14
Laurel	sprays of leaves	21–28
Mahonia	leaves	21–28
Maidenhair Fern	single fronds	12–16
Maple	leaves and 'keys'	14–18
Oak	leaves and acorns	14–21
Old man's beard	leaves and seedheads	10–14
Portuguese Laurel	sprays of leaves	21–28
Pyracantha	clusters of berries	18–21
Raspberry	sprays of leaves	12–14
Rose	leaves and hips	14–21
Rosemary	sprays of leaves (retain scent)	12–14
Rowan	leaves and berries	14–21
Sycamore	leaves and 'keys'	8–12
Willow	sprays of leaves	12–14

Skeletonising Leaves

Students often ask about skeleton leaves. These may be purchased through the market sundriesmen, but it can be fun to try and make your own. Skeletonising leaves was a very popular pastime in Victorian times. Use a strong leaf which will stand up to the treatment well. Magnolia grandiflora is ideal. This is the method you should follow:

1　Boil gently in water for 30 minutes. A teaspoon of washing soda should be added to each quart of water.
2　Let the leaves cool off in cold water.
3　Remove from liquid and spread very carefully on a piece of paper on a flat surface. With the back of a knife scrape off the green, but do not tear or split.
4　Place in very weak bleached water for one hour.
5　Rinse in clear cold water.
6　Wipe dry — very carefully.
7　Press on blotting paper.
8　Mount on wires when dry.

Artificial Flowers

In floristry artificial flowers are usually referred to as 'silk' flowers, though the term 'silk' is not truly correct. One should be careful when talking to customers, and explain this to them. Most of the so-called silks are a polyester/silk mixture. Another point to be careful about is that not all artificial flowers will wash. Some have washable petals, but fabric foliage which does not wash, so when buying for the shop all these things must be considered and very carefully noted. See that all the staff know about these problems.

At one time I could not bring myself to do anything with silk flowers, but I am now changing my ideas. Where fresh flowers cannot be used, and there is a chance to have something, 'silk' may well be the answer. They are now well made in good colours, and often well shaped to make them look extremely realistic, provided you pay the right price. Many cheap supplies are nasty and impossible to identify with any real flowers, and are best left well alone. For make-up work, however, the better quality artificial flowers may be used. Often they are too large, but if taken to pieces, carefully wired, and a little imagination used, they can be quite acceptable.

My advice to you would be to keep to the true colours of the plant or flowers. Anything that is not a natural colour immediately gives it away. I would also suggest that you keep to seasonal things — we do not want Hyacinth and Tulips all the year! Most of these flowers and plants have been made in the Far East, and one cannot expect them to be realistic unless they have had something really good to copy. Once the manufacturers master a good shape and get the foliage right, they introduce outrageous colours because they do not know any different. What the florist must do is to discourage this, and only buy those that are true to life. 'Fun flowers' — those that do not conform to any true name or pattern — may well be all right for a splash of colour at a party, but for everyday use they are no good.

I also believe that you can mix artificial and real flowers at times. Provided you soften the lines by bending the stems, etc. and get the colour right, they can be mixed and may go unnoticed. It is when something stands out because it is unnatural looking that a second look is taken, and then the cat is out of the bag. At home I have a large wooden tub in which I have been growing real plants for many years. At the base some of the leaves of the taller plants are missing, so I have introduced a few artificial plants with the other short-trailing ivies, and they go in extremely well. I have had people ask quite naturally 'Oh, please let me have a cutting of that', and they have not believed me when I have had to tell them 'You will have difficulty in rooting that one!'

It is true to say that a knowledge of horticulture is a great asset when working in a flower shop. This applies especially when handling artificial plants because if they are shaped up into their natural form they will look so much better. The same applies to the stems of flowers — always manipulate these to get some life into them. So often, perhaps in an effort to make them more interesting and realistic, there are extra appendages to the flower sprays. These must be removed straightaway if you wish to keep the secret. Arrange them exactly as you would fresh stems, all radiating from a central point. Grade your shapes, sizes and colours, and try to forget that you are working with anything other than real flowers. Of course, you will use oasis sec, and it may be worthwhile having an oasis pin holder or a 'frog' for extra weight.

6. CHRISTMAS DECORATIONS

At Christmas time flower arrangements fall into two very distinct groups; namely, fresh and artificial. In my mind there is no comparison between the two, and I would never use the artificial plastic ones from choice — they are usually glittered in some way, and once that is in the house it gets carried on clothes and keeps appearing for months afterwards all over the place; yet they are extremely popular, and must certainly be available on sale for two to three months before Christmas. The hand-made flowers which we used to produce were quite wonderful and these, in conjunction with hand-made foliages, were very realistic. Some of the 'silk' available today can look excellent mixed with fresh winter foliages, if viewed from a little way off.

Many florists today sell the raw materials, together with other Christmas sundries, for customers to make up arrangements themselves. Candles are always required and if you do not offer them, the clients will have to go to the nearest shop to purchase, so have a few on offer. One point to remember is that they are fragile and will not sell if cracked; also they fade quickly if left out in bright light in the shop window.

I think the ideal large arrangement at Christmas time is one comprising of Holly, both green and variegated, Garrya elliptica, Ivy trails and Ivy berries, Norwegian Spruce, Elaeagnus pungens aurea, with perhaps a centre cluster of Mahonia japonica. To add extra interest, a group of Pine cones and some branches of Larch with its small cones or branches covered with Lichen. For my dining table, I use a small low bowl with Ivy, variegated Holly, Christmas Roses, Winter Jasmin and a little Mistletoe.

You may be lucky to find an odd early Camellia or spray of blossom; it does so depend on the season. Many years ago plenty of the little red Ranunculus or Roman Hyacinths were available from France, but these now seem to be a thing of the past.

A door knocker or wreath is a must for me (see Plate 11). You can work all sorts of interesting material into it, such as Eucalyptus seed pods, different shaped cones, berries and small fruits with mixed foliages, but one of just fresh Holly with a large red bow can be most attractive. Here again, why spoil an excellent piece of workmanship by using inferior ribbon? The bows made from water repellent ribbon are never good. Use a wide (2in or 5cm) ribbon with a wired edge as this remains crisp and the loops to the bow stand out. It is expensive, but you can wash and iron it for another time. The one and only time that I added artificial materials to my own door wreath disaster struck. A gang of hooligans, on leaving a neighbouring public house, and, I may say, well under the weather, struck a match and set light to the ends of the ribbon. This in turn flared up and the whole door was soon enveloped in flames — a costly business and the last time that I will include any plastic materials!

Another favourite item on the decoration list is the Christmas Tree. It need not be large, but it should be a good shape and a good colour. I always feel that the trees are available far too early, and they are dried out long before they are on sale. Try, if buying for your shop, to get a good batch lifted for you in the last two weeks before Christmas. There are rules and regulations now about rooted trees, so you may need to have the stem set in a good log, but if you can keep the roots so much the better. Rooted trees should be potted in soil and kept moist to try and avoid the needles shedding. The problem is that the atmosphere in the house at Christmas is far too dry for most living material, and you cannot spray a decorated tree. See that the pot is large enough to balance the decorated tree. Perhaps a spray of leaf shine before decorating may help to keep down transpiration.

Set up the tree away from any direct heat, and trim out a few branches if it is very bushy. Remove a few of the 'feathers' down the branches and main stem so that you can see the structure of the tree. To my way of thinking there is nothing prettier than tiny white lights on the tree, but it is not everybody's taste, so you may need to have coloured sets for selling ready-decorated trees. I like to see trees decorated to a colour scheme — red and silver, green and gold, or all in one colour — rather than multi-coloured. If you are having lights I believe it is best to set up these first; and do check that they work before starting on the tree. Once these are on, now fix the top. It can be a star, a group of tinsel feathers, or you may like a well-groomed fairy. The fairies made by Constance Spry were out of this world and simple to make if you are artistic and able to paint a pretty face. The rest was just a wire framework draped with pretty fabric for the dress, and jewels added to give an extra sparkle.

You can also have a group of ribbon bows and streamers of different lengths coming down through the tree. Every attached bell or bauble (and these should be graded out for size as you go down the tree) should be tied on and finished with ribbon ends as a small bow.

Get some weight into the centre of the tree by going in deep with such things as little made-up posies of flowers in the colour scheme. Finish the base with a large bow of ribbon lined with tarlatan. Small gifts can be added to the tree, or placed around the base.

Pot plants are always most useful at Christmas and there are a number to choose from: Azaleas are normally just coming in; Cyclamen and Begonias in strong reds and pinks are at their best; and Chrysanthemums are readily available. Solanums, with their red and orange fruits, make a bold display, and can be used in window boxes if the temperature does not drop too low. In hard weather I have seen these stripped by pigeons, but normally they will last three to four months outside.

Cut flowers are always available, and Chrysanthemums in reds and bronzes look well with the Christmas foliages. In fact, most colours can be used to fit in with the room decoration. See that your vases are well topped up because the water loss with central heating and fires can be quite considerable.

Mixed reds are fun to do, and at this time of the year you have a good range of materials available. Somehow they fit in with Christmas, whereas at other times of the year many people do not like them. The use of ribbon and candles can really add just the extra touch for special party decorations.

Table Centre With Candle

You will need:

A candle and candlestick or bottle
A candlecup and oasis or wire netting
Small pieces of interesting foliages and flowers in fresh and artificial materials
Thin florist's wire

First, fix a candlecup firmly into a candlestick or bottle and then secure either a small piece of 2in (5cm) wire netting or a small piece of oasis in it. Wire netting and oasis should be secured by florists wire. At this stage, a candle taller than 12in (30cm) should be added. This also helps to hold the netting or oasis firmly in position. The flowers are then built around it.

See that the candle is well above the flowers, especially if you are using artificial materials because they burn so quickly.

Arrange by grouping your pieces, bringing through the colours and different shapes, getting some deep down and other pieces at different heights so that everything shows well and 'sits' comfortably in the container. All stems should radiate from the candle. Remember to have some stems flowing over the rim of the vase.

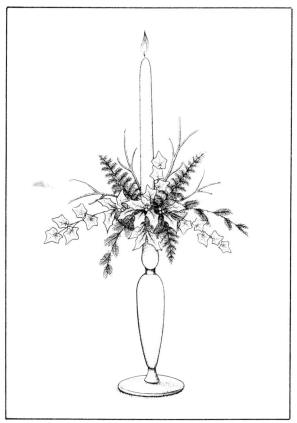

Figure 6.1: A Christmas candlestick decoration, made entirely of artificial flowers and foliages

Door Knocker Or Door Ring

You will need:

An assortment of fresh or artificial foliages (Holly, Ivy, Blue Pine and Spruce with Fir Cones)
Thin florists wire
One heavy piece of wire (or a wire coathanger)
Crepe paper ¼ to ½in (7.5mm to 1.25cm) wide
1 metre of ribbon

Cut a selection of foliages (fresh or artificial) using Holly, Ivy, Blue Pine and Spruce with Fir Cones. You will need approximately 72 pieces to make an average-sized door ring.

Wire the material on thin florists wire, placing the wire at the neck of the stem and twisting securely.

Make the frame with a heavy piece of wire (a metal coathanger could be used). Bend into a round shape and fix a loop of wire on to the frame to hang the ring by. Wrap the wire with crepe paper. Start at the loop and secure the pieces to the frame by twisting the mounting wires around the frame. Make sure there are no sharp ends of wire on the back which may cause damage by scratching. Work around the frame in a pattern, keeping it the same width all the way round and add in the cones at regular intervals. Work round back to the hook.

Figure 6.2: Working on a door wreath

Take a metre of ribbon. Cut approximately 2in (5cm) off the end. Fold the ribbon to form two loops and two streamers, making the streamers the length of the inside diameter of the ring. Wire the centre to form two loops (bow) leaving two equal ends of wire at the back of the bow. Tie the remaining piece of ribbon across the centre of the bow to hide the wire. Trim both ends of the streamers at an angle.

Attach the bow to the ring with the florists wire or a nylon thread.

Fun Flowers

You will need:

1 sheet of green metallic crinkle paper for stem and leaves
1 sheet of red metallic crinkle paper for 'petals'
Thin and thick florists wires
Silver reel wire (or fuse wire)
Glue
Yellow crepe paper
Pair of scissors

Cut out the pattern for the bracts (petals) in cardboard. Make several cardboard patterns of different sizes varying from 2–3in (5–7.5cm) in length. Take the red crinkle paper and fold the longest side to make a double layer, a little wider than the larger bract, making sure that the stretch of the paper is across the bract.

Cut the length of the paper. Cut the strip of paper to the length of the bract allowing a little extra each end. You will need five of the larger bracts and three of the smaller ones. For simplicity these can be of two sizes. Actual flowers are all different sizes.

Take the glue and apply it to the inside of the folded piece taking care not to get any on the coloured side as it will lift the colour. Take a thin gauge wire and place it in the centre of one side about half an inch (1.25cm) down from the top. Fold the other side over and press down firmly ensuring that the wire is firmly glued in between the paper folds.

Make up all pieces in this way.

Place the cardboard pattern piece on the wired paper and cut out around it. Cut out the five large bracts and three small ones in this way.

To make the centre stamens cut a strip of crepe paper ¼–½in (7.5mm–1.25cm) wide. Twist the crepe paper around the top of a thin wire which has been looped at the top and go round several times on the same spot to make a thick piece at the top, then continue twisting the crepe paper down to cover the wire for 2–3in (5–7.5cm). Glue the crepe paper at the bottom of the wire. Make five stamens for each flower.

Take a length of silver wire (or fuse wire). Place five stamens together with the tops level and bind together about 2–2½in (5–6.5cm) from top.

Bind in three small bracts on the stem of paper. Place in the large bracts around these and bind round. Bind in some of the heavier florists wires to the thinner wires of the bracts using enough to make a suitable thickness of stem. Take silver wire down to the ends of all wires to hold them tightly together. Bind down over the wires with crepe paper from just below the flower.

Cut a narrow strip of green crinkle paper and twist down the stem, over the crepe paper. Then shape the petals by running your fingers along the wire in the centre of the bracts.

If you wish to add leaves to the stem, cut them out from green crepe paper exactly as you would do for the red bracts, and bind these on to the stem, placing them in naturally.

Festival Tree

You will need:

3 pieces of artificial hemlock (a type of conifer tree) or similar
Thick florists wire
Crepe paper
Crinkle paper
Plaster of Paris or cellulose filler
Small pieces of artificial holly (or similar) to decorate base
Glitter
Cotton wool
Assorted Christmas decorations

Cut the hemlock into various sized pieces to represent the branches of a tree. Mount each piece of hemlock on two or three florists wires by twisting the florists wire around the base of the hemlock, and allowing at least 3in (7.5cm) of the wire to hang freely. Cover all the florists wire with strips of crepe paper.

Cut crinkle paper into strips and twist round over the crepe paper, stretching as you twist to make a good firm covering.

Place two pieces of the wired hemlock together, just overlapping at the stem. Join together with a florists wire and cover with crepe paper and crinkle paper. Make up a minimum of three of these double pieces.

Figure 6.3: An artificial festival tree for Christmas

Begin to put the tree together using the smaller single pieces towards the top. Join in each branch with a wire, then cover the wire and all stems with crepe and crinkle paper. Work down and round the main stem gradually using longer stems to form a natural shape; bring some movement into the main trunk by bending the wires a little. Continue down and use the double pieces towards the bottom. To get thicker stems towards the main trunk bind in some strips of cotton wool and cover with crepe paper, followed by crinkle paper.

Form the trunk to 2–3in (5–7.5cm) below the lowest branch and then bend the wires at right angles to the trunk so that the tree will balance. Bend the ends of the wires round to form a smaller base.

Make up some Plaster of Paris, cellulose filler or quick-drying cement and set the wire base of the tree into it to make a good 'snow bank'. While the filler is still moist, sprinkle over with glitter and decorate as desired. Leave to set. Decorate the branches with bells or cones, or other small Christmas decorations.

7. WEDDING AND CHURCH DECORATIONS

(See Plates 13 and 14)

I often find that people get carried away when the chance arises and overdo things. I have in mind flower festivals when there are so many arrangements that you cannot see the church and its interior. Every corner, nook and cranny is just overflowing!

Many churches are extremely beautiful, and the flowers that are used within the church should add to this beauty and not detract from it. A few large arrangements will be much better than a lot of small ones, and I would suggest — taking it on an average — that six to eight arrangements will do the job admirably for a normal church.

Let me say, straightaway, that before going into a church and making arrangements to do flowers, it is correct to ask permission first from the vicar. He will immediately put you in the picture, and tell you who is in charge of this aspect of the church. Many churches today have connections with Flower Clubs and Guilds, and these good ladies like to do the flowers themselves. If you have been asked by the bride to do the flowers, there is a reason for it, and you have every right to ask for permission to carry out her wishes.

Once you have the go-ahead, I suggest you meet up with the bride or bride's mother and go through the church making notes, discussing any particular flowers, colours, etc. Start at the altar. Here there will be some rules. Some people allow flowers on the altar, some prefer them to each side. I would never suggest or agree to flowers over the back of the altar, and in a small church perhaps a single group to one side is enough.

I always feel it is a good idea to use the church vases for those flowers on the altar, and to suggest that these arrangements remain in the church after the service until they are ready to be thrown away. Often these vases will be of brass and have narrow necks so only three to four stems of Lily can fit into each — ideal because this is where simplicity comes in. Many altar

frontals have Lilies embroidered into them, and there is nothing better than to follow this guideline.

From a distance these flowers will stand out better than anything else, and can be seen from the back of the church. Mixed colours and fussy arrangements may well be lost at a distance. You can, if necessary, put another container such as a candlecup on top of the church altar vases to get a bigger area in which to arrange the flowers, but I would always leave things well alone, if possible.

The next important area — and this is where the very large groups come in — is at the chancel rails, usually either side of the pulpit and lectern. It is here that a large part of the wedding service takes place, and is the area where your flowers really will be seen by the whole of the church congregation. These groups should be backed well with foliage, so that the true value of all the flowers shows up well. If only a light background is used many of the flowers on the outer area of the vase may be lost. These two arrangements should be a matching pair, with the colouring and flowers linking up with the bridal party. (Remember here that when doing a pair of vases each needs exactly the same materials, so always divide up first so that no mistakes can be made.)

If you are in a small church, perhaps only one group will be needed at the chancel rails, on the opposite side to the one at the altar. Many churches have their own pedestals for this position, but often the vases will not be to your liking for a really large group. If you are not happy, bring in your own equipment (carefully marked) because if the vase is not 'right', you will not achieve the effect you want. This is where a large washbasin or washing-up bowl comes into its own — a large wide area in which to spread the stems and enough room to put in a block of oasis for extra weight at the back, and still have plenty of room for the water. (You should, of course, hide the bowl with your arrangement, but to be on the safe side apply a coat of paint to match the pedestal.) The wrought iron stands available often have a tiny dish in which a block of oasis just fits, and this is out of the question for a long-lasting, large group.

Arrange the flowers in exactly the same way as you did your small groups in the house. Aim to have fairly long stems on everything because you cannot achieve flowing lines with short pieces of foliage stuck up in tubes. Remember when doing groups here that the lectern and pulpit will be used on occasions around the time of the wedding, if not during the service itself, and room must be left for easy access to both. Although the florist is trying to put on a big show, the vicar may not be too happy if barred from his territory!

The next area for a pair of vases, but on a much smaller scale, is just at the start of the aisle, in the main body of the church. The same style and flowers will be perfect, but the vases will need to be more of an all-round shape as the arrangements will also be seen when coming out of the church.

An attractive group in the entrance to the church is welcoming, and may be prominent in photographs taken around the porch after the service. Sometimes a hanging basket can be a feature in the porch. On occasions photographs will be taken in the vestry, and a small table bowl may add to the picture.

This amount of flowers will usually suffice — just make the groups the correct size for the church in question. However, if it is a very large wedding, window vases will give more colour to the body of the church, and are in ideal positions for all to see. The important point to remember here is to use low containers, well weighted and secured to the back of the sill, so that as the flowers open they do not throw the weight forward and tip over. When arranging these I would go right to the back of the vase with the outline flowers. Remember too, it is not a Flower Festival, so do not put flowers on the pulpit and lectern.

Another place which can often benefit from flowers is at the back of the church — that area so often used for collecting items that are not in regular use, resulting in organised untidiness. A pedestal vase here shows up well as the guests leave, and makes a nice finish to the service.

You may be requested for flowers on the font — this may be a good position, but do remember that they must not be *in* the font. They must be able to be moved easily if a christening is to take place before the arrangements are cleared from the church.

Pew ends can be extremely pretty, but must be the correct size and not look too overpowering (see Plate 15). They should be fixed to each or alternate pews, or may be even every third pew end. Sometimes you will find they are only at the front of the church, and this looks rather odd — it is better to spread them out evenly along the whole bank of pews.

Difficulty arises when it comes to fixing them because in no way should the woodwork be defaced. They are best made on a block of damp oasis covered with silver paper, or in a round oasis tray. Small holes may be burnt into the plastic through which to thread a cord to hang them by. Bows and ribbon tails will add to the attraction of these and fill up the area without adding weight.

I have seen pew decorations used many times, even graded in colour from white at the altar coming right through cream, apricot to deep red at the back of the church, but this to my mind was overdone. They should be in keeping with the bridal flowers and colours, and be simply arranged. Of course, they can be just natural bunches or posies, but with everything to get done for the wedding, any flowers that can be started earlier in water or oasis with no fear of their wilting, are a great help.

I always like to feel that the flowers remain in the church until they die, but this does mean a visit to clear them later in the next week. Sometimes arrangements can be made for the vases not belonging to the church to be returned to you, but you must set a deadline, otherwise when more jobs come in you have nothing of the right shape or size with which to work. How often people promise to return the vases by a certain time, but in the end excuses are made and you may still have to go and fetch them yourself.

Sometimes your customer will ask for the flowers to be cleared and arranged back at the home, or may request that they be sent to friends/relatives absent from the wedding ceremony. This is a service which does require extra cash payment, and you will have to box the flowers to make them look attractive.

It is not advisable to be seen taking the flowers away straight after a wedding. You may get a name for hiring, or taking the flowers back for selling again! Never agree to remove arranged vases from the church to enable them to be used at the reception. It is almost impossible to get them out of the church and away in time. Even if there is the time available, they never really travel well. If they do not look good at the next function, they are no credit to you.

Remember, when discussing flowers, to make notes of any real likes and dislikes. Also note the water supply, and — nearer the time — see that you are aware of any services taking place when you are hoping to do the work.

If possible, talk to the flower lady and let her know you will wire-up any vases you use — thus avoiding the embarrassing situation that I experienced one day.

On that occasion I had agreed to use the vases in a particular church — it was in Northamptonshire — and I suggested that if I left London early, I could do it all myself, going on into Warwickshire for the weekend, and I would clear the necessary vases on the way back on the Monday. When I reached the church, the flower lady came up to me all smiles saying, 'I have washed all the vases and put new netting in for you.' However, she had used the very small mesh. As I was working with stripped Lime, Lilies, Delphiniums and Paeonies, you can just imagine my thoughts with all those thick stems. To her dismay, it all had to come out!

I am not a lover of garlanding. It has to be very well done to look really good. It is expensive on time and material, and can fade so quickly, and furthermore you have the problem of fixing it up in some places. So often people suggest using it to hide something when, in fact, it seems to make whatever it is you want to hide more prominent. I remember on one occasion having to fix garlands to the main columns in the aisle of St Margaret's, Westminster — a beautiful church. None of the columns are exactly the same size, and when garlanded this was more noticeable.

With garlands it is imperative that the distance between each twist is exactly the same. To get this right, drop a piece of string as a plumb line, marked out with tape in equidistant lengths, both sides of the column, but half a step up on one side to get the drop on the garland. In theory, by doing this to each one they should be the same.

Figure 7.1: Decorating the poles for a Jewish wedding canopy. Foliage at the top and another at the base (not shown), with three posies/ribbons evenly spaced between

Jewish Weddings

Jewish weddings and synagogue decorations differ very slightly from those of other denominations. The layout of the synagogue follows a set pattern, and all appear much more modern in their furnishings and interior design than some of the older Christian churches. Colours may be a problem.

It is the canopy (chuppah) that is different, and as this is the focal point of the wedding service, it needs particular attention. It may well be very ornate, or can be quite simple, but always consists of four pillars and an awning. I have seen it with a complete flower cover, with bunches of flowers at each corner and with no flowers at the top at all, but some decoration on the poles seems to be a must. These uprights can be wrapped round with a garland of flowers or have Smilax twined round them with flowers tucked in at regular intervals.

One arrangement that I have in mind, and would like to suggest, was done simply with bunches of spring flowers on a rather 'trellis-like' structure for the canopy supports. (You could have a narrow trellis in white to tie to each pole, if you wanted a change from the normal brass pole effect.) At the top and bottom we just tied small posies of mixed greens, Ivy trails, Ivy berries, variegated Box and Laurustinus. Three mixed bunches of spring flowers in different Narcissi and spray Carnations in white, cream colourings with Ivy foliage and berries were tied to the centre area. Once fixed to the poles, they were tied at the front with a white wired ribbon bow, and the back of each bow had a cluster of ribbon ends of different lengths to finish off and hide the mechanics. The same applied for the green bunches at the top and bottom.

The whole effect was most pleasing, very quick to do, and the flowers (as tied bunches) had been in water right up to going into the synagogue. They took little time to make, and no extra material was needed.

Flowers In A Marquee

It is great fun to hold your party within your own property, and a marquee can give you the extra room required. There are certain areas that you can decorate, but, remembering the low ceiling level at the sides, it is better to get your main flowers to the centre. These flowers can either hang from centre points between the poles, or from special half baskets fitted to the poles. If you are having chandeliers for lighting, the latter is your only place. Do not garland the poles, but cover them in the same material used as a lining to the tenting, and fix the flowers up high so that everyone can see them.

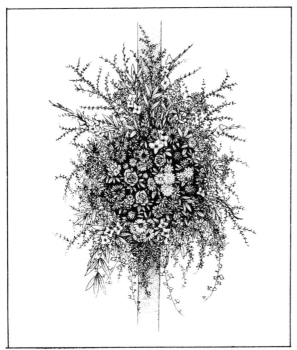

Figure 7.2: Flowers for a marquee — in a half basket fitted on a tent pole

When using hanging baskets it is of the utmost importance to get the necessary chain or cord with loops fitted before the marquee goes up — otherwise there is nothing to hang the basket from; a line across from pole to pole looks as if you have borrowed the washing-line! Make your arrangement down at table level resting the basket in a bucket, and then use meat hooks for quick hanging.

Individual table vases are usually lost once the marquee is filled with people, and there is little room for them on the small tables. For proper sit-down occasions, a few table centres can still be used, together with those up high. Extra colour can be obtained by hanging more half baskets, or lanterns, round the inside of the marquee — get them up as high as you can, and allow the flowers and foliages to flow from the container.

If the function is taking place during the day and the weather is warm and sunny, then one side of the marquee may be opened to bring the garden into the picture. The flowers round the sides can still remain, but a rapid backing operation may be necessary to hide the mechanics. The entrance to the marquee from the house may also need a little decorating, but this will depend on its length — if short, flowers may be seen through the tunnel, and then nothing will be necessary.

If there is a buffet table, flowers may well be included and these should be fairly high up above the food level. An ideal vase for this is a large meat cover, inverted and set in a stand (see Plate 16). Sometimes a cake table will be set up in the marquee and this can be a pretty feature. Make a real flower cake top, and here I do agree that garlanding hanging in loops from the table side looks attractive, with perhaps a thick band of flowers round the cake base.

Large groups on pedestals are not easy to do — so often the height is not enough to get the proportions correct, and even then you may take up a lot of floor space getting the groups set either side of the cake table. If groups it has to be, do see that the bases on which they are to stand are really firm and level.

Trees In Tubs

Topiary work, such as flower trees in tubs, also looks good in marquees.

These can be made up from just foliage, or foliage and flowers when they take on a much more interesting form. They are also excellent for Christmas time in mixed Christmas foliages with berries and red ribbons.

How to make trees in tubs
You will need good 8–10in (20–25cm) pots for the bases — they must be large enough to be heavy, so that they are really stable standing firmly on the ground with little chance of falling over. Line these pots with brown paper and set in one tree trunk or broomstick 3ft 6in–4ft (1–1.2m) high in the centre of each pot. Use quick-drying cement to form a ball of 'soil' which can then be dropped in any container of

Figure 7.3: A flower tree in a tub

the correct size. If you do not line the pots with paper you will find the cement expands and will certainly crack clay pots. You can use Plaster of Paris, but this is not so heavy and the trees are more likely to fall over.

The broomstick should be painted green and then bound with ribbon to suit the colours of the occasion. When dry, add a little soil, peat or gravel to the top of the pot. On to the top of the pole bind a good ball of well-teased moss. This should be fixed firmly and when bound on be the size of a ball approximately 5–6in (12.5–15cm) in diameter. Some people use oasis holders, but I find I get a better shape with a round sphere of moss. A round ball of oasis is good, but expensive. If you are using oasis, it is useful to put wire netting over the sphere to give more strength and support. Fix the netting to the top of the pole for security.

Into this you set your double legged mounts of foliages first and then your flowers which are wired down and mounted. (See Floristry Terms, p. 71.) Trees of white, pink or yellow single daisy Chrysanthemums with pretty bows and ribbon tails look charming for the entrance to the marquee at a wedding reception or at a party. They, of course, can also be used inside.

For small table decorations you can do similar arrangements. Place a block of oasis sec into your vase

— either cylinder or square-shaped tubs are ideal. Set a piece of dowling bound with ribbon into this for the stem. On to the top of the stem fix a block of wet oasis and into this place Rose stems with extra foliage to hide the oasis — you will have charming 'Rose trees' which last well. 'Carol', 'Cecile Brunner', 'Iceberg' or the small old-fashioned roses look most attractive. Use a ribbon for bows and tails which blends with the Rose colour.

Swags

Often students mix up these with the term garlands, but there is a very big difference. Swags are made on a frame, whereas garlands are on a string or rope. The modern way to make a garland is to use a length of oasis-filled plastic tube in the form of a string of sausages. The stems are pushed in through the cover and remain moist in the soaked oasis.

For a small swag often wire netting shaped to the correct pattern will suffice, but any really big structure will have to be made on a proper iron framework to stand the weight. The frame is then mossed with ordinary sphagnum moss. Cover the frame with shaped pieces of wire netting to hold the moss in place, and back the frame with plastic sheeting. Swags are normally only seen from the front and sides. The work will be done in exactly the same way as you would do wreath work, keeping the shape of the frame carefully, and getting fullness and depth to the work in the widest part. First pin on the foliage to achieve the green background and then secure the flowers on to this base.

When we were asked to do the flowers in the Royal Opera House, Covent Garden, for the 'Entry into Europe' in 1973, we had to have frames made to fit between the light brackets around each of the tiers. These had to last some weeks and were made of artificial roses and foliage. When completed they were very heavy — I cannot think what fresh material would have weighed. Probably the most difficult part was treating everything with fire-proofing, drying all the material and getting the swags to the job. We had to hire a large furniture van and carry them to the theatre hanging on meat hooks from the roof. Another difficulty was having to do the work through the night because there was no break in the theatre programme, so it was a case of in after the evening performance when the last theatre-goers had left. It was great fun but you must be able — if you are asked to do these 'one-off' jobs — to muster extra help and be a good organiser. Time is a great problem, and also finding the room to work as close by as possible. There can be no mistakes, and everything must run smoothly.

Just one word of warning when working with swags. It is important that the moss or oasis base is well soaked, but that it is not too wet. Here is a true story of what happened many years ago when Spry's had to decorate all the tiers at the Opera House for a Gala Performance.

The swags (made especially to fit between each light bracket) were mossed and watered well in advance. Fixing the fresh flowers naturally had to be done at the last moment. Well, the apprentices had been so well schooled into seeing that everything was moist before leaving the premises, that they had damped down the swags again before fixing the fresh materials. The swags seemed fine, but once in position in the Opera House they started to drip down muddy water on to the seats below! Nothing could stop it — the weight of the flowers seemed to press on the moss

and it was as if someone was squeezing a sponge. Frantic mopping up followed; rolls of cellulose wool, then used for keeping bouquets moist in transit, and tissue paper, were called for, and quickly wedged behind and under the swags. The trouble with this material was that when really full of water it would drop 'plonk' like a custard tart to the floor below! Imagine a tiara below suddenly covered in a great swathe of wet cellulose wool! Luckily the trouble stopped just in time, and the surplus water was held by the wool swabs fixed at the last moment. I mention this incident because you learn from mistakes, and this really taught us a lesson.

The last very big job involving garlanding was the ropes of artificial flowers and real foliage used in Parliament Square when HRH Princess Margaret was married in 1961. All the poles — standing some 30ft (9m) high, bearing gold crowns at their top — and there were many of them — had at their base about 6ft (1.8m) from the ground large platforms on which were planted real Hydrangea, Genista and Ivies. From three equal points around the perimeter of each platform right up to the crown base were ropes of flowers and foliage, and a wider rope was wrapped around the centre pole.

Cake Top

A fresh flower cake top should be light and dainty, and pick up the colourings of the bridal party, or just be in greens and white when it will go with anything.

This is where the much maligned silver trumpet vase comes into its own in a miniature form (see Plate 17). If you do not have a silver one available, a liqueur or small upright sherry glass filled with cellulose wool will be suitable. I prefer to see the flowers up a little above the cake from choice, rather than when they appear as a small posy pad right down on the cake top. When a posy pad is used, however, the base can be a ball of moss or oasis covered in silver paper.

Proportion is extremely important, and it must be correct to look smart. If too small the cake top will look miserable, and if too large and flat on the top the whole elegance will be lost. If you are using oasis or moss, although covered in silver paper, I would still suggest you put a disc of polythene or wax paper under them.

You do see just a few stems of Freesia, for example, standing in a small vase on the top tier, and that is far better than the plaster 'bride and groom' or horseshoe that so often come as a top to the cake, but to look

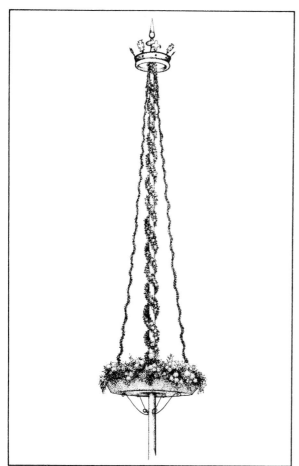

Figure 7.4: Garlanding of central pole and supports

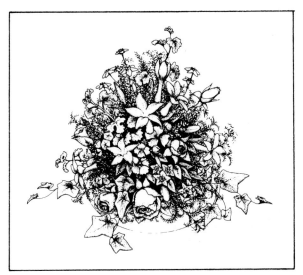

Figure 7.5: A cake top posy pad made on oasis. Small flowers have been used, including Hoya, Stephanotis, Rose buds, Ivy, Geranium and Hydrangea

really special the cake top should be properly wired. Each piece is wired up very carefully with the lightest possible wires, and then made as you would do a loose posy bouquet; when it stands upright in the vase, however, the sides are pulled down to get a nice flow over the vase edge. Remember to allow a few more flowers to fill the gaps that may well occur towards the centre when the outline flowers droop over the sides. Some containers do have a special fitting to go into the icing. See that this is given to the people doing the cake so that the necessary hole can be made at the time. The florist should not have to be responsible for this. There are often a few pieces left over from doing the bouquets and sprays, etc., so to be able to use them on the cake top avoids waste and, what is more important, gives a better return on the money spent at the market!

When using the little pad of oasis, mount any natural stems on 24 gauge × 7in (.56 × 180mm) wire, and the pieces which have already been sprayed up can be just pushed into the oasis to hold them in position (see method on p. 81). Everything must be light and open in appearance; there's nothing worse than an overcrowded mass of colour just sitting on top of the cake. Sometimes, trails of flowers are arranged to flow from the top of the cake down the sides; this, to my way of thinking, spoils the shape of the cake and makes everything look too heavy. The flowers can be bound on to a length of baby ribbon to make the trails, or on a fine silk cord, or again on a wire working exactly in the same way as described for a baby's all-round headdress (see p. 98).

If trails of flowers are required, I prefer to see them as a thicker garland round the base of the cakestand pinned to the cake tablecloth in loops caught up with posies at each point where it drops from the table edge.

Many florists work in conjunction with caterers, and there may be a special table on which to stand the cake with a number of different round cloths to give the desired effect and colour range.

Be prepared for the unexpected — you may be asked to use a special container such as a christening mug or old salt cellar to go on the top of the cake. I am sure that you will manage it, but for preference I still go back to the elegance of a vase on some sort of a foot because this lifts the flowers up higher and gives a lighter effect to the top of the cake.

Font Decoration

This is often referred to as a font top. These decorations are used for christenings and at other festivals such as Easter, Christmas, etc. The font is an ideal area to decorate, usually showing to good advantage as people pass through the church (see Plate 18). Let us consider it in the light of a commercial order and imagine that we are decorating for a christening. The other times are usually taken over by the flower ladies of the church.

Now the most important point to remember is that the font itself will be used, so nothing must cover the top. For ordinary decorations you may use the base and perhaps stand a big arrangement on the top of the font (rather using it as a pedestal for a large all-round arrangement). Never arrange flowers in the font itself, unless you are resting a bowl inside to hold the flowers which can be moved easily.

The first way to deal with a decoration of this kind is to make a frame the size of the font top. This is mossed as for a wreath and then covered with foliage or bun moss leaving five bumps on which to secure the flowers. One bump is large, but the other four can be the same size, or two medium and two smaller. The large bump on the frame should be directly opposite to the place where the minister will stand.

For a christening simple flowers are the best to use, and at certain times wild flowers can be quite lovely. White, cream, blues and pinks and mixed pastel can all be used together with Ivy trails, Fern fronds and light foliages. You can work with just five clusters or posies on the top of the frame, but usually, if there is room, have the large group coming down off the frame and trailing down to the base of the font, rather like a large pew end in shape. Much will depend on the style of the font. Some churches have their own special fitting, and it may only be necessary to place a few flowers in small containers, while others will have to be wired to make them stay in the correct positions. What is so important, and can easily be forgotten, is that the font itself is required for the service, and should not be completely hidden with masses of trailing foliages and flowers.

If the decoration has to be wired, try to see that as much as possible is done internally so that the finish will look natural. Small flowers supported by thick wires make for a stiff and unnatural look.

Figure 7.6: Flowers for a new baby, arranged in a cradle

Keeping Wedding Flowers And All Made-up Work

There is no doubt in my mind that having a coldstore is a very great asset. The cost of installation may appear high, but over the years there should be a very great saving on flower purchasing. Flowers take up a fair amount of room, but they must be put somewhere, and at least it does mean all flowers (or the majority of your flower stock) can be kept in a set place. In fact, a coldstore provides the ideal conditions for holding the flowers so that their development is slowed up. A few flowers (Gentians, for instance) should not be kept in the coldstore, however, because once they close up, they do not seem to open again.

Flowers made up into bouquets or wreaths should be covered with a fine film of moisture then a thin cover of cellulose wool, or tissue paper, which is again

damped, and this should remain moist all the time. They can be boxed down and stacked in the coldstore without coming to any harm — in fact, they are better like this. Bouquets can be started, or rather the foliage pieces may be wired up, two days before they are needed. Just wire up and mount into sprays. Place these between layers of moist tissue, or on moist cellulose wadding, and box down. They will be perfect when required. This does mean that you can get ahead with work, evening out the pressure and not leaving everything to the last moment. Of course, some flowers should not be damped overhead, and some Narcissi and Sweet Peas are examples where the petals go papery and are soon useless.

It is important to keep the materials in strict order of purchase, and see that old stock is brought forward to the front for use first. Keep the coldstore clean and tidy, and do not put infected materials away for storage. Botrytis (grey mould fungus) or Tulip fire (spot) will slowly spread if it gets a hold in the store. The only disadvantage that I can think of with having a coldroom is the noise from the motor, but you may be able to site this away from the working area.

Tinted Flowers In Bouquets

Occasionally, you may be requested to 'tint' flowers to get a special colour effect. This is done by dusting the 'dry' petal surface with a powder containing a dye — applied with a fine paint brush. If this has to be done, there can be no spraying overhead or placing the treated flowers in a damp place, because the powder will pick up the moisture and the colour will run. Never do this from choice — it causes problems!

8. POT PLANTS FOR DECORATION

The use of indoor plants for room decoration has been popular for many years, but it has grown by leaps and bounds during the last few years. While the traditional flowering pot plants — Cyclamen, Azalea, Hydrangea, Heathers and others — are still very popular, we have been given a much wider choice by the large-scale cultivation of evergreen plants.

Collectively these are known as House Plants because they are tolerant of indoor conditions, and are easy to look after in most cases if certain guidelines are followed. Remember, plants are alive and are sensitive to environments. They are not just ornaments in a room requiring occasional dusting; they are living material.

House Plants

For permanent effect, foliage plants with smooth, fairly thick leaves are generally the most satisfactory. Softer plants (e.g. Coleus) and flowering plants may also be used for temporary colour effect in their season.

The placing of plants in rooms calls for careful consideration. Windows facing north, east and west uncurtained by day throughout the year are suitable, also south-facing windows lightly curtained during the brightest hours of summer days. Plants with green foliage should be used for north windows. Few plants will tolerate the poor light conditions in the interior of normal rooms, but some may be grown there if large windows exist on two or three sides of a room. Fluorescent lighting has been used successfully to provide light during normal daylight hours. No plant should be stood directly over a radiator of any type without the insulation of a 'moisture tray'.

'House plants' sent to market and sold through retail shops have been grown in greenhouses, and care is necessary in acclimatising them to room conditions. In order that plants should suffer as little as possible, the best time to buy is from the end of May until the end of August when conditions during transport and in markets and shops are nearer the original growing conditions than at other times. This, of course, cannot happen, and they are wanted all the year round. Plants selected should be sturdy, without drawn straggling growths, and furnished with healthy leaves to the base.

Many plants may be grown in unheated rooms if established in them before winter, e.g. Hedera, Ficus pumila, Saxifraga sarmentosa. Many more may be grown in rooms which can be kept a few degrees above freezing point — e.g. Begonia rex, Tradescantia, Maranta — while the range of plants which is successful in centrally heated rooms is limited only by the minimum temperature which is maintained during cold spells. Whatever the room conditions, windows should be heavily curtained at night during cold spells. The temperature in all cases should be kept as even as possible, allowing a rise of a few degrees during daylight.

The main causes of ill-health and death of pot plants are:

(a) faulty watering
(b) draughts and other bad atmospheric conditions
(c) damage caused by insects, pests and diseases.

A plant should not be given water at the roots until the soil is almost dry. The old method of ascertaining this is to tap the pot with a stout stick or small metal rod. A ringing sound indicates that the plant needs water, a dull one that the soil is moist. For this test it is essential that the pot should not be cracked. However, today with nearly all plants in plastic pots, the test has to be visual (by colour), by weight and the look of the plant. Water should be supplied either from the spout of a watering can or a jug, completely filling the space between the soil and the top of the pot, or by immersing the pot to the rim in water until the soil surface is moist all over. With the exception of one or two plants — e.g. Cyperus, which appreciate boggy conditions —

pot plants should never be stood permanently in water containers. Water will be needed more often when plants are growing freely in hot, bright weather than in the autumn and winter when the soil should be kept on the dry side.

Draughts should be avoided, especially when outside temperatures are low. Ideally, windows as well as doors should be fitted with draught excluders. Windows should not be left open when winds are high, or when the outside temperature is considerably below that of the room.

The atmosphere in a normal house is too dry for really healthy plant growth. Pots should be stood, if possible, on trays of sand, gravel, weathered ash or moss kept moist in dry weather, and when fires are burning in the room. This is essential where central heating is installed.

Fumes from gas appliances are injurious to most plants, and rooms with gas fires are usually unsuitable for pot plants. Where gas is used for cooking, the kitchen door should be kept closed as much as possible when the cooker is in use to prevent the spread of fumes. Atmospheric pollution in some areas often makes for extreme difficulty of cultivation, and frequent spraying or sponging of the foliage is necessary. The most effective cleanser is probably a white oil insecticide.

The most useful insecticide for keeping plants free from pests is liquid derris, plants being either sprayed or dipped. Mildew on foliage plants can be controlled by spraying or dipping in a solution of $\frac{1}{4}$oz (7g) of washing soda in one gallon of water.

When plants have filled their pots with roots, they will need to be moved into pots one size larger. John Innes Potting Compost is a suitable potting medium, and potting-on should not be done in winter.

When in active growth plants will benefit by feeding once a fortnight with a complete fertiliser such as John Innes Liquid Feed. Care should be taken with leaf cleaning sprays; they can block the breathing pores if used in excess. Try to keep the temperature from fluctuating too much; and we are told today that it helps if you talk to your plants (Jock Davidson of Thomas Rochford Limited is a great believer in this therapy).

The following is a short list of suitable plants, which may be obtained from reputable florists:

Aphelandra squarrosa 'Louisae'
Begonia in variety
Bilbergia in variety
Chlorophytum capense variegatum

Cissus in variety
'Crotons' (Codiaeum)
Cyperus diffusus
Elettaria cardamomum
Fatshedera lizei
Fatsia japonica
Ficus in variety
'Ivy' (Hedera) in variety
Maranta in variety
Monstera deliciosa
Neanthe bella
Pellionia in variety
Peperomia in variety
Philodendron in variety
Pilea in variety
Rhoicissus rhomboidea
Sansevieria in variety
Saxifraga sarmentosa
Scindapsus in variety
Spathiphyllum vallisii
Tradescantia in variety

I came across this poem when looking through some books on horticulture and flower arranging, and it amused me. I believe it does cover many important points.

House Plants

You take us from our habitat in countries far
    remote.
You bring us to your chilly isles by aeroplane or
    boat.
Ferns from humid forests, and cacti from hot
    plains,
Orchids from the tropics where fall the heavy
    rains,
Alpines from the mountain tops among the
    melting snow,
Little sapling conifers from rocky slopes below.

You transport us to your nurseries, and put us
    under glass.
In rows of little plastic pots, where people as they
    pass
Can gaze at us with interest, while experts who
    are able,
Discuss our Latin names and print them neatly on
    the label.
You buy us for your homes — but with no
    knowledge what to do,
You plant us in a substance called John Innes
    number two.

In your rooms with central heating, the Alpines
    are kept hot.
The Orchids from a warmer clime are in a
    draughty spot.
You are mystified and worried if our green leaves
    fail to grow,
So you water us and water us, until we overflow.
You give us weekly doses of a thing called liquid
    feed,
And chase off phantom aphids with sprays we do
    not need.

You leave us in the sunshine, when all we want is
    shade,
We're a disappointment to you if our flowers
    droop and fade.
But down below, our rootlets, in Wedgwood bowl
    confined
Are longing for the freedom of the soil they left
    behind.
We are not botanic specimens, but plants of God's
    creation.
Designed to be a part of this world's natural
    vegetation.

But a few of you are gardeners, who treat us with
    respect.
For you we blossom freely, and hold our heads
    erect.
Poinsettia and Cyclamen relieve your winter
    gloom.
Streptocarpus and Saintpaulias will brighten up
    your room.
You supply our needs and treat us as if we are
    your friends.
For you alone, the pleasure which we bring you,
    never ends.

(By kind permission from *Poems for Everyone* by
Dorothy A. Wise, published 1982 by Arthur H.
Stockwell Limited, Ilfracombe.)

Plate Or Dish Gardens

Extremely popular, these are a good way for florists to
sell both flowering and foliage plants during the
period from December through to April. At this time
of the year many of the smaller plants are about, and
together with bulbs and small flowering shrubs, they
work in well together to make an 'arrangement'. The
rest of the year plants in flower are normally too large,

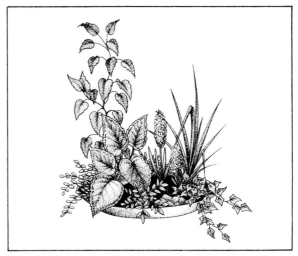

*Figure 8.1: A garden on a plate, including Cissus, Hyacinth,
Ivy, Sedum, Begonia rex and Chlorophytum*

but mixed foliage and ferns can be used.

    Shallow, oblong troughs, old meat dishes (espe-
cially those with a well area for fat), round flat dishes
and large plates are all good for planting. Plastic cat-
trays also serve a useful purpose. I have often smiled
to myself when a shop order has come down to the
workroom for a 'sweet smelling cat-tray' — I know
exactly what the assistant meant, but it is difficult to
put it over to the customer! It is a good idea to have
your container on little raised feet to stop any damp-
ness on the base from condensation. I would always
recommend they stand on some form of mat.

    These decorations usually look best on a low coffee
table, and make a point of interest in a room. Think of
them as a flower decoration and plan them carefully,
bearing in mind colour, shape of leaves, height of
plant and habit. When they are made up in all mixed
greens, they may last for a long time if carefully handled; but if you have, for instance, flowering bulbs,
these will have to be changed all the time to keep the
'garden' going.

Making your plate or dish garden
This is what you will need:

(1)   One fairly large dish or plate (it needs to be able
to hold seven to nine different plants to look
interesting).
(2)   If deep enough, a little broken crock at the base
and some pieces of charcoal will help to keep the soil
sweet.
(3)   Good compost — John Innes No. 1 is the best to
use — not soil out of the garden (see p. 62).

(4) Interesting pieces of shaped rock or stone. Cork bark from the Spanish Cork Oak. Shingle. Moss. Slate and Gravel, and maybe a branch or two covered in Lichen.

Never use artificially coloured gravel or white marble chips. The addition of one or two Japanese ornaments, such as shrines and temples, needs to be done with care and imagination. If you want to have a pool, a piece of clean glass over moss looks much better than an old broken mirror, but do remember that it normally should be placed at a fairly low level in the container.

(5) Flowering plants — such as Iris reticulata and other small ones. Hyacinths. Miniature and small-flowered Daffodils. Primulas in different types. Polyanthus. Azalea. Dwarf Tulips and Crocus. For special occasions maybe a pot of forced Lily of the Valley. Small Cyclamen. Foliage plants such as Ivies, Begonias, Peperomia, Sedum, Cissus antarctica, Chlorophytum, and you can also do similar ones in Cacti and succulents.

These are just a few of the plants from which you can choose. Remember, those that grow too vigorously or are too temperamental are best left out, or grown on their own.

First, see that your container is watertight and not cracked — when filled it will be quite heavy, and a crack could give under strain.

Place the gravel, crocks and charcoal pieces on the base of the dish, then a layer of good compost. This should be just moist enough to hold its shape when squeezed in the hand.

On the previous day you should have well soaked the plants you are going to use. After knocking them out of their pots, mould the 'ball' of soil carefully to fit into the container. Open up the root run a little, especially if they are a little pot bound. Stand the plants in position keeping the taller plants to the back of the dish for a facing arrangement, and to the centre if to be seen from all round. See that the plants stand well — in other words, get a nice, flat base to the ball of soil. Pack round more compost, and make sure that it is firm. Do not overcrowd — allow them room to spread a little, and a breathing space. Now fix in the larger pieces of stone to add interest. A little more soil may be needed perhaps, and then a little tap on each side of the dish to settle the soil well. Now add the gravel, slate, moss, etc. Do not finish up with a great mound of soil that looks as if you have buried the cat under it! It should not be flat, but have interesting contours. One or two patches of gravel are good as watering spots — moss tends to dry out and then the water

runs off, if you are not careful. Keep the garden fairly moist, spray over from time to time, and allow plenty of light and an even temperature of about 55–60°F (13–15°C). The temperature can rise a little with the light intensity. Remove dead leaves as they occur and prune back any long weak growths. See to staking when necessary. Flowering and bulbous plants should be lifted carefully from the dish and replaced by others of the same pot size.

Hanging Baskets

These are quite popular as a form of decoration — using growing plants when they are required for a long period, and cut flowers and foliages when it is just for a special event, such as a wedding party or a dress show in a marquee.

Plants and cut materials

It is a good idea to arrange the basket at the height from which it will be seen. If you have good curving branches which, of course, are ideal, you can arrange them in a bowl placed within the basket. I would suggest you have a block of oasis in the base, and wire netting on the top. If your material is shorter, then you may have to work with a couple of blocks of oasis, just resting on a shallow saucer to prevent drips of water falling to the floor surface. The stems are then stuck in at all angles around the basket, but it is more difficult to get elegant shapes and flowing lines. I know some people work with blocks of oasis wrapped in tin foil or placed in a polythene bag, but I prefer the method I have suggested. Simplicity is really the key to success. Plenty of colourful daisy-type flowers and grasses with light foliage look well, or branches of Rambler Roses just on their own. Certainly garden-type flowers are needed.

If you are working within a marquee, you must consider the lining colour when choosing flower colours. The baskets when purchased are normally painted green, but a coat of white paint may make them more attractive when used with cut materials. Remember also to paint the meat hook and chain from which the basket hangs.

Planting a hanging basket

First hang the basket at a convenient height at which to work. The ordinary wire baskets are much more pleasing than the plastic ones with saucers attached, but they do need more attention as they dry out more quickly.

You will need good, fresh carpet or bun moss to line the basket — working from the base up towards the rim. The moss is placed top facing the wire bands, that is, facing outwards. Press so that the wire cuts into the moss, and do not leave any gaps. Fill up to about half way with good moist compost. Now fit a collar of metal about 1in (2.5cm) wide round the top of the basket. It is now time to introduce your plants.

Depending on the size of the basket, the number of pots will vary. You will need something tall for the middle, then three plants around the centre one, and then another row of maybe five or six round the outside area, which will trail over the basket rim. All the pots should have been well watered before planting. Place compost round the ball of roots and press firmly with your fingers. The compost should be in excellent condition and just fill all the space between the root balls. Fill with compost up to the metal collar in the basket. This acts as a water retainer when the plants are established, and the soil has firmed up. Without it, when watering overhead, the water just runs off the surface. A collar makes a false rim to retain 1in (2.5cm) of water which runs through the basket rather than off it, and it avoids your having to bring the basket up and down to soak it in a large bowl. It also saves the plants from getting damaged in doing so.

Once planted up, it pays to leave the basket in a cool greenhouse for a few days to become established. Spray overhead and keep the moss really moist, but do not over-water at this stage — encourage the roots to leave the balls of soil in search of moisture in the new compost.

For a quicker display, you can plant up the sides of the basket as well as the top. This is how you can do it.

Put a layer of moss in the base of the basket and up the sides for an inch or two (2.5–5cm). Fill this area with compost, then place through the wire from the outside some plant material, rooted well but washed so that the soil is nearly gone. Plants ideal for this are Ivy, Lobelia, Tradescantia, Ivy Leaf Geranium and Petunia — you need something which trails naturally.

Lay out the roots carefully over the compost. Now follow with another band of green moss round the basket, then more compost. Follow this with another row of rooted plants — between the first row, but 2in (5cm) above. Now add a little more compost, then plant up as before. This just means that the trailing plants have got a start and you should, with luck, achieve more colour from a given area early on in the season.

Treat your hanging baskets as you do any decoration, and remember colour, shape of leaf, different height and habit of the plants, so that you may work in to an overall scheme.

Hanging baskets can be used all the year, but they are most successful with summer displays when they should grow rapidly and not be checked in any way. They require feeding regularly once the plants have become established. Remove dead heads all the time — once a plant has set seed, it has fulfilled its purpose in life and tends to die off. By not allowing it to set seed, it keeps on growing and producing flowers.

Watch out for aphids, mildew, slugs and snails, and treat straightaway. Do not allow any weeds to grow — they may appear in the moss of the basket wall.

Baskets can be made of one plant or of a number. Do remember that with luck everything will grow, so allow room for this in your planning and planting. Pinch out trailing plants once they have started to keep them bushy.

If you look after the basket well, you can grow very many different plants in them. I list here a few of the most suitable for every need:

Ageratum	blue
Alyssum	white and mauve
Begonia	
Chlorophytum	
Cineraria maritima	silver foliage
Fuchsia	
Geranium	trailing and upright in many colours
Heliotrope	
Impatiens	
Ivies	
Lobelia	blue in two colours, and white
Marguerite	
Nemesia	
Nepeta	trailing and variegated
Petunia	many shades and sizes
Phlox drummondii	
Salvia	
Tradescantia	

Window Boxes, Tubs And Urns

It is amazing how many people have a window box of some sort or another, but only a few really understand how to look after them and get the greatest value from them.

Let me say straightaway that to do them well can be expensive, with up to six 'plants' per year for maximum colour and interest. To really see window boxes at their best visit Switzerland and Austria — they are magnificent and all colours seem to go well with the wood of the chalet-type homes.

Many so-called window boxes should not be in use. Often you can see them precariously perched up high on a narrow ledge with no form of fixing. My first suggestion is do see that permission has been granted from landlords or architects that the boxes may be safely fixed before you get involved with planting them on a contract basis.

The boxes themselves are important, and should be suited to the building. There is no doubt that the old lead ones, now so valuable, were superb, and they never look out of place. There is no upkeep on these, but you would need a good insurance policy today to cover them!!

Imitation boxes in fibre glass are very long-lasting, but they are light and may need extra weight in the base. Stone is expensive to buy in the first instance, but long-lasting; stone blends in very soon, and looks excellent. Modern-looking boxes in a form of asbestos are also made, but I do not consider they look so pleasing. Wood today is so seldom seasoned, so you will find that the boxes soon become warped. Soft wood rots very quickly; hard wood is longer-lasting. Both would benefit from having a lining, and need regular painting or treating with preservative. Plastic, however well done, I do not find complementary to the plants. The colourings are hard when new, and soon discolour and, with fast-growing plants, pressure from the roots can easily split the containers. You will find all manner of objects used, and I so well remember all the ammunition boxes which we filled with Hydrangea for the decorations along the route at the Coronation. One very important consideration is drainage. No plant will live long in a waterlogged soil, so you must see that there is some form of drainage. Second, you must ensure that the size of the box is large enough to give the effect required — a box 4in (10cm) wide and 6in (15cm) deep is far too small unless you are going to be attending to it every day with water and plant foods. When making boxes, do see that they are made up in units which can be easily handled, otherwise when it comes to the time for emptying them you will have problems.

John Innes Nos. 1 or 2 are ideal composts normally, if you follow up with regular feeding once the plants are established. Aspect is another thing to be borne in mind, and protection from severe wind and cold, or very strong sun for long periods, is something you should think about. In Britain there are not normally extremes of weather conditions to contend with, but I would say that most of the bulbs and permanent plants will stand 0° to −10°F (zone 6) for a few weeks — provided the soil is not too wet.

Planting can be done as a complete change each time or you can, with the use of larger boxes, have some permanent plants and just remove those that are temporary during the season. As with all decoration work, thought must go into the colour scheme, the shape of the foliage, the different heights of plants next to each other, and the use of flowing material over the edge of the box to soften the line. My own window box at home has had the same Ivy plants in it for ten years now; everything is changed regularly, but not all at once. This then does not leave the box without some colour and interest.

When planting up, it is well worth first putting a layer of good crock over the drainage holes, and then some fibre over this before filling up with compost. Today crock is seldom put in a pot — the plant will be potted on so quickly that perhaps it is not worthwhile, and a waste of time when the compost used is open and free draining, but with permanent planting I would always use crock.

It may be a good idea, if you have room and the strength to do it, to have two sets of boxes so that you can get plants established in the garden after planting before you have to put them on display. Bulbs and plants can go back into the garden after a session in the box — only the annuals will be useless. Take cuttings of Fuchsia, Marguerite, etc. and, with the aid of a propagating frame, grow on more plants. It is important as a sales assistant that you are enthusiastic about growing, and that you encourage the customer to try all these ideas.

Try to keep the plants moving. Change the soil every other year unless it is a very small amount when a yearly change would be easy. If you do not change the soil, feed it with a good, general fertiliser and check for acidity — a pH of 6.5 is a good level to aim for overall.

The following would be a guide from which to plan your boxes. Six changes are the minimum if your boxes are always to look good.

Early winter
Plant small conifers and green plants such as Acuba, Euonymus, Ivies and Hebe — these remain during the year. Put Solanum in the front in drifts, or Heathers.

Early spring
Replace the Solanum/Heather with Polyanthus and groups of pot-grown Daffodils or Hyacinths.

Late spring
Plant Cineraria or, in a sheltered spot, pot Hydrangea. Also pot Tulips.

Early summer
Plant a selection from Lobelia, Alyssum, Ageratum, Cineraria maritima, Helichrysum petiolatum, Impatiens, Fuchsia, Petunia, Geranium, Nemesia and Heliotrope.

Late summer
Chrysanthemums in pots.

During the growing period it may be necessary to stake some of the plants neatly. Do this before they fall over because it will keep the boxes neat. Once over, you cannot get them back. If some permanent plants are present, prune back from time to time to keep them in good proportion and shape.

Bulbs

I believe all florists should carry bulbs in small amounts in the autumn. They are always popular, and if the sales assistants know a little about them and are keen on growing things, I am sure that they will sell well. Another point of sale is through containers. A few good bowls, perhaps some glass hyacinth vases, and a number of bags of bulb fibre, all turn over money. These items could make up a window display, together with colourful posters from the Bulb Growers' Association. Do not go in for specialist bulbs, only those suitable for growing in the house, tubs and window boxes. I believe, if you arrange a display of how to go about growing them, you will certainly find an interest.

Constance Spry loved the early bulbs, and I quote from a 'housewife' magazine article, 'There is nothing more enchanting in the dark days of Winter than one of the earliest of Spring's flowers — the fresh, delicately scented Roman Hyacinths which bloom before the larger, fatter more handsome Dutch varieties.' I love them all, but if I had one choice, I should plump for the white Romans. These are essentially flowers for indoor growing.

Regretfully today Roman Hyacinths of good quality are not available, but a lot of work is going on to clean up stocks of bulbs which over the years have been infected with virus diseases. Those who remember them hope that new stock will be available in the years to come.

The 'Paper White' Narcissi were also withdrawn from reputable bulb catalogues for a time, but now they are becoming more readily available in excellent quality. They are grown, I believe, in Israel and if planted in early September flower as early as late October with superb flower spikes. The great secret is to sell only top quality bulbs — you will not have room for lower grades for garden planting and naturalising. The large-flowered Hyacinths should be 'prepared' — this is a special treatment they go through to make them flower early, and naturally this process will cost a little more money.

I would suggest that you only carry prepared Hyacinths, early flowering Narcissi, miniature Narcissi, early Tulips, and of the small bulbs, Crocus, Snowdrops, Iris reticulata, Chionodoxa. As part of your advertising campaign, prepare a small leaflet on how to get the best results from your bulbs. It should be something on the lines of showing how simple all will be if the correct instructions are followed.

Incidentally, if you are buying bulbs in the market yourself, check to see that the outside coat of the bulb is free from fungus, mildew, etc., and that the basal plate of the bulb is firm. Try to get your bulbs planted before any sign of shoot growth appears — if you are late purchasing them, the shoot growth will have started and careless handling can badly damage the growing point.

How to grow bulbs for indoor decoration

1   Select even-sized bulbs, and to be certain that all flowers will come out together, keep to all the same variety in each container. If you wish to have mixed Hyacinths in a large container, grow on in separate pots and plant them up just as they are coming into colour. You can time all different varieties to flower together, but it is difficult and one out can spoil the whole effect. The bulbs should be clean and firm to the touch.

2   Soak your bulb fibre so that it is moist, and then squeeze out any surplus water before filling the bowl, pot or half pan. If you have attractive containers, try to stand the flower pots inside without showing — flower pots have good drainage and will not be damaged by outside conditions whereas fancy containers may be. Otherwise place the bulbs in shallow boxes (3–4in, 7.5–10cm deep) and then plant in containers later, though this, I feel, checks the roots. To allow continuity, start batches into growth every two to three weeks.

3   Place Hyacinths and Narcissi under the compost with just the noses showing. Other bulbs need to be buried deeper (two to three times their depth). The bulbs should be evenly placed in the pans, pots or decorative bowls. In boxes they may be closer, but they should not be touching. As they

will be moved into other containers while growing, they can be given more room later on.

4   All bulbs, once planted in soil or bulb fibre, should undergo a period in the dark and be kept cool for up to nine weeks, so that good root development will take place. The temperature should remain even at somewhere between 35 to 40°F (2 to 4°C). At the end of this period the growing tip to bulb should be about 1in (2.5cm) out of the bulb. If left too long the foliage becomes too elongated and unbalanced growth results.

5   All the containers should be stood out on a level base, be just lightly covered with silver sand, and then completely covered to a depth of 7–8in (17.5–20cm) with damp peat or clean, open soil free from stones and other rubbish, or leaf soil and old ashes. The silver sand will allow the soil to fall away cleanly from the bulbs when the container is tipped, and the fibre below will remain undisturbed. If you have no standing out area available in the garden, a balcony or coalshed floor will be all right, or, better still, a cellar, but do see that the soil covering the bulbs is kept damp. Label everything carefully with the planting dates, so as to be able to identify and bring them on in the correct sequence.

6   Crocuses and Narcissi ('Paper White' and 'Soleil d'Or') will grow well in moist gravel. Half fill your shallow bowl with gravel, then firmly place the bulbs in position and cover up with more gravel. Keep the base of the bowl wet. Bulb glasses, in which to grow individual Hyacinths, are also useful. Stand the bulb on the ridge just above the water level (add a little charcoal to the vase) — and watch the roots grow down into the glass. Leave these containers in a cool shaded place until the flower spike is just through the neck of the bulb. If you buy good fat bulbs they will be full of plant food, so all that they then need is something to hold them in an upright position and moisture for the roots. Always buy new bulbs for growing in water culture and forcing for indoor use. Once they have been forced they are better then planted in the garden to grow on naturally.

7   Bring your bulbs into the light gently, covering them with newspaper for the first day. Check for water and see that they are damp. Gradually increase the temperature and lightly spray overhead. Stake them if you feel it to be necessary — do this before your stems fall over, because they never go back up again properly. You can place little twigs of Hazel Catkins among the Crocus and taller pieces with the Narcissi. As they grow, the buds on the branches will also develop, so you can having living 'trees' for stakes with catkins and small foliage, which can be quite pretty.

8   Another bulb which is worth stocking is the Hippeastrum, commonly known as Amaryllis. Ideal for indoor cultivation, Amaryllis never ceases to amaze people when they grow one. Its large striking flower is long-lasting, and very decorative.

Compost

One of the most important factors in the growing of plants is the soil mixture in which the plants are grown. A good compost should have the following qualities:

1   Correct physical condition so as to ensure good aeration and drainage, and adequate water retention.
2   A sufficient and balanced supply of plant nutrients.
3   Freedom from weeds, pests and diseases.

In the old days every gardener had his own idea about compost, and each crop grown in seed trays and pots had its own special mixture — a great many were secret to the famous old gardens around England, and made up under strict supervision. Today, thanks to the work carried out at the John Innes Horticultural Institute, we have arrived at some standard composts which give good results with the majority of pot plants. There are others, but I think for our purposes we cannot go far wrong by using John Innes No. 1, which is readily available for purchase in sacks and small packets. Remember, it is better to use fresh supplies, so bulk buying is not advisable although, of course, it does have a bearing on the cost.

The composition is as follows:

7 parts sterilised loam
3 parts peat
2 parts sharp sand

Add to each bushel of compost
$\frac{3}{4}$oz (21g) chalk (carbonate of calcium)
4oz (112g) John Innes Base

The base fertiliser is made up by weight of
2 parts hoof and horn meal	13 per cent N
2 parts superphosphate	18 per cent P_2O_5
1 part sulphate of potash	48 per cent K_2O

There are three potting composts — all the same except for the food content. A potting compost containing the above quantity of John Innes Base is known as JIP No. 1. JIP No. 2 contains twice the quantity of John Innes Base (8oz, 228g) and chalk $1\frac{1}{2}$oz, 42g) per bushel, and JIP No. 3 three times the quantity (12oz, 336g) Base and ($2\frac{1}{4}$oz, 64g) chalk.

I would not entertain the idea of mixing your own compost, unless you are using large quantities, as great care must be given to getting the correct main ingredients — loam, peat and sand. However, here are some guidelines should you wish to do so.

Loam

Not every kind of loam is suitable for making composts. It should preferably be of medium-heavy texture, with a pH of 6.3, but if it is more acid, sufficient lime should be added when stacking to bring it up to that figure. It should contain enough phosphates and should be fertile. Limey loams should never be used, nor should extremely acid ones. It is desirable that loam should be stacked, by placing 2in (5cm) (loose) of strawy stable manure between alternate layers of sods. Since all loams contain weed seeds, it is advisable that they should be steam sterilised.

Peat

The peat should be of horticultural quality, either a moss or sedge peat. Fine and dusty ones should be avoided. Bracken peat, which contains silt and sand, is suitable for ericaceous plants, but should not be used in making up composts for the general run of pot plants.

Sand (grit)

The sand should be sufficiently coarse, with particles up to $\frac{1}{8}$in (3mm) in diameter. If it is clean, it need not be sterilised.

Sterilisation of compost

Freedom from pests, diseases and weed seeds is essential for a good seed or potting compost, and this can easily be achieved by following the correct sterilising procedure. The most efficient method is to heat the loam by means of steam. It should be noted that it is the loam alone which requires sterilising. Trouble can be caused by sterilising mixtures of loam and peat, and of loam and fertilisers.

I believe that, after reading these notes, you will decide it is better to purchase the compost ready made, but it is useful to know a little of the work carried out on the preparation of some of these products. The customer who comments on, say, for example 'The high cost of a sack of JIP No. 2' can be politely told a little detail of what goes into making it such a price!

PART TWO

FLORISTRY

9. MATERIALS USED IN FLORISTRY

The wiring of flowers and foliage is a very important factor in floristry. Wiring is essential if the proper shape is to be kept, and if the flowers are to stand up to what is required of them, but care should be taken to avoid over wiring.

Where possible the wiring should be hidden (internal), and the flowers and foliage should remain natural looking. Your flowers, when made up to wear, should look like a beautiful piece of jewellery — they should have movement and be as light as possible.

Wires

Today, with the very haphazard supply of wires available, it is difficult to lay down laws as to what you should use. All I would suggest is that the finest wire that will do the job satisfactorily is the best. You are not *staking* a stem, you should be *just lightly wiring* it down to support it. I believe it would be true to say, except for Christmas decorations, that we seldom use a heavier wire in the school than a 20s.w.g. (0.90mm), and the majority of our mounting wire is 22s.w.g. (0.71mm). Wiring down the stems would be mostly 22 or 24 (0.71mm or 0.56mm). So often I find that very pleasing work is spoilt by unnecessary and too heavy a wire being used. See Table 9.1 for a useful chart, issued by the Institute of Iron and Steel Wire Manufacturers, which shows old and new identification numbers for florists supplies. Remember, the higher the gauge number the finer the wire.

Table 9.1: Metrication of Florists Wire

UNIT OF WEIGHT
Price £X per 25 kg

SIZES

Recommended sizes	Replacing
1.25mm	18s.w.g.
1.00mm	19s.w.g.
0.90mm	20s.w.g.
0.71mm	22s.w.g.
0.56mm	24s.w.g.
0.46mm	26s.w.g.
0.38mm	28s.w.g.
0.32mm	30s.w.g.
0.28mm	32s.w.g.
0.24mm	34s.w.g.
0.20mm	36s.w.g.

LENGTHS

Recommended lengths	Replacing
90mm	3½in
130mm	5in
180mm	7in
230mm	9in
260mm	10in
310mm	12in
360mm	14in
460mm	18in

BUNDLES
Weight per bundle = 2½kg

REELS
125 grams per reel
10 reels per box
20 boxes per 25kg pack

Types of wires

STUB WIRE
20s.w.g. × 10in (0.90mm × 260mm)
20s.w.g. × 7in (0.90mm × 180mm)
Used for mounting wreath work and for wiring down heavy flowers, e.g. large Chrysanthemum blooms.

22s.w.g. × 14in (0.71mm × 360mm)
22s.w.g. × 12in (0.71mm × 310mm)
22s.w.g. × 10in (0.71mm × 260mm)
22s.w.g. × 7in (0.71mm × 180mm)
Used for wiring down medium flowers, e.g. Asters,

Daffodils and some Roses, mounting flowers for bouquets and for pinning and securing some foundation work onto wreaths.

24s.w.g. × 10in (0.56mm × 260mm)
24s.w.g. × 7in (0.56mm × 180mm)
Used for wiring down thinner stemmed flowers, e.g. small Roses and Border Carnations, wiring and mounting of some foundation work onto wreaths, and bouquet work.

28s.w.g. × 7in to 32s.w.g. × 7in
(0.38mm × 180mm to 0.28mm × 180mm)
Silver stub wires. Used for wiring down smaller flowers, e.g. Violets and Snowdrops.

Wires are sold by weight and packed in boxes of ten bundles. Each bundle weighs $2\frac{1}{2}$kg.

SILVER REEL WIRE. Made in various gauges 26–36s.w.g. (0.32mm–0.20mm). Used for wiring down smaller flowers, e.g. Lily of the Valley, preparing and mounting flowers and foliages for corsages, buttonholes and head-dresses. Also used for binding bouquets, buttonholes and head-dresses. Reel wires are sold by the box of ten reels.

BLACK OR BLUE ANNEALED WIRE. Various gauges — used for mossing and in some flower wiring.

GREEN WIRE. Used for tying bows of ribbon as it does not rust. Sometimes used for mossing fancy designs as it is less conspicuous than string.

Wire tidy

This is a must — it may cost a little to purchase a proper one, but it will save money in the long run. Wires should never be laid down on a wet surface — they soon rust and can make dirty marks if used in this state. You can make a wire tidy easily by nailing different sized tins on to a strip of wood. One tidy in the centre of the work table should be enough. Wires should be labelled to identify them, and the full range should be available, if possible. With a home-made tidy see that the base is wide and heavy enough to stop the containers over-balancing. Always keep your wires in their correct gauge groups. They are very expensive and difficult to obtain, so do not waste them.

String

MOSSING STRING. Used for binding moss onto funeral designs. String is sold by the packet of one dozen reels.

PACKING STRING. Used for tying flowers, bouquets and funeral designs into boxes.

3-PLY STRING. Used for garlanding and tying up outside of boxes. Sold in large balls.

GREEN STRING. Used for tied bunches.

Other Materials

Boards for wreathwork
A board 8in × 4in (20cm × 10cm) made of hardboard or 3-ply wood is used for a spray on a board. A 4in × 4in (10cm × 10cm) size board is used for a posy pad. Oasis trays and bowls can take the place of these boards and are very successful.

Cycas leaves
Natural foliage from the Cycas Palm is used in wreath work. They can also be purchased in a plastic form today.

Florists scissors
These are special scissors with a serrated edge. They cut heavy stemmed foliage wires and also wire netting. Keep them oiled and they should last for years.

Flower spray or Springer
Used for spraying bouquets, sprays, etc., with fine spray of water. Use clean water only.

Gutta percha
This is a rubber substance used for covering stub and reel wires to make them water and rust proof. The gutta is cut in half lengthwise to make it thinner. It is sold in various colours: white, natural, green, etc.

I shall never know why gutta cannot be made in two widths. The normal is fine for some work, but for wedding or corsage spraying up, it is far too wide and when split in half gives a much neater thinner stem cover which in turn makes for less weight and neater work.

Don't buy too much at a time. It does not keep if

you store it in too hot a place: once perished you will do well to throw it out because it has no stretch to it and breaks all the time.

There are other tapes on the market, but you will find this by far the best for your purposes.

Lichen or reindeer moss
Used in funeral work as a foundation on the frame, this is now very expensive but still good for certain designs.

Oasis frames
These come in wreath, cross and other shapes. The manufacturers of oasis keep adding to their ranges and they are very useful to have for quick work, but to my way of thinking never give the same results as when a well mossed frame is used.

Posy frill
This is a doyley-like frill which is sometimes placed round the flowers on a Victorian posy. Don't forget to cut the edge to get the correct shape. They are stamped out and the contours are not always followed accurately.

Ribbon
Used for putting on handles of bouquets and for tails of ribbon on head-dresses, loose and Victorian posies. Not much is used in decorating, but with discretion it can sometimes fill a gap or supply just the correct colour.

Shadow leaves
Skeletonised Magnolia leaves are used in bridal work. The small leaves are most attractive but must be kept dry. Also used in dried arrangements.

Silver paper
This is sold in rolls, with sheets to the roll. Cut it into thin strips. Cover stub and reel wires with silver paper instead of gutta percha which is difficult to get. Fine household foil will do but, before cutting it into narrow strips, put tissue paper between the sheets. It will then separate and can be used singly.

Wire frames for wreath work
Round wreath, cross and chaplet frames are bought by the dozen, in sizes 12in (30cm), 14in (35cm), etc. going up in stages. Cross frames go to 6ft (1.8m) in length: these are known as coffin crosses. Unusual designed frames are made to order and are bought singly.

Flowers Suitable For Spray Work

Achillea	Hydrangea
Agapanthus	Lachenalia
Alchemilla	Larkspur
Alstroemeria	Lilac (small clusters)
Anemone	Lily of the Valley
Astrantia	Mignonette
Azalea	Muscari
Border Carnations	Myosotis
Carnation petals	Narcissi
Chincherinchee	Nerine
Delphinium flowers	Nigella
Erica	Orchid
(small pieces of heather)	Pieris
Eryngium	Polyanthus
Escallonia	Primrose
Freesia	Ranunculus
Fuchsia	Rhododendron
Galanthus (Snowdrop)	Rose buds and petals
Galtonia	Scilla
(Summer Hyacinth)	Stephanotis
Gnaphalium	Stock
Heliotrope	Tuberose
Hellebore	Violets
Hop flowers	Zinnia (baby flowers)
Hyacinth pips	

Foliages Useful For Spray Work

Use only the small leaves. Remember if they are too young they will just not last, so in some cases it is better to use small pieces of older materials. I do not like cutting down leaves to size. I know that it is done in the trade, but careful selection will keep this to a minimum. Cut leaves usually show — a bruised leaf margin soon becomes apparent. Pick the foliages to blend with your flower colours. Wire as lightly as possible with the neatest of stitches.

Andromeda	
Artemesia	(Southernwood).
Begonia	Very small leaves from the indoor plants.
Berberis	Some varieties have useful small leaves and dark colouring.
Cyclamen	Many marbled varieties are most useful — get a return on your old pot plant.

Eucalyptus	The small-leaved varieties are best, e.g. Gunnii.
Euonymus	Variegated forms useful.
Geranium	Very good range of coloured foliage: creams, pinks, etc.
Hebe	See Veronica.
Hedera helix in variety	Excellent range — some very hard.
Heuchera	Good coloured leaves (venation attractive) in autumn and through the winter.
Ivy	See Hedera.
Ilex — Holly	Small variegated are interesting.
Myrtle	Small leaf — long-lasting tips.
Osmanthus	Different forms — long-lasting tips. Holly and Olive leaf form.
Osmaria	A small, dark green, 'firm' leaf.
Peperomia	A number of house plant foliages can be used.
Pilea	Another house plant — good leaves.
Pittosporum	Some good-coloured leaves in variegated form.
Rosemary	Grey-green spiky foliage.
Ruta (Rue)	Grey-green parsley-like foliage.
Salvia (Sage)	Purple and grey-green.
Sedum	
Senecio	Silver-grey — white back to leaf — can use upside down.
Stachys (Lambs Ears)	Soft grey foliage — do not get wet.
Thyme	Various good-coloured shoots — strong scent.
Tradescantia	A number of colours — only use tips, not individual leaves.
Veronica (Hebe)	Choose the small leaved forms.

10. FLORISTRY TERMS AND METHODS

Backing funeral frames
All work going out should have the moss area covered. This may be done by using Laurel leaves, Cupressus, oiled paper or some form of plastic wrap. This is pinned on before any work is commenced on the top of the frame. The use of oasis in some form of a 'tray' automatically gives a neat back to the work.

Binding
This is used to hold the flowers and leaves into position when making bouquets, sprays, head-dresses, buttonholes, etc. Silver reel wire is used, usually 36 gauge (.20mm) for sprays, head-dresses and buttonholes and 30 gauge (.32mm) for bouquets.

Double leg mounts
For wreath work and bouquets. Hold the flower in the left hand, the head of the flower being on the top of the hand. Place the stub wire vertically at the back of the stem approximately ¾in (1.8cm) from the base of the stem. The part of the wire below the stem is 1in (2.5cm) longer than the part above the stem.

Bend both ends of the wire down to form a hairpin, keeping the wires to the width of the stem.

Hold the hairpin stem very firmly with the finger and thumb of the left hand and with the right hand wind the longer lower wire around the upper shorter wire and stem two or three times. Always wind away from yourself. The two legs should now be of equal length.

For sprays and head-dresses. When making a double leg mount on smaller flowers such as for sprays and head-dresses, wire with 32 gauge (.28mm) or 30 gauge (.32mm) silver reel wire, making the double leg mount in the same way as for the mounts on large flowers and foliage.

Sometimes when the flower is being mounted, the wire may be pushed through the flower or the stem before it is bent to form a hairpin, and then twist the wire round the stem three times.

Extended legs
This is used in floristry when flower stems are too short and need to be made longer. The wired flower is mounted with a single leg mount with appropriate wire, the mount and wire then being covered with gutta percha.

False legs
This is the term used when a wire replaces or extends a natural stem.

Feathering
This is when separate petals are taken from a Carnation and two or three wired together. Take one large petal, one medium and one small one. Have the large one at the bottom, then the medium and the small one on the top.

Make a pleat in the centre of these three petals holding them together. Push a 32 gauge (.28mm) silver wire

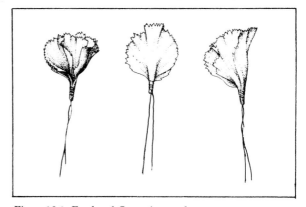

Figure 10.1: Feathered Carnation petals

through to hold the pleat in position and twist the wire three times round the Carnation petals. Bring the wires down as a single or double leg, depending on use.

Cut off the ends of the petals below where the twists of wire finish.

Foundation work
Also called Based Work or Block Work. All flowers used are removed from their natural stems or left on very short stems. They are mounted or pinned to the frame in a flat mass. Cover the moss with tissue paper before pinning. This keeps the work clean. The smaller the flower the better the result will be.

Garlanding
Ropes of flowers made for decorating pillars in a church or draped round tables at a wedding reception, etc. The flowers are wired with a single leg and the wire is twisted round three-ply string.

Take care that all the ends are on top of the string in order to prevent the scratching of furniture.

'Greening'
In wreathwork the small pieces of green which have been wired together in threes with a double leg and the pieces placed into the moss on a frame, to cover the moss. For further details see wreathwork section in Chapter 15.

Grouping
The term grouping is used when different flowers, foliage or a particular colour is gathered together to make a 'group' rather than have bits and pieces spotted about through the decoration. It applies in vases, funeral work and all make-up. Over-grouping can result in blocks of colour and can be too definite. It is better to have the colour, shape or what have you in 'sweeps' rather than blocks.

Guttaring
This term is used for covering wires. Various materials are used and there are many different 'tapes' on the market. In the majority of cases gutta percha is used, this being obtained in green, white, brown and natural colours. It is a tape of rubbery texture which grips the wires and stretches slightly when gripped between the fingers. The warmth of the hand helps to soften it and, although not glued in any way, it does stick to itself.

The secret of covering any wire is to get the material to lie flat on the wire and to run it down as quickly as possible. Always start on the stem of the flower where the mount begins and hold the material in the left hand between the thumb and first finger, with the wire between the thumb and first finger of the right hand. Place the gutta at an angle of 45° to the mount and start twisting the wire with the right hand, stretching the tape slightly with the left hand. Twist the covering down quickly to the base of the wire, and finish off by twisting it onto itself. Thin strips of silver paper can be used instead of the gutta but you cannot stretch them because they will break. Otherwise, the same method of covering is used — the narrower the strip the neater the cover.

Loose work
Used in funeral designs, the flowers stand away from the frame and each line around the frame is a different length. The in-between spaces are filled with foliage and the frame itself is lightly greened.

Mossing
A term used in wreathwork. The moss is bound on to a funeral design with either string or wire. See the section on wreathwork in Chapter 15 for the full explanation on how to moss various frames.

Pinning flowers
For wreathwork, when the heads of flowers are pinned to cover the moss on a funeral design. The pins are usually 22 gauge × 3½in (.71mm × 90mm). This is explained fully in the section on wreathwork in Chapter 15.

Pinning Roses
Used to hold roses at the bud stage. Make a small hairpin about ½in (1.25cm) long, and pin the sepals against the petals. This keeps the petals from opening. Insert the pin through the chubbiest part of the bud.

Pipping
When individual flowers are taken from the main stem of the flower, for example Hyacinth Bells from the stem of the Hyacinth. Use a double leg mount, usually 32 gauge (.28mm), and cover with gutta percha.

Return end This term is used in funeral, bouquet, spray, head-dress and buttonhole work. It is composed of the flowers which are placed in after the centre of a bouquet has been reached. The flowers after the centre of a bouquet, etc. are placed in and face back to the top flowers.

Single leg mounts Place the appropriate wire behind the natural stem. The upper wire should not be longer than the natural stem. Close the wires to form a hairpin and wind the lower wire two or three times around the upper wire and natural stem, the last twist being at the end of the stem. Straighten the long wire — this forms the single leg mount. The upper shorter wire must not extend past the base of the natural stem.

Spray or corsage Flowers worn on the shoulder of a dress or coat are called either a spray or corsage.

Spraying up Spraying up is used in bouquet work when compound flowers and leaves are too heavy to place in as a whole. Take separate leaves or flowers from the main stem and wire the flowers with silver reel wire with a double leg. The leaves have a stitch and double leg of silver reel wire. The double leg of both the flowers and the leaves are covered with gutta percha from where the wire is twisted, to the bottom of the double leg which needs to be approximately $2\frac{1}{2}$in (6.25cm) long.

When the flowers and leaves have been prepared in this way, they are then attached to a 22 gauge × 14in wire (.71mm × 360mm). Always have the same type of leaf or flower and have three, five or seven leaves or flowers as a spray. It is better to have uneven numbers on the stub wire. Choose varying sized pieces; in the case of flowers begin with buds and work to larger flowers with leaves, small ones to larger ones.

Take the 22 gauge ×14in wire (.71mm × 360mm) and the smallest flower or leaf and place its false leg against the stub wire so that it overlaps the top of the wire by 1in (2.5cm).

Bind with 36 gauge (.20mm) silver reel wire from the top of the stub wire down $1\frac{1}{2}$in (3.75cm) of the false leg of the flower or leaf. Take the next-sized flower or leaf and place it to one side of the top one, letting the tip of it reach just beyond the base of the first flower or leaf. Binding the leaf or flower into position about an inch (2.5cm) away from the natural stem and with the same piece of binding wire, travel down with it to attach the false leg of this one to the stub wire.

Take the third flower or leaf to the opposite side to the second one and again an inch (2.5cm) away from the natural stem, bind to the stub wire. If more flowers or leaves are required, alternate them side to side, binding them to the 22 gauge × 14in (.71mm × 360mm) wire. When the last piece has been placed in position, travel an extra inch (2.5cm) with the binding wire to hold firmly, before cutting the binding wire away.

Cover the stems with gutta percha by bending the pieces downwards, with the exception of the first one. Begin the gutta where the binding has begun at the top of the stub wire. When the gutta has travelled down to where the second flower has been bound into position, bend the flower or leaf back into its original position.

Gutta to the next flower in this way and then continue to the bottom of the 22 gauge × 14in (.71mm × 360mm) wire. When gutta percha is used it is not always necessary to bind on with reel wire first, but use the gutta percha to bind and to cover the 22 gauge × 14in (.71mm × 360mm) at the same time. In this case the pieces are not bent down but left in position all the time.

Stitching leaves A term used when wiring leaves. The leaf needs to be supported for floristry. Take the leaf with a small stem attached and, keeping the back of the leaf uppermost, make a stitch three-quarters of the way up the leaf across the centre vein with silver reel wire, the gauge depending on the size and weight of the leaf. The stitch should be small so that it is hardly visible from the front.

Bend the two ends of the wire down to form a loop at the back of the leaf.

Have one of the ends of the wire coming down against the stem and twist the other wire round the wire against the stem of the leaf. If a double leg is required, leave the wire which goes down the stem fairly long. If a single leg is required, this should be no longer than the natural stem of the leaf.

When using large leaves for wreath work, such as Megasea or Hosta or large Hedera canariensis, a 24 gauge wire may be used as a support. The 24 gauge (.56mm) wire is hooked through the main vein on the reverse side of the leaf, the longer wire being brought down close to the main vein and wound around the stem.

Stitching Carnation leaves (two stitches) Another method is adopted for thin pointed leaves, for example Carnation grasses.

Cut the bottom of the grass at an angle.

With a piece of silver reel wire, usually 32 gauge (.28mm) make a stitch in the grass approximately halfway up the leaf at the back and going at an angle across the centre vein.

With the same piece of wire, make a second stitch where the grass tapers before the point at the top, again at an angle across the centre vein and at the back of the leaf.

Bend over the tip of the wire so that it does not stand away from the grass. The piece of wire left at the bottom of the leaf is twisted round the part that has been cut at an angle.

Stringing A term used in wreathwork. String is twisted round to hold the moss onto a frame.

Swagging Swagging has more shape to it than garlanding and is wider at the centre. Done on a mossed flat backed base, it is seen only from the front.

Teasing moss When preparing moss to place on a frame, pull out the moss making it looser and remove any pieces of stick or foreign bodies.

Wiring down This is placing a wire into the head of the flower and wiring either on the inside or outside of the stem to give it support and to stop it from breaking. Various gauge wires are used depending on the thickness of stem and the weight of the flower. Examples are given in Chapter 11.

Care must be taken that flowers are wired into the seed pods or else breakages may occur. The wire should not show through the head of the flower.

11. THE WIRING OF FLOWERS

General Wiring Of Flowers And Leaves

Flowers have to be wired very neatly, keeping the wire out of sight as much as possible. The wire is used to support the flower and should be just strong enough to do this, but not so thick as to make the finished work look heavy and rigid, a very common fault with many florists. The length varies as to how long you require the flower to be. Never bind over the foliage on the stem of the flower, but make sure the wire twists go between the leaves.

Hollow and soft-stemmed flowers have wires placed inside the stems but when the stem is hard, for example Carnations, the wire has to be on the outside of the stem. Here it is essential to twist the wire round the stem, not the stem round the wire, keeping the wire close to the stem. Wire down quickly with not too many twists.

Great care must be taken so as not to damage the flower by bruising, because with soft stems, such as Tulips, this will cause discoloration which will quickly show up in the finished work.

Examples of wiring flowers

ALSTROEMERIA. Flowers with a compound head are wired with 22 gauge (.71mm) from the top of the main stem and twisted down the outside of the stem to the bottom. Each flower is wired down by placing a 32 gauge (.28mm) silver reel wire into the base of the seedbox and twisting quickly down the thin stem and once round the main stem. Each flower is treated in this way, making sure that the twists of each flower go in the same direction. The ends of the wires are cut short and tucked into the main stem.

ANEMONE. A hollow-stemmed flower. A 22 (.71mm) or 24 (.56mm) gauge wire can be used depending on the thickness of the stem. Holding the flower with the left hand and the wire with the right hand, push the wire up inside the stem. When the green collar of foliage is reached near the head of the flower, watch that the stem does not break, and carefully guide the wire through the solid piece here and then up into the head of the Anemone. Make sure that the wire does not come through the black centre. Many Anemones have a twisted stem, so gently bend them straight as the wire is being pushed up.

ARUM LILY. A soft-stemmed flower. If the flower is small a 22 gauge (.71mm) wire is heavy enough, but if it is large a 20 gauge (.90mm) is needed. Push the wire up inside the stem, from the bottom of the stem to the head. Make sure that the wire cannot be seen from the centre of the flower.

CAMELLIA. As with Gardenias, the petals will bruise if touched by hand. Use cotton wool or cellular wadding. Remove the Camellia from the main stem and insert the two silver wires criss-crossed through the base of the flower. Place a cotton wool 'bud' at one end of a 22 gauge × 14in (.71mm × 260mm) wire and place into position at the base of the flower in order to replace the natural stem. Secure in place by bending down the rose wires and twisting around the 22 gauge (.71mm) stub. Cover with gutta percha.

CARNATION. A hard-stemmed flower, so the wire goes down the outside of the stem. Push a 22 gauge (.71mm) wire into the stem at the base of the calyx, making sure it goes in at the back of the flower. Twist once round under the head of the flower and then take the wire quickly down the stem, twisting as you go. Do not have too many twists.

CHRYSANTHEMUMS AND DAHLIAS. These are hard-stemmed flowers. Generally a 22 gauge (.71mm) wire is heavy enough, but for exceptionally large Chrysanthemum blooms use a 20 gauge (.90mm). Push the wire into the inside of the stem approximately 3in (7.5cm) from the head, and push it up to the head. The bottom of the wire can then be twisted down the remainder of the stem on the outside. Buds of Dahlias and smaller flowers and buds of spray Chrysanthemums can be wired on 24 gauge (.56mm) wire which is taken down to join with the main stem and then cut away.

DAFFODIL. This is a hollow-stemmed flower. Use 22 gauge (.71mm) wire. Hold the flower in the left hand and the wire in the right hand, and push the wire into the hole at the base of the stem and carefully up the stem. You will find a slight difficulty when you reach the dried-up papery tissue (spathe) because the stem of the flower is much thinner here and becomes more solid. With an even pressure, guide the flower carefully between the thumb and first finger of the left hand, with the flower resting on the top of the hand. The wire should just reach into the seedbox, and not, as often happens, come out into the Daffodil trumpet, where it will show.

EUCHARIS LILY. This exquisite flower requires careful and delicate wiring. Remove from main stem. A hollow tube 'stem' now remains. Cover the tip of a 22 gauge × 14in (.71mm × 360mm) wire with a bud of dampened cotton wool. Insert the wire into the throat of the flower until the cotton bud is lodged snugly into the top of the tube 'stem'. The flower will be more securely wired if the seed pod is left intact; however, in order to obtain more depth for use the seed pod may be removed.

Pass a thin silver rose wire through the stem just below the petals. Bring both ends down and twist around the 22 gauge (.71mm) wire. Put gutta percha over the base of the flower and down the false stem.

FOLIAGE. Large leaves are wired singly, usually with a single stitch of reel wire at the top of the leaf and a large loop of wire at the back for support which is bound onto the base of the leaf stalk. For very wide leaves, such as Hosta or Megasea, two or three stub wires may be fanned out from the leaf base, ending in a small stitch on the leaf perimeter. The gauge of wire depends on the weight of the leaf.

For compound leaf sprays such as Roses see Figure 11.5c (p. 79).

Small fleshy leaves such as Tradescantia are best used as growing tips; do not strip them down to the individual leaves. Wire with a fine silver reel into the growing point then down the stem, mounting onto a fine stub for use in a bouquet.

Ivy leaves can be sprayed up into groups of three

and five but again leave natural tips if you can for inclusion in bouquets.

See spraying up details in Chapter 10 (p. 73).

FREESIA. Freesia flowers need to be supported as well as the stems. This is done by taking a piece of 36 gauge (.20mm) silver reel wire and attaching it by twisting it on the main stem at the base of the bottom flower, twisting the wire up the flower to where it begins to bulge and then taking it down to the main stem. Thus giving the shape of a figure of eight.

When at the main stem, twist the wire up this stem to the next flower and wire it as for the first flower. Do this to all the open flowers but it is not necessary to wire the buds. Twist the wire up the main stem at the base of the buds until the top bud, then twist the wire round the base of it and cut the wire away.

Take 30 gauge (.32mm) silver wire and push it into the stem where the 36 gauge (.20mm) binding wire began and twist down to the base of the stem.

GARDENIAS. The flowers of the Gardenia, whether used for spray or bouquet work, need to have a support of cardboard at the back of the petals. Never touch the petals of the Gardenia with your hand as their petals are so delicate they will immediately bruise and go brown. Move the petals with a piece of cotton wool or cellular wadding.

Take the Gardenias from the main branch. Cut a circle from a piece of cardboard and then cut a star shape in the centre of it.

Three leaves are required for backing the cardboard and they need to be the same size and wired with 32 gauge (.28mm) silver single stitch, leaving a single leg with spike. Push the cardboard over the stem of the flower and up to the back of the petals to support them. Move the petals into position with the cellular wadding, to make a well-shaped flower. Break the calyx from the stem, push a 22 gauge × 10in (.71mm × 260mm) wire through the stem under the cardboard and bend it down to make a hairpin with one long leg and one short leg; this should be level with the stem of the Gardenia. Push a 36 gauge (.20mm) silver wire through the stem and then place the three leaves round the cardboard, the short spike pushed into the stem, the single leg going straight down the side of the stem.

The leaves should show beyond the flower. Bind them on under their natural stems with 36 gauge (.20mm) silver wire and then down the stem of the Gardenia and a little way down the stub wire. Cover with gutta percha from where the binding wire begins down to the bottom of the stub wire. If the outer ring of petals are damaged, they can be removed.

Plate 1

Plate 2

Plate 3

Plate 4

Plate 5

Plate 6

Plate 7

Plate 9

Plate 8

Plate 11

Plate 10

Plate 12

Plate 13

Plate 16

Plate 14

Plate 19

Plate 15

Plate 17

Plate 18

Plate 20

Plate 21

Plate 22

Plate 23

Plate 24

Plate 25

Plate 26

Plate 27

Plate 28

Plate 29

Plate 32

Plate 30

Plate 31

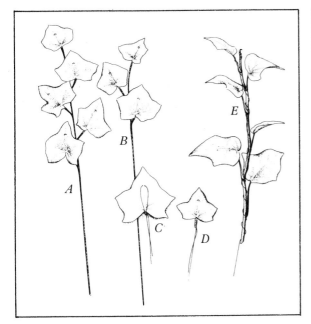

Figure 11.1: Ivy in different forms
A. *Five-spray of leaves*
B. *Three-spray of leaves*
C. *Back view of single wired leaf*
D. *Front view of single leaf, wired single mount*
E. *Wired natural spray*

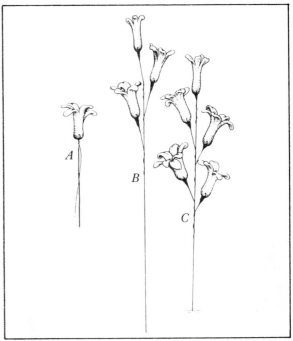

Figure 11.2: Hyacinth — spraying up bells
A. *Single bell or pip*
B. *Three-spray*
C. *Five-spray*

GERBERA. For a bouquet, wire internally as far as possible. For long stems go into the stem about 3–4in (7.5–10cm) below the flower and quickly twist the remaining wire down the outside of the stem. Do not come out through flower head. Use a 22 gauge (.71mm) wire.

GLADIOLI. The large flowers will need an 18 gauge × 14in (1.25mm × 360mm) for wiring down the stem. Place the wire into the stem just below the first flower and twist rapidly down the stem. A silver reel wire can be taken up round the flowers to the tip but normally this is not necessary.

Bridal Gladioli should be wired on 22 gauge (.71mm) or 20 gauge (.90mm) up the stem and a silver wire from the first flower to the tip. Individual flowers are wired on double leg 32 gauge (.28mm) or 30 gauge (.32mm) silver reel — or if very heavy a single or double leg 24 gauge (.56mm) or 26 gauge (.46mm) wire.

HYACINTH. This is a soft-stemmed flower. Hold the flower with the left hand and the wire with the right, and push a 22 gauge (.71mm) wire up inside the stem until the top bell is reached. If the flower is extra heavy a 20 gauge (.90mm) wire can be used.

LACHENALIA. These have fleshy stems and are not more than 6in (15cm) long normally when purchased from market. Try to wire internally using 24 gauge (.56mm). If it is too spindly, go into the stem just under the first flowers and wire down the outside, getting the wire up into the head as far as possible. Wire outside between the bells with 32 gauge (.28mm) silver wire.

LILIES. Push a 22 gauge (.71mm) gauge wire into the stem a few inches from the head of the flower and twist the wire down to the bottom of the stem. If there is more than one flower on a stem, wire the longest flower right the way down the main stem. Then wire the side flower to where the stem joins the main stem; twist round once on the main stem to hold it firmly in place.

LILY OF THE VALLEY. This is wired from the base of the stem with 36 gauge (.20mm) silver reel wire, twisting very neatly up the stem between the bells and finishing with a twist round the base of the top bell. This needs great care as the wire can easily cut off the top bell.

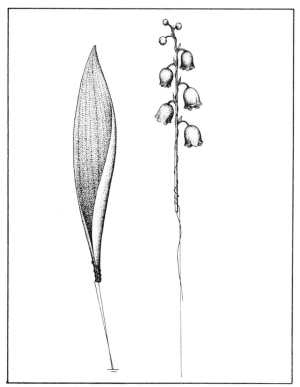

Figure 11.3: Lily of the Valley — wiring

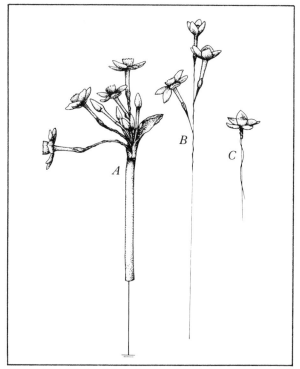

Figure 11.4: Wiring Polyanthus-type Narcissi
A. *Complete stem with 22 gauge (.71mm) wire inside the stem up to the spathe; external silver wire down each individual flower stem*
B. *Individual flowers mounted in a spray*
C. *Individual flower with seedbox removed*

NARCISSI. When a Narcissi has more than one head on a stem, it needs to have a 22 gauge (.71mm) gauge wire inside the stem until the spathe is reached and then a 32 gauge (.28mm) silver wire pushed into the seedbox of the individual flowers and twisted down the stem to where the small stems reach the main stem. Then twist the wire round the main stem, cut it away and push the end into the main stem for a neat finish. All the wire from the small stems must be twisted in the same direction. If the individual flowers are fairly heavy, a 30 gauge (.32mm) wire can be used. It is not necessary to wire all the buds.

The spathe is removed for bouquet work, but it is not necessary to remove it for wreathwork.

Sometimes for some varieties of Narcissi such as 'Cheerfulness', the 22 gauge (.71mm) wire can go beyond the spathe up into the stem of one of the compound flowers and the rest is wired with silver wire down to the main stem.

NIGELLA. These stems are often wiry. Pierce into the hollow part with a 22 gauge (.71mm) stub and secure the thin area with silver reel, going up into the flower head first and working down the stem to the heavier stub wire.

ORCHIDS. When using for bouquets and sprays, cut the orchid, leaving about ³⁄₄in (1.8cm) of stem. Wire up inside the stem with a 22 gauge (.71mm) or 24 gauge (.56mm) wire, length depending whether it is for a bouquet or spray. The wire needs to be 14in (35cm) long for a bouquet and 7-10in (18-25cm) long for a spray. Push a 32 gauge (.28mm) silver reel wire through the stem and twist down the stub wire a little way. Cover with gutta percha from where the binding wire is twisted to the bottom of the stem.

RANUNCULUS. Often these are hollow stems, but they do have difficult joints where the leaves are attached. Try to wire internally going up into the flower head. The heavy flowers often bend over at the neck and need support. Use 22 gauge (.71mm) or 24 gauge (.56mm).

ROSES. Roses are hard-stemmed flowers, so the wire needs to go on the outside of the stem. The gauge used depends on the size of the flower, either a 22 gauge (.71mm) or 24 gauge (.56mm), and also

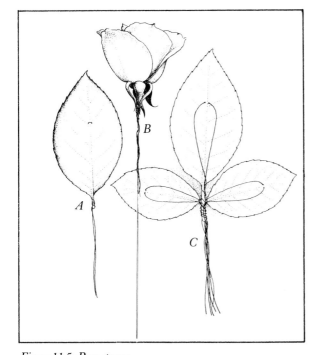

Figure 11.5: Rose sprays
A. Single wired leaf
B. Individual Rose mounted
C. Three-spray of Rose leaves

whether it is for wreathwork or bouquets. If the rose is in a bride's handspray a thick silver stub wire is used. Push the stub wire into the base of the seedbox at the back of the flower, close to the stem and twist it round once near to the head, then continue twisting the wire down to the bottom of the stem. Take the twists down quickly and do not have them close together.

SCABIOUS. Where possible, wire internally, but often, after the first pair of leaves down the stem from the flower head, the stem becomes thick and the wire may well then have to be external.

Go well into the flower head but make sure that the wire does not show. Use a 22 gauge (.71mm) wire, 10–14in (25–35cm) in length.

SNOWDROPS. Wire them as for Violets (see below) but push the wire into the base of the seedbox and quickly twist down the outside of the stem. If the stem is very weak, bind in the little paper sheath to give it extra support.

STOCK OR LARKSPUR. These have small flowers up the stem. You will have difficulty in trying to wire to the top of the stem, so use the following

method. With Larkspur push a 22 gauge (.71mm) wire up the centre flower stem, and with Stock push the wire into the inside of the stem, a few inches from the top and then twist down the outside to the bottom of the stem. In both cases go as near the top as possible, then finish off the tip with 32 gauge (.28mm) silver reel wire to connect with the 22 gauge (.71mm) stub wire. Pierce the 32 gauge (.28mm) wire into the base of the first flower or bud.

TULIPS. A soft-stemmed flower, it is difficult to push a wire inside the stem of a Tulip when a long stem is required. So, push the wire inside the stem just below the first leaf on the stem, and then up the stem to the head. Twist the bottom part of the wire round the outside of the stem below the first leaf and down to the bottom of the stem.

VIOLETS. These are wired usually with 36 gauge (.20mm) silver reel wire. Push the wire into the top of the head, bend it round the stem and twist the wire down the remainder of the stem. Do see that the wire follows the contour of the Violet 'neck'.

WATER LILY. These make wonderful flowers for a special summer table setting. They do not travel well so should be obtained locally and treated straight-away.

The flowers close once the light fails so to keep them open, carefully wax the base of the petals; then they cannot close. This is done by placing drops of warm (not too hot because it damages the petals) wax, but it must be warm enough to run through the base of the petals before setting.

Wire the thick fleshy stems for make-up with a 22 gauge (.71mm) or 20 gauge (.90mm) wire internally.

Wiring Of Flowers For Head-dresses, Sprays And For 'Spraying Up'

Flowers may be used whole or, if too large, in smaller sections when making a spray or head-dress, but it is important that these are not too small. One reason is that they do not last so well and another is that the effect is lost and the spray or head-dress looks over-wired and bitty.

With most flowers the wire is pushed through the flower just above its base and the wire is twisted two or three times round the stem to form either a single or double leg mount. Some very small flowers are 'clumped' together and then mounted and some flowers need to be wired up the stem first and then mounted.

The following describes the wiring of various flowers. If a certain flower is not described then wire as for a flower of similar shape.

ALSTROEMERIA.   Take a single flower from the main stem, leaving a small stem on it. Push a 32 gauge (.28mm) or 30 gauge (.32mm) silver wire, if the flower is heavy, through the base of the flower and mount it.

BLUEBELLS.   Some of the flowers are wired singly with 32 gauge (.28mm) silver wire through the base of the flower and then mounted.

The buds can be wired in a clump, especially the tip end of the Bluebell, with 32 gauge (.28mm) silver wire pushed through and then mounted.

CHINCHERINCHEE.   Some flowers are wired singly with 32 gauge (.28mm) silver wire through the base of the flower and then mounted.

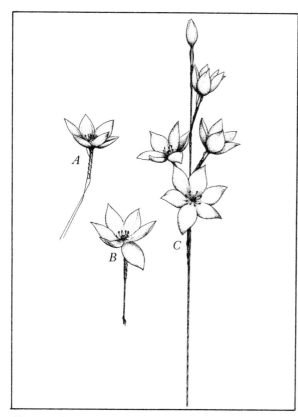

Figure 11.6: Chincherinchee
A. Individual flower wired
B. Individual flower wired and covered in gutta percha
C. Five buds and flowers sprayed up

The buds can be wired in a clump, especially the tip end of Chincherinchee, with 32 gauge (.28mm) silver wire pushed through the buds and then mounted.

DELPHINIUM PIPS.   Wire with 32 gauge (.28mm) silver wire through the base of the flower and mount.

ECHEVARIA.   These are usually wired in clumps with 32 gauge (.28mm) silver wire pushed through the flowers and then mounted.

They can also be wired singly with 32 gauge (.28mm) wire through the base of the flower and then mounted.

FORGET-ME-NOTS   (MYOSOTIS). Wired   in clumps, these are tightly bound together with 32 gauge (.28mm) silver wire which is then taken down the stems to form a mount.

FREESIA.   These can be wired as single flowers with 32 gauge (.28mm) silver wire and then mounted. Sometimes they are left at their full size or they may need to be cut shorter.

When shorter flowers are needed, cut them off above the stem and gather them together at the base. Wire with 32 gauge (.28mm) silver and mount.

Freesia buds have a 36 gauge (.20mm) wire twisted up the main stem between the buds on a spray, beginning at the larger buds at the bottom and working to the smaller buds at the top. To finish, twist the wire round just beneath the smallest bud and cut the wire away.

Mount with 32 gauge (.28mm) silver wire.

GENTIANS.   32 gauge (.28mm) or 30 gauge (.32mm) silver wire is used depending on the weight of the Gentian. The wire is pushed through the base of the flower and then mounted.

HYACINTH.   32 gauge (.28mm) or 30 gauge (.32mm) silver wire is used depending on the weight of the flower. The wire is pushed through half way up the bulge on the bell of the Hyacinth.

HYDRANGEA.   Use two or three florets together keeping the flowers fairly level at the top. With 32 gauge (.28mm) silver wire have one piece of wire going straight down the stem, and twist the other piece of wire immediately beneath the florets and then three times round the stems.

LILY OF THE VALLEY.   This usually needs to be cut in half and the two pieces used separately.

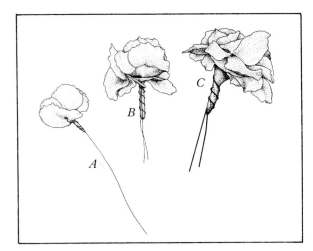

Figure 11.7: Hydrangea florets
A. Single leg mount for a head-dress
B. Double leg mount for spraying up
C. For use in foundation work

Each piece is then wired from the base and the wire twisted up between the bells on the main stem finishing with a twist round the base of the top bell. This needs great care as the wire can easily cut off the bell. Each piece of Lily of the Valley is then mounted with 32 gauge (.28mm) silver wire. Two pieces of Valley can be mounted together or a piece of Valley and a leaf can be mounted together if required.

MICHAELMAS DAISY.   Take the flower from the main stem leaving a small stem on it. Push a 32 gauge (.28mm) silver wire through the base of the flower and mount it.

MIMOSA.   If the flowers are close together on the stem, they can be clumped together and bound tightly with a 32 gauge (.28mm) wire. Then make a mount.
   If the flowers are more spread out, twist a 36 gauge (.20mm) wire up the main stem, and then mount with 32 gauge (.28mm) silver wire.

NIGELLA (LOVE IN A MIST).   Push a 32 gauge (.28mm) silver wire through the base of the flower and mount it.

'PAPER WHITE' NARCISSUS.   The Narcissi are best left with the seedbox on, but when they are going to be cut very short to give depth to the spray or headdress they need to be cut just above the seed pod. The 32 gauge (.28mm) silver wire should be pushed through the seed pod, so that the flower is left natural, and then mounted.

When the seedbox has been removed the 32 gauge (.28mm) wire is pushed through the flower a little way up from where it has been cut.

ROCK CYCLAMEN.   Push a 32 gauge (.28mm) silver wire through the base of the flower and mount it.

SNOWDROP.   Push a 32 gauge (.28mm) silver wire through the seedbox and mount it.

STEPHANOTIS.   These are usually left with a small piece of stem, but are sometimes cut above the base of the flower to give shorter flowers. This is to give depth to sprays and head-dresses. Push 32 gauge (.28mm) silver wire through the base of the flower and mount.

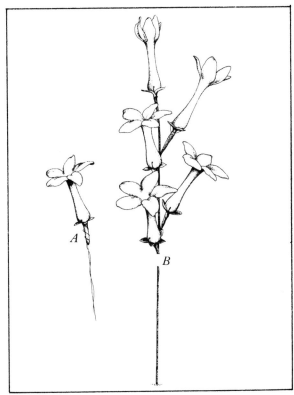

Figure 11.8: Stephanotis
A. Individual flower mounted
B. Five pips sprayed up

STOCKS.   If the flowers are large take a 32 gauge (.28mm) silver wire and twist it round close to the petals to hold them into position.

12. BUTTONHOLES AND SPRAYS

Rose Buttonhole

Choose a fairly small well-shaped Rose bud which has had a good drink — the pointed buds are better to use than those of the fat cabbage type.

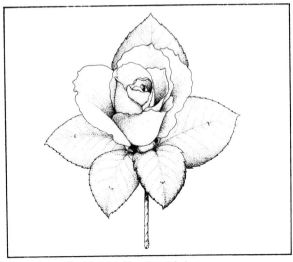

Figure 12.1: Gentleman's Rose buttonhole

Materials needed:
24 gauge (.56mm) × 7in (180mm) wire for stem
32 gauge (.28mm) silver reel for mounting leaves
36 gauge (.20mm) binding wire

Remove the stem and sepals only if these are large and untidy, mounting the bud on a double leg 24 gauge (.56mm) × 7in (180mm). I prefer to leave the sepals; if necessary, pin these down with small hairpin-shaped pieces of 32 gauge (.28mm) wire to stop the bud opening — this can be a problem in hot weather.

Select five good clean, firm leaves — one a little larger than the others. Wire these singly with a loop at the back and a small stitch, but have a single leg to

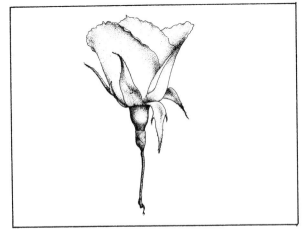

Figure 12.2: Rose bud, with sepals pinned (on the left) to hold the bud in its tight form

keep the stem thin. Cover three mounts very carefully with gutta percha. The two at the front go in deep and gutta is not normally used for them. Gutta the base of the seedbox — this helps to hold the binding wire up high.

With the face of the Rose towards you, place the largest leaf at the back of the flower. Bind at the base of the seedbox. Place two leaves on either side and encircle the bud, binding these mounts tightly right down the stem. Bend the two lowest leaves slightly to form a return end. (These from choice should be the smallest of the leaves.)

Finish off by covering the false stem by binding with gutta. The stem should be about 1½–2in (3.75–5cm) long.

Carnation Buttonhole For A Man

Generally, men are very reluctant to wear any form of buttonhole and, unfortunately, decline the chance, except at weddings or some special function when they will wear something fairly small, compact and not too showy. The Carnation is ideal for this purpose, and has good lasting qualities. Here are instructions for making a Carnation buttonhole correctly.

You will need:

a 24 gauge (.56mm) × 7in (180mm) wire for
   mounting
2 pieces of 24 gauge (.56mm) × 1½in
   (3.75cm) long approx.
32 gauge (.28mm) wire for mounting backing leaves
36 gauge (.20mm) silver for binding
one piece of plain cardboard for backing the flower

Choose a well-shaped flower which has had a long drink — a Carnation which has split will do well for this work. Rose leaves, or small leaves like Pittosporum or Box will be needed to cover the back of the flower. Take the flower, remove all but ½in (1.25cm) of the stem and carefully tear away the calyx and any thickness at the petal base. Now, take out the seedbox — this is most important because it is this part which causes the bulge in the base, stopping the flower from going through the buttonhole. It is not the correct thing to have displayed a long silver paper stem on the coat lapel. Unfortunately today many suits do not have a buttonhole and to provide for such cases the short stem must be covered in a dark gutta percha.

Now that the petals are free, hold the flower upside down to allow them to fall into place, and then secure with the cardboard collar. (This is a circle of white cardboard cut to support the petals, but just small enough not to show from the front. Some people prefer a star shape, cut to the centre because they say it remains firmer.) Push up the collar as far as you can, and then secure with the two cross wires of 24 gauge (.56mm) × 1½in (3.75cm) approx. (so much depends on flower size).

Now place the 24 gauge (.56mm) × 7in (180mm) wire through the flower and bend down to make a double leg — again some florists will give just one twist on to the little piece of stem left at the base of the petals.

Now prepare leaves for backing the cardboard. Supposing Rose leaves are to be used, select approximately six and bend them over double, then mount by making a stitch in the top of the double leaf surface. Secure wire round the small stem left on the leaf and make a double leg mount — one short leg and the other long. The short piece of wire at the base of the leaf is then pushed under the cardboard to help keep the leaf in place — this is done on 32 gauge (.28mm) silver reel wire.

Back the whole surface of cardboard with leaves, bringing down the wire mounts in a neat straight plane and binding each in tightly with 36 gauge (.20mm) silver as close to the card as possible.

Adjust the petals carefully into shape so as to give a round flower. Pinch the base of the petals to make this area flat to enable it to go easily into the buttonhole.

Finish by cutting off the wires short, and binding down the false stem with dark green gutta percha. Face the Carnation slightly by pressing at the base of the flower and tilting it forward.

It is not usual to have any foliage, but should this be

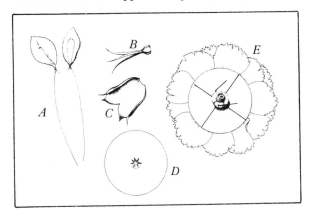

Figure 12.3: Making a Carnation buttonhole
A. Single leaves mounted for backing the card
B. Stigma, style and seedbox removed
C. Calyx
D. Card for backing, with star shape cut in the centre
E. Card in place and secured with two cross wires

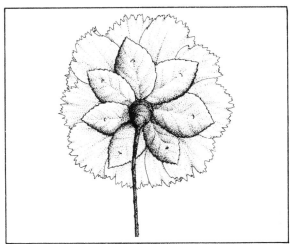

Figure 12.4: Completed Carnation buttonhole, back view.
Single Rose leaves of ideal size — no need to double over in this instance.

required, three leaves of different lengths are permitted to show just above the back of the flower. These are made up in a spray of three. Each one is wired with a small stitch at the back of the leaf and then the three wire mounts twisted together and covered with gutta. The leaves should start from the top of the calyx.

Damp lightly and box up until required.

Gardenia Buttonhole

These are sometimes asked for, and when well made can look very pleasing, but today they are very difficult to find in the market. (Many men are against the heavy scent which can be rather overpowering.)

Gardenias bruise very easily, so the greatest care must be taken when handling them — they are better kept damped down between cellulose wool in the market box when not required. As they become past their prime they turn a creamy brown colour.

Always work with a small pad of wool on the bench so that the flower can be laid on a soft surface.

Materials needed:

3, 24 gauge (.56mm) × 7in (180mm) wire
32 gauge (.28mm) silver for leaves
36 gauge (.20mm) silver binding
Cardboard

Remove the flower head from its foliage and carefully cut off just below the calyx. Take a small circle of card with a star cut in the centre and insert this over the base of the stalk pushing it up carefully under the petals to give a firm backing. The points formed by the star should be enough to hold the card up but two 24 gauge (.56mm) × 7in (180mm) wires can be pushed through at the back of the card as for the Carnation buttonhole if necessary. Place out the petals very carefully as they bruise easily; so often the outer ones tend to curl. The cross wires will be approximately 1½in (3.75cm) long.

Five Gardenia leaves are necessary for backing the flower. These should be firm and a dark green colour. Clean them over with a soft piece of wool to remove water stains. Wire on 32 gauge (.28mm) silver wire, single leg with a loop at the back of each leaf.

Mount the flowers on a double leg 24 gauge (.56mm) × 7in (180mm) which is inserted right under the cardboard collar and tapered to make the false stem. Bind on the backing leaves with 36 gauge (.20mm) silver reel wire as for the Carnation, then cover with gutta percha from just under the flower head to the base of the 2in (5cm) stem.

Violet Buttonhole

This is a pleasing and not too pretentious buttonhole made from seven Violets. These are cut short and mounted on single leg 32 gauge (.28mm) rose wire. Gutta lightly and then place one at the top, two below this, then four in the bottom row, twisting the mounts to hold them firm. Wire a small leaf to place at the back, mount and bind in. Cover the base of the wire with gutta percha. The leaf at the back is usually a well-shaped Ivy leaf — Violet leaves are too large.

Rose Sprays

Roses make an excellent corsage or spray. They can be made up into various sized sprays with two, three and five roses. Some have their natural stems and others are pipped. Try to use the foliage belonging to the Rose itself and not from another variety.

Two-spray of Roses
Natural stems

Materials needed:
2 Roses (different sizes) and as a guide
    2 three-sprays of leaves and 3 single leaves but with some varieties you may have to adjust this
2, 22 gauge (.71mm) × 10in (260mm)
32 gauge (.28mm) and 36 gauge (.20mm) silver reel wires
green gutta percha

Wire the Roses with 22 gauge (.71mm) × 10in (260mm) as described in Chapter 11. If the Roses have particularly thin stems 24 gauge (.56mm) wire can be used.

The three single leaves are wired with 32 gauge (.28mm) silver, with a loop and a stitch at the back of the leaf and double leg. The two three-sprays of leaves, which are the top three leaves on a leaf spray, are each wired with a stitch, loop and a double leg; the six legs form the false stem. Gutta from below the last two leaves. When using single leaves, grade for size and keep the larger ones to the centre.

Take a length of 36 gauge (.20mm) silver reel wire and the smallest Rose with a single leaf behind it.

Figure 12.5: Two-spray of Roses on natural stems

Attach the binding wire about 2in (5cm) down the stem of the Rose and bind the single leaf into position with a small part of the leaf showing above the Rose.

Travel quickly down with the binding wire and place a three-spray of leaves on the top of the stem of the first Rose, so that the top of the first leaf of the spray is half way up the Rose and slightly to one side.

The second and slightly larger Rose is placed under the first very slightly to one side. The top petals of the second Rose are just beneath the seedbox of the first.

The binding wire stays in one place after the second Rose has been placed into position. Bind a single leaf on either side of the second flower; the widest part of the spray is here.

The spray has a return end of leaves, either a three-spray or three single leaves. Make sure the false legs do not cross each other.

Cut the false legs and wires from the Rose stems to the binding wire. Cut the two Rose stems at different lengths. Cover the binding under the second Rose with gutta percha.

Three-spray of Roses

Materials needed:
3 Roses, each a different size
2 three-sprays of Rose leaves and 5 single Rose leaves
2, 22 gauge (.71mm) ×10in (260mm) wire
1, 22 gauge (.71mm) × 7in (180mm) wire
32 gauge (.28mm) and 36 gauge (.20mm) silver reel
  wire
green gutta percha

Wire the two smallest Roses with 22 gauge (.71mm) × 10in (260mm) as shown in Chapter 11. If the Roses have particularly thin stems 24 gauge (.56mm) wire can be used. The third and largest Rose is mounted on a 22 gauge (.71mm) × 7in (180mm) single leg, the stem of the Rose being as short as possible. The 22 gauge (.71mm) × 7in (180mm) wire is pushed through the seedbox about half way up. Gutta the twist of the single leg mount.

The five single leaves and two three-sprays of leaves are as for the two-spray of Roses.

Attach 36 gauge (.20mm) silver binding wire about 2in (5cm) down the stem of the smallest Rose. Place a single leaf behind it, the petals of the Rose being in a line with the stitch on the leaf. A three-spray of leaves is placed to one side on the top of the stem of the first Rose, the top leaf of this coming to about half way up the Rose. The second Rose is placed on the opposite side to the three-spray of leaves, the petals of it forming the base of the sepals of the first Rose. The stem of this Rose goes down the side of the stem of the first Rose.

The third and the largest Rose is placed in next. The single leg is pushed between the stems of the first two Roses and the wire is twisted round the stems, just

Figure 12.6: Three-spray of Roses for evening wear

beneath the stem of the third Rose, one and a half times. Then cut the remaining wire away at the top of the spray. The third Rose is in a line with the first Rose. Place leaves on either side of the third Rose to get the widest point.

The return end can be a three-spray of leaves or three single leaves. Finish the spray as for the two-spray of Roses.

Five-spray of Roses for day wear

Materials needed:
5 Roses, one small, two a little larger, one a little larger still and one open Rose
about 3 three-sprays of leaves
4 single leaves
3, 22 gauge (.71mm) × 12in (310mm) wire
2, 22 gauge (.71mm) × 7in (180mm) wire
32 gauge (.28mm) and 36 gauge (.20mm) reel wires
green gutta percha

The first three Roses are left on natural stems; they are the smallest one (number 1), one of the next-sized ones (number 2), and the next largest (number 3). These three are wired as described for the wiring of Roses in Chapter 11 with 22 gauge (.71mm) × 12in (310mm). The two remaining Roses, that is the largest one (number 4) and the second-sized one (number 5) are cut, leaving about ¼in (.6cm) of stem. A 22 gauge (.71mm) × 7in (180mm) wire is pushed up into the stem and a piece of 32 gauge (.28mm) silver reel wire pushed through the seedbox and twisted down the stem and the stub wire. Gutta down from where the silver wire has been twisted and go to the bottom of the stub wire.

Wire the leaves with 32 gauge (.28mm) silver as for the two-spray of Roses. Use a piece of 36 gauge (.20mm) silver reel wire for binding and attach it to the smallest Rose about 3in (7.5cm) from the top of the Rose. Place a medium-sized leaf at the back of it, so that it just shows above. A three-spray of leaves is placed to one side and then the second Rose to the other side; a second three-spray of leaves is placed in the opposite side to the first one and the third Rose is placed in the opposite side to the second three-spray.

The fourth and largest Rose is placed in a line with the first one and faces upwards; it is placed into position with the false leg on top of the natural stems of the other three Roses. Place leaves on either side of this Rose as the widest point is at the fourth flower. All the binding is now in one position under the fourth flower.

The return end is placed in next; this consists of the fifth Rose which is the same size as the second flower and is placed in on the same side. Place a single leaf under this Rose so the tip just shows beyond the Rose. Place a three-spray of leaves in the centre of the return end.

Cut false legs away to just beneath the binding wire, cut the three natural stems at different lengths so they are longer than the return end. Gutta the binding wire under the fourth flower to make a neat finish.

Five-spray of Roses for evening wear

Materials needed:
5 Roses similar sizes as for the five-spray for day wear
3 three-sprays of Rose leaves and 4 single Rose leaves
3, 22 gauge (.71mm) × 12in (310mm) wire
2, 22 gauge (.71mm) × 7in (180mm) wire
32 gauge (.28mm) and 36 gauge (.20mm) silver reel wire
gutta percha (colour according to colour of Roses)

Cut all the Roses to a ¼in (.6cm) of stem. The first three Roses have a 22 gauge (.71mm) × 12in (310mm) and the last two are wired with 22 gauge (.71mm) × 7in (180mm). Push the wire up into the stem, then push a 32 gauge (.28mm) silver through the seedbox and twist down the Rose stem a little way to hold securely. Gutta from where the wire is twisted to the end of the stub wire.

Wire the Rose leaves with 32 gauge (.28mm) silver as for the two-spray of Roses. The making of the spray is the same as for the five-spray for day wear, but all are bound on false legs instead of natural stems. The placing of the Roses is exactly the same. To finish the spray taper the false legs to the binding wire. Make sure the false stem does not show beneath the return end.

A Cabbage Rose

This uses up petals from blown roses. Depending on the variety used it usually takes three to four Roses. 'Pink Sensation', 'Sonia' and 'Bridal Pink' are good varieties, but handle them with great care to save bruising. Once made this lasts well.

Remove the petals from the Rose carefully and keep in size groups. Use 32 gauge (.28mm) silver wire for larger petals and 36 gauge (.20mm) for smaller ones.

Carefully pleat a petal or two smaller petals together (mostly single) and mount as for a feathered Carnation on a single leg (see p. 71). Wire up two three-sprays of leaves on 32 gauge (.28mm) silver double leg and five or six single leaves.

Figure 12.7: Cabbage Rose

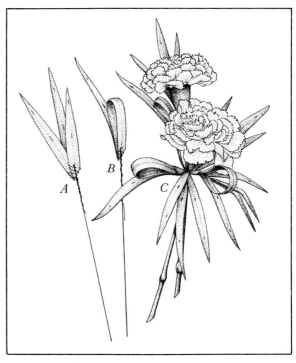

Figure 12.8: Two-spray (corsage) of Carnations
A. Three-spray of straight grasses
B. Straight and looped grasses
C. Natural stems with return end of grasses

Take one good seed pod, remove the sepals and leave ½in (1.25cm) of stem. Wire on 24 gauge × 10in (.56mm × 260mm) single leg. Cover the natural stem with gutta percha.

To make
Attach the binding under the seed pod using 36 gauge (.20mm). Bind on a row of small petals, binding at the base of the petals. Now face the flower. Keep binding in one place. Make petals stand away from the centre, and keep adding more to get a fully open flower. Place the sprays of leaves with one on the left behind the flower and the other as a returned end. Place single leaves in reverse to back the flower and hide the wires. Bind. Then taper the stems and cover with gutta percha.

Carnation Sprays

The leaves of the Carnation are known as grasses. For sprays these need to be removed from the stems and wired for use in the spray. Many florists use Asparagus Fern in Carnation sprays, but it is preferable to use the foliage of the flower wherever possible rather than another variety. The grasses are more clean cut and less 'fussy' than Asparagus Fern.

Two-spray of Carnations

Materials needed :
2 Carnations (different sizes)
12 grasses
5, 24 gauge × 7in (.56mm × 180mm) wire
2, 22 gauge × 12in (.71mm × 310mm) wire
32 gauge (.28mm) and 36 gauge (.20mm) silver reel wire
green gutta percha

First wire the Carnations with 22 gauge × 12in (.71mm × 310mm). Wire nine grasses with single stitch and single leg; then bend three grasses in half with the right side of the leaf at the top. Pierce a 32 gauge (.28mm) silver through the two ends to make a double leg mount. The bottom of the grass should be cut at an angle.

Take three of the straight grasses at three different lengths. With the longest one in the centre, fit the base of the three grasses to one point. Take a 24 gauge × 7in (.56mm × 180mm); holding the three grasses in the left hand, pierce the wire through the three grasses a little way from the base and make a single leg mount.

Twist the three false legs of the grasses a little way down the stub wire, then cut them away. This is known as a spray of three grasses. Cover with gutta percha from where the 24 gauge × 7in (.56mm × 180mm) has been pierced through the grasses. Make two of these three-sprays.

Mount a double and a straight grass with 24 gauge × 7in (.56mm × 180mm) in the same way and gutta it. Three of these are needed. This is known as a straight and doubled spray. When all the grasses and Carnations have been prepared, take a length of 36 gauge (.20mm) binding wire; then take the smallest Carnation and place a three-spray of grasses behind it so that it shows above the Carnation by about ½in (1.25cm). Attach the binding wire 2–2½in (5–6.25cm) down the stem of the flower to hold the grass in place.

Travelling down with the binding wire all the time, place a straight and doubled grass spray to one side, so that the top of the spray goes half way up the small Carnation. When the binding has travelled approximately 1in (2.5cm), the second Carnation should be placed in position; it goes slightly to one side. The petals rest just beneath the calyx of the first flower. The binding stays in one position now, just beneath the second flower.

Grasses need to be placed in to give a definite width to the spray; this should be across the second flower so place a straight and doubled spray on either side of the spray. The spray has a return end which can be made by placing in a three-spray of grasses, facing back to the top of the spray.

Finish by bringing the binding wire up between the false legs and the stems. Take the wires from the lower part of the Carnation stems up to the binding wire which is under the second Carnation and cut the false legs away to here. Leave the natural stems about 3in (7.5cm) and cut them at different lengths at an angle. Cover over the binding wire at the centre with gutta percha.

The amount of grasses used can vary according to the size of the Carnations or the size of the grasses.

Three-spray Carnations

Sometimes a three-spray may be requested, but these are rather large to wear.

Materials needed:
3 Carnations each a different size. 17 grasses
7, 24 gauge × 7in (.56mm × 180mm) wires
2, 22 gauge × 12in (.71mm × 310mm) wires
1, 22 gauge × 7in (.71mm × 180mm) wire
32 gauge (.28mm) and 36 gauge (.20mm) silver reel wire
green gutta percha

Wire the two smallest Carnations with 22 gauge × 12in (.71mm × 310mm) as shown in the general wiring section in Chapter 11. The third and largest one should be cut to a ¼in (.6cm) of stem; then pierce a 22 gauge × 7in (.71mm × 180mm) through half way up the calyx and bring it down to form a single leg mount. Gutta where the wire is twisted over the stem.

The grasses are wired in three straight, and straight and doubled, as wired for the two-spray of Carnations. Three sets of three straight are needed and four sets of straight and doubled grasses. Take a length of 36 gauge (.20mm) silver reel wire and attach the wire about 2–2½in (5–6.25cm) down the stem of the smallest Carnation.

Bind a three-spray grass at the back of the Carnation so the tip just shows above the Carnation. Travel down with the binding wire and place another three-spray of grasses to one side of the Carnation, so the tip goes half way up the first flower. Place the next-sized Carnation on the same side of the grass so the two Carnation stems are parallel, and the top of the second Carnation is at the base of the first Carnation. Place in a straight and doubled grass on the opposite side to the second Carnation.

At this stage the third and largest Carnation is placed into position and sits on the top of the spray. Push the false leg between the stems of the first and second Carnation and twist the wire round the stems one and a half times. Cut away the false leg on the top of the spray so as not to leave a spiteful wire at the back. The third flower is in line with the first. The binding wire stays in one place under the third Carnation after having travelled 1–1½in (2.5–3.75cm).

Place the grasses in to make the widest point at the third Carnation and make a return end of grasses, using the last three-spray and a straight and doubled one. Cut the false legs away and the wires from the first two Carnations up to the binding wire. Trim the stems at an angle, with one slightly shorter than the other. Cover over the binding wire with gutta percha.

Malmaison

Sometimes one large Carnation is required for a spray; when this is needed make two or three Carnations into one large one.

Materials needed:
3 Carnations
6 Carnation grasses
7 or 8 small leaves, e.g. Rose or Pittosporum leaves
3, 22 gauge × 7in (.71mm × 180mm) wires
3, 24 gauge × 7in (.56mm × 180mm) wires
32 gauge (.28mm) and 36 gauge (.20mm) silver reel wire

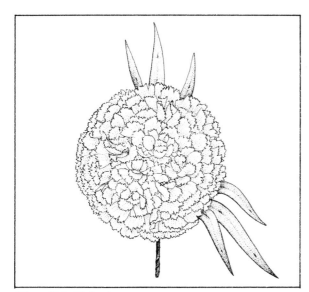

Figure 12.9: Malmaison

a piece of cardboard 3 × 3in (7.5 × 7.5cm)
green gutta percha

First prepare the small leaves for backing the cardboard which holds the flowers together. Each leaf has a single stitch and a double leg, with the short leg being about ½in (1.25cm) below the stem and wired with 32 gauge (.28mm) silver.

The grasses are wired as for the three-spray for Carnation sprays. Two three-sprays are needed. Take the piece of cardboard and cut it into as large a circle as possible. In the centre cut a small circle large enough to take the petals of the three Carnations.

Remove the seedbox from each Carnation by pressing at the base of the seedbox with the finger and thumb. The seedbox will then come up through the petals and can be taken away. Remove the calyx and the sepals. Cut the stems very short and put a 24 gauge × 7in (.56mm × 180mm) through the base of the petals. Bend the two ends down to form a hairpin. Try to keep holding the three Carnations downwards to keep the group together.

Before placing the Carnations through the hole in the centre of the cardboard, push the large outer petals of each flower to the sides and make the three Carnations look as one with the small petals on the inside and larger petals on the outside. Pull the petals into shape. Push the three Carnations through the hole of the cardboard and push the cardboard as close under the petals as possible.

Secure the cardboard into position by putting three cross pieces of 22 gauge (.71mm) wire across the back of the cardboard at equal distances apart, about 2in (5cm) long.

Take a length of 36 gauge (.20mm) binding wire and place leaves round to cover the cardboard by pushing the small piece of wire on the leaf into the petals just beneath the cardboard and binding them into position just beneath the natural stem of the leaves. Bind on the false legs of the leaves.

Taper the stem and false legs to about an inch (2.5cm) and twist the binding wire to the end of the false stem. Gutta the false stem half way down before placing in the grasses, one on either side of the Carnation. Cut the binding wire away and cover with gutta percha from where the grasses have been placed into the end of the false stem. Then face the Carnation by pressing at the base of the flower and tilting it forward.

Lily Of The Valley Spray On Natural Stems

Lily of the Valley is usually left with natural stems for a spray. Their own foliage is also used.

Materials needed:
1 bunch of Lily of the Valley (10 stems in a bunch)
5 fairly small leaves
36 gauge (.20mm), 32 gauge (.28mm) and 30 gauge (.32mm) silver reel wire
green gutta percha

Wire ten pieces of Lily of the Valley as explained in Chapter 11. Cut two pieces in half and mount two pieces together with 30 gauge (.32mm) silver double leg. Cover with gutta percha.

Wire two of the leaves with a 32 gauge (.28mm) silver single stitch and twist the two wires down the natural stem.

The remaining three leaves have a piece taken from the top of the leaf for a straight piece, and the base of the leaf is bent down for a looped piece. Place the straight piece behind the loop and push a 30 gauge (.32mm) wire through the leaves and make a double leg mount. Cover with gutta percha.

Use 36 gauge (.20mm) silver wire for binding; keep the binding wire in one position. Select a straight piece of Lily of the Valley and attach the binding about 5in (12.5cm) down the stem. Place shorter flowers on either side of it, each being a different length. The stems on this spray can cross each other to give the required effect. Gradually make the spray wider, until the widest flowers are placed into position, in a line with the binding wire.

The flowers in the middle should be placed in at different levels, some being fairly long and building up to a tallest flower in the centre of the spray. The mounted Valley are placed in over the binding wire to give a slight return end. Then place the two straight leaves at the back of the spray, keeping them below the flowers and at different lengths. The mounted leaves are arranged attractively through the spray, some coming over the binding wire and giving a slight return end.

Take the wires away from the natural stems up to the binding wire. Cut the false legs away up to the binding wire. Cover the binding with gutta percha. Trim the natural stems, leaving the longest in the centre tapering towards the sides; these should not be cut too short.

Freesia Spray For Day Wear

Freesia sprays for day wear may be made in mixed colours or of one colour only. They are left on their natural stems and the spray is made to look as natural as possible.

Materials needed:
8–10 stems depending on the size of the flowers
30 gauge (.32mm), 32 gauge (.28mm) and 36 gauge (.20mm) silver reel wire
24 gauge (.56mm) × 7in (180mm) stub wires

Wire the flowers as explained in Chapter 11. If some of the stems have a particularly large flower at the base, this can be removed and wired separately with 32 gauge (.28mm) silver wire with a double leg mount and covered with green gutta percha.

Use 36 gauge (.20mm) silver wire for binding the flowers into position. They are bound in on their natural stems. Begin with a small, straight and fairly pointed Freesia. Place a slightly larger flower to one side of this, just a little lower down. Place a third Freesia to the opposite side of the first one; it can again be slightly larger but needs to be a little shorter than the second flower.

If you are using mixed coloured Freesias they should be grouped through in colours, the yellow and white one way and the pink and mauve the opposite way.

Attach the binding wire approximately 5in (12.5cm) down the stem of the first flower and keep it in one place the whole time the spray is being made. Bind the other two Freesias into position. Try to use

Figure 12.10: Straight spray (corsage) of Freesia
A. Large individual flower wired
B. Stem mounted
C. Flowers wired and stem mounted

the curved stems as much as possible at the sides and also have some on the return end. Gradually get wider on the sides of the spray, at the same time placing some Freesias in the centre at various lengths, some gradually getting higher to the centre. The larger flowers which have been wired separately can be placed in very low to give extra depth. The widest part of the spray is where the binding wire is. Place a flower either side to give the widest point; these two flowers must be the same length. The stems in this spray are allowed to cross each other where they are being bound into position, in order to obtain the correct shape. Place the tallest flower in the centre of the spray; this should be a fairly small flower and the rest of the flowers build up to this centre flower.

Make a return end of flowers by using the curved stems, carefully bending them back to form the returned end. The longest flower on the return end is in the middle, and is roughly half the length of the top of the spray. Place flowers on either side of this Freesia to meet the widest point. Also place some in the centre to meet up with the centre flower.

To finish the spray, take away the twisted wire from the natural stems up to the binding wire. Cut the false legs away to the binding wire. Cut away the binding wire, and cover with green gutta percha. Trim the natural stems, but leave them quite long with the longest ones in the centre.

Gardenia Sprays

The Gardenia is not often seen now, other than as a pot plant. There are no specialist growers who market Gardenias as cut flowers today to my knowledge so if you have a supply it is a very worthwhile asset to your business.

Gardenias are made in sprays of twos and threes. It is best to use their own foliage. If the leaves are too large they can be trimmed at the base to make them smaller, but never trim them at the top as they will bruise and go brown. The flowers also bruise very easily and soon go brown. The fresh flowers are a perfect white and as they age so they become cream in colour.

If there are buds attached to the Gardenias these can be wired with a 24 gauge (.56mm) × 7in (180mm) up inside the stem and a 32 gauge (.28mm) silver wire pushed through the calyx and twisted around the stem and a little way down the stub wire. Cover with gutta percha from where the wire has been twisted down to the bottom of the stub wire. Never touch the petals of the Gardenia with your hands, but use cellular wadding.

Two-spray of Gardenias

Materials needed:
2 Gardenias of different sizes with 3 leaves round each flower
Gardenia leaves of various sizes to be placed through the spray
2, 22 gauge (.71mm) × 10in (260mm) wires
32 gauge (.28mm) and 36 gauge (.20mm) silver reel wire
If there are buds these should be used and then a 24 gauge (.56mm) × 7in (180mm) wire is required

First, wire the two Gardenias with 22 gauge (.71mm) × 10in (260mm) as shown in Chapter 11 and tip the faces. Wire the leaves for the spray with 32 gauge (.28mm) silver single stitch and double leg and cover them with green gutta percha.

Bind the spray together with 36 gauge (.20mm) silver wire; take the smallest Gardenia and place a medium-sized leaf behind it and bind about 2½in (6.25cm) from the head of the flower. Travel down

with the binding wire and then place a leaf to one side of the Gardenia; the tip is roughly half way up the side of the Gardenia.

Place the second flower very slightly to one side of the first flower, on the opposite side to where the leaf has been placed. Do not bind too near the natural stem of the flower. The binding wire stays in one position when the second flower has been placed into the spray.

Put leaves on either side of the second flower to make the widest point of the spray. The return end leaves are placed in and face the top of the spray. Approximately three leaves are needed for the return end. Taper the false legs, so they do not show beneath the return end leaves. Take the binding wire down the false legs to hold them into position. Cover the false stems with green gutta percha.

Three-spray of Gardenias

Materials needed:
3 Gardenias each a different size with three Gardenia leaves around each flower
8–9 Gardenia leaves to be used through the spray
2, 22 gauge (.71mm) × 10in (260mm) wires
1, 22 gauge (.71mm) × 7in (180mm) wires
32 gauge (.28mm) and 36 gauge (.20mm) silver reel wire
If there are buds these should be used and a 24 gauge (.56mm) × 7in (180mm) wire will be needed

First wire the three Gardenias as shown in Chapter 11. The largest Gardenia should be wired with 22 gauge (.71mm) × 7in (180mm) wire. Tip the faces. Wire the leaves with 32 gauge (.28mm) silver wire, single stitch and double leg, then cover with green gutta percha.

Bind the spray together with 36 gauge (.20mm) reel wire. Take the smallest Gardenia and place a medium-sized leaf behind it, so that some of the leaf shows above the flower. Begin the binding wire about 3in (7.5cm) down the false stem of the flower. The method is the same as for the Gardenia two-spray. Travel down with the binding wire and then place a leaf to one side and also a bud if you have one.

The second and slightly larger flower goes to the opposite side to the leaf and the bud. A leaf can be placed to cover a part of the false stem of the first flower.

Place the third and largest Gardenia into position; it sits flat on the false legs and is in a line with the first Gardenia. The binding wire stays in one place under the third flower. Place leaves on either side of the third flower to make the widest part of the spray.

Place in three return end leaves, the largest being placed in the centre. Cut the false legs away just beneath the return end, take the binding wire down to the end of the false stem and cover with green gutta percha.

Orchid Sprays

There are many varieties of Orchids; the one most used in sprays used to be the Cymbidium but today the Singapore Orchid is widely used. Orchids used to be made into a one-spray, two-spray or three-spray but now it depends on the size. As Orchids have not a suitable foliage for use in sprays a houseplant foliage, such as Ivy, Peperomia, Scindapsus, etc., is used.

One-spray of Orchid

Materials needed:
One Orchid and a few leaves
1, 22 gauge (.71mm) × 7in (180mm) wire
32 gauge (.28mm) and 36 gauge (.20mm) silver reel wire
gutta percha

Wire the Orchid as described in Chapter 11 with 22 gauge (.71mm) × 7in (180mm) wire.

The leaves are wired on 32 gauge (.28mm) silver single stitch; you should double leg and gutta them. If some leaves are particularly heavy a 30 gauge (.32mm) silver could be used.

Bind the spray together with 36 gauge (.20mm) silver. Keep the binding wire in one position under the natural stem of the flower. Arrange the leaves attractively around the Orchid, keeping the spray fairly narrow at the top with the width going across the centre of the Orchid. Some of the leaves should form a return end. Taper the false legs to just above the return end, take the binding wire to the bottom of the stem and cover it with gutta percha.

Two-spray of Orchids

Materials needed:
2 Orchids, each a different size, if possible
a few leaves in various sizes
2, 22 gauge (.71mm) × 10in (260mm) wires
32 gauge (.28mm) and 36 gauge (.20mm) silver reel wire

gutta percha (usually natural)

The Orchids are wired as described in Chapter 11 with 22 gauge (.71mm) × 10in (260mm) stub wires. Wire the leaves in the same way as for a one-spray of Orchids.

Bind the spray together with 36 gauge (.20mm) silver, place the smallest Orchid in first with a leaf behind it and bind about 2½in (6.25cm) down the false leg.

The second Orchid is placed beneath the first slightly to one side, leaving a small space between the two Orchids. Arrange the leaves through the spray gradually working to the widest point at the second flower. The binding wire stays under the second flower. Finish as for a one-spray of Orchid.

Three-spray of Orchids

Materials needed:
3 Orchids, each a different size
a few leaves in various sizes
2, 22 gauge (.71mm) ×10in (260mm) wires
1, 22 gauge (.71mm) × 7in (180mm) wire
32 gauge (.28mm) and 36 gauge (.20mm) silver reel wire
gutta percha (usually natural)

Wire the Orchids as described in Chapter 11, the two smallest with 22 gauge (.71mm) × 10in (260mm) and the largest one with 22 gauge (.71mm) × 7in (180mm). The leaves are wired as for a one-spray of Orchid.

Bind with 36 gauge (.20mm) silver reel wire. The smallest flower is placed in first. Begin binding about 2½in (6.25cm) down, place a leaf behind the first Orchid and arrange leaves through the spray making the widest part of the spray at the third Orchid. Place the medium Orchid to one side and bind just beneath the natural stem. The third and largest Orchid is placed facing back for the return end; some leaves are also needed for the return end.

The binding stays under the natural stem of the third flower. Cut false legs leaving the false stem just under the return end and cover the stem with gutta percha.

Violet Sprays

These can be made in various shapes and ways: a spray for day wear, a cluster for day wear, a spray for evening wear and a cluster for evening wear. These sprays can also be made using Snowdrops or Rock Cyclamen.

Violet spray for day wear

Materials needed:
2 bunches of Violets
2 Violet leaves
32 gauge (.28mm) and 36 gauge (.20mm) silver reel wire
green gutta percha

Wire the Violets as described in Chapter 11, but leave a length of wire at the bottom of the stem. Wire the two leaves with 32 gauge (.28mm) silver stitch and twist it round the natural stem.

Bind with 36 gauge (.20mm) silver wire. Choose a small, long-stemmed Violet and attach the binding 3–4in (7.5–10cm) down from the flower head. Place two shorter flowers on either side of this flower, a head shorter than each other, and working up to larger flowers.

Do not bind too tightly or you may cut the stems. Travel down with the binding wire for about 1in (2.5cm) but in doing this place Violets in at the sides, gradually getting wider. Also place some in the middle of the spray, getting some higher and putting some in deeper. Place a leaf to one side among the Violets. The widest point comes when the binding has travelled the 1in (2.5cm). The tallest flower should also be at this point in the centre of the spray; make it between 1–1½in (2.5–3.75cm) high.

Measure a flower for the return end; this should be half the length of the longest flower at the top of the spray. Untwist the wire from the bottom and cut the stem to the required length, then retwist round the stem three times at the base to hold it firmly in position. Cut the wire to 2in (5cm) below the stem. All the flowers for the return end are done in this way, cut to the length required. Push the wire at the end of the Violet through the stems where the binding wire stays after travelling the 1in (2.5cm) and bend it down at the back with the natural stems.

Bind into position with the binding wire. Make a rounded return end placing the flowers into position in this way to the required lengths they are needed. Build round to meet the widest flowers and also build up to meet the tallest in the centre. Also place some short Violets in for depth. Place a leaf in the return end, among the Violets on the opposite side to the leaf at the top of the spray.

Finish by untwisting the wire from the stems up to the binding wire and cutting it away. Cut away the wires which have been pushed through. For the return end, up to the binding wire, cover the binding at the centre with green gutta percha. Trim the natural stems, leaving the longer ones in the centre, the short towards the sides.

Violet cluster for day wear

Materials needed:
1½ bunches of Violets
3 Violet leaves
32 gauge (.28mm) and 36 gauge (.20mm) silver wire
green gutta percha

Wire the Violets as described in Chapter 11. Wire the leaves with 32 gauge (.28mm) silver wire, stitch and twist the wires down the natural stem. Bind with 36 gauge (.20mm) silver, keeping the binding in one place. The cluster is fan shaped. Take a small flower and bind about four inches (10cm) down the stem. The widest flowers are when the binding wire is in one position.

The centre flower should be three-quarters the length of the first flower and lean towards the top. Arrange the Violets at various lengths throughout the cluster, with some flowers building up to the centre flower, and some very short to give depth. Have an uneven or broken line along the bottom of the cluster, but this is not a definite return end. Place the leaves into position; these form a collar around the cluster.

The stems are left natural, with the wires removed from them, up to the binding wire. Taper them on either side, with the longest in the centre. Cover the binding wire with green gutta percha.

Violet spray for evening wear

Materials needed:
2 bunches of Violets
2 Violet leaves
32 gauge (.28mm) and 36 gauge (.20mm) silver wire
gutta percha — green or natural

Cut the Violets at various lengths from 2in (5cm) to ½in (1.25cm). Wire them all as explained in Chapter 11 and then mount with 32 gauge (.28mm) silver double leg and cover with gutta percha from where the mount begins.

Wire the two leaves on 32 gauge (.28mm) silver single stitch and double leg and cover with gutta percha. Bind with 36 gauge (.20mm) silver; begin the binding 3in (7.5cm) down the first Violet which is a small one. Always bind on the false legs and not on the natural stem. The making of the spray is as for a *straight spray*, but the two leaves are placed into positions, one in the top of the spray to one side and in the return end on the opposite side.

Taper the false legs, take the binding wire down to the bottom, and cover the false stem with gutta percha.

Violet cluster for evening wear

Materials needed:
$1\frac{1}{2}$ bunches of Violets
3 Violet leaves
32 gauge (.28mm) and 36 gauge (.20mm) silver wire
gutta percha — green or natural

Wire the flowers as explained in Chapter 11. As the cluster is being made, the Violets need to be mounted on 32 gauge (.28mm) silver double leg mounts and covered with gutta percha from the beginning of the mount to the length they are needed in the cluster; all the Violets are bound in on the false leg, directly beneath the natural stem.

The leaves are wired on 32 gauge (.28mm) silver, single stitch and double leg to the length required as for the Violets.

Bind with 36 gauge (.20mm) silver into a fan shape, making it as for the cluster for day wear keeping the binding in one place.

Taper the false stem to about 1in (2.5cm), take the binding wire down to the bottom and cover it with gutta percha.

Straight Spray

Straight sprays can be made from various flowers; for example, Hyacinth, Freesia, 'Paper White' Narcissi, Chincherinchee, Stephanotis.

These flowers need to be pipped to make the spray. Foliage such as Ivy leaves can be used, but usually the flowers and buds of the flower are sufficient to make an attractive spray.

The amount of flowers you will need will vary according to the size and type you are using. To give a rough guide, if Hyacinths are being used then between 30 to 40 pips are required for an average-sized spray. 32 gauge (.28mm) and 36 gauge (.20mm) silver reel wire is needed and if the flowers are particularly heavy 30 gauge (.32mm) silver. The colour of the gutta percha depends on the colour of the flower being used.

White gutta should be used for white flowers, natural for coloured flowers. Silver paper is also used to cover the wires for some sprays.

Wire the flowers with 32 gauge (.28mm) silver with a double leg, or heavier flowers with 30 gauge (.32mm) silver. For details of the wiring see Chapter 11, and cover them with gutta percha. Take a length of 36 gauge (.20mm) silver reel wire for the binding. Choose a small flower or half-open bud, and then a slightly larger flower. Place the second flower selected about a head shorter than the first flower. Attach the binding wire about 3in (7.5cm) down the false legs. This helps to keep the spray flexible and not looking too stiff. Place a third flower, slightly larger than the second to the opposite side of the second flower, about half a head shorter, then bind it into place with the binding wire.

Gradually travel down about 1in (2.5cm) with the binding, keeping it going down at an angle, and then keep the binding in one place. While doing this, place the flowers into the spray so it gets wider and builds up higher.

When binding the flowers into position, do not bind too near the head of them, but let them extend on their false legs to make the spray look light and not too solid. Only the flowers placed in very short for the depth are bound just under the natural stem. All the false legs must go beyond the centre of the spray. When the centre is reached, the binding wire stays in one position. The two widest flowers are placed in at right angles with the false legs. Also place in the tallest flower in the same line as the widest flowers, but in the centre of the spray; this stands up straight and is approximately $1\frac{1}{2}$in (3.75cm) tall. It should be a small flower or a bud.

There should be plenty of variation of length; never place two flowers in side by side at exactly the same length. Have an uneven or slightly broken line down the edges of the spray. Include some short flowers for depth. Place all the flowers in from the top and sides and not from the back of the spray. The spray has a return end, which is half the length of the top of the spray and forms a semi-circle to meet the widest flowers. Still keep the binding wire in the same position.

Use fairly small blooms for the longest ones on the return end. Build up the flowers in the return end to meet the centre flower of the spray. Have variation of length in the return end as for the top of the spray. To finish the stem of the false legs, cut the false legs away to about $1–1\frac{1}{2}$in (2.5–3.75cm) below the binding wire at the centre, and taper them to make a nice slender false stem. Take the binding wire down the false stem to the bottom and cut it away. Cover the false stem with gutta percha. If buds or leaves are being used in the straight spray these should be grouped through.

Curved Spray

Similar flowers can be used in this as for the straight spray; the same materials are needed.

Wire the flowers with 32 gauge (.28mm) silver with a double leg. For details of the wiring see Chapter 11 (head-dress and spray section). Cover them with gutta percha.

Take a length of 36 gauge (.20mm) silver reel wire for the binding. Choose a small flower or half-open bud, and then a slightly larger flower. Place the second flower selected about a head shorter than the first flower. Attach the binding wire about 3in (7.5cm) down the false legs to keep the spray flexible. Place a third flower slightly larger than the second to the opposite side of the second flower, about a head shorter than it; bind into place with the binding wire.

When these flowers are in position, you need to travel down with the binding wire and at the same time build the flowers higher on one side than the other. The side you build higher depends on which way you want the spray to curve. If the spray is a left to right curve then more flowers and longer ones are needed to be built on the left hand side. In the case of a right to left spray, more flowers and longer ones need to be placed on the right hand side of the spray.

Travel with the binding about 1in (2.5cm). As you are building out to the sides with the flowers you must also be placing some in the middle of the spray at various lengths. Keep the larger flowers shorter and the smaller flowers higher, and gradually build up to the centre.

Keep the binding wire in one place when it has travelled approximately 1in (2.5cm); this is considered the centre of the spray and is also the widest part. On the side which has been built up more you have a long flower for the widest point, and on the opposite side a very short one. Do not get the outline too solid, but have a broken line along the edge. The tallest flower in the centre of the spray is a small flower or half-open bud and should be three-quarters the length of the longest flower at the widest point. The centre flower leans towards this point.

When the centre flower has been placed into position, the return end is then formed. Place the longest flower of the return end at an angle to form the curve. It goes in at the side where the shorter flower of the widest point is placed and is half the length of the top

of the spray. A flower half a head shorter goes to one side of it, and a flower half a head shorter than the second flower can go to the other side of it.

Fill in with flowers to meet the widest points on either side of the spray. Also fill in with flowers in the centre of the return end and build up with flowers to meet the centre flower.

Curve the false stem with the return end, and cut to about 1in (2.5cm). Taper the false stem and twist the binding wire down to the end of it. Cut the binding wire away. Cover the false stem with gutta percha. If buds and leaves are used, these should be grouped through. (See Plate 20.)

'L'-shaped Spray

Similar flowers can be used as for the straight spray; the materials needed are the same.

Wire the flowers with 32 gauge (.28mm) silver with a double leg. For details of the wiring see Chapter 11. Cover with gutta percha.

Join the sprays together by bending one of them at a right angle where the binding has stopped after travelling ½in (1.25cm), and bind it to the other spray where the binding has stopped after travelling the ½in (1.25cm).

Fill the corner of the spray with flowers to form the 'L' shape and place a flower in the centre of it just over 1in (2.5cm) in length for the tallest point of the spray. Build up to this with small flowers or buds. Put larger flowers in at shorter lengths to give depth.

Finish by cutting the false stem to about 1in (2.5cm) and tapering it. Take the binding wire to the bottom and cut it away; cover with gutta percha.

Posy Spray

Similar flowers can be used as for a straight spray; the materials needed are the same.

Wire the flowers with 32 gauge (.28mm) silver double leg. For details of the wiring see Chapter 11.

Select seven fairly small flowers or buds and place them so that the tips of the flowers are all at the same level. Using 36 gauge (.20mm) silver, bind the seven flowers together on their false legs about 2in (5cm) from the top of the flower, for an average-sized spray. If you want a smaller spray do not bind as low down; if you want it to be larger, bind lower down. When the flowers are bound into position, these are the outline flowers. Keep the binding wire in one place all the time you are making the cluster. Spread the flowers out to form a circle, keeping the flowers an equal distance apart. The back must be kept flat so it sits well against the clothing.

The false stem goes down at the back of the cluster. Place the centre flower, which is three-quarters the length of the outline flowers, into position; it leans towards the top flower.

Place the remainder of the flowers into position, working from the outside to the centre. Make sure some of the flowers are nearly the same length as the outline flowers; this will help keep the shape of your circle and avoid a 'spoke' effect. Fill the centre of the cluster, building up to the centre flower. Place some of the larger flowers in low to give depth. Vary the lengths as much as possible so that you do not have two flowers which are exactly the same length side by side.

Cut the false stem to about 1in (2.5cm) and taper it. Twist the binding wire down to the end of the false leg and cover with gutta percha.

Mixed Sprays

These can be made in various shapes, such as a straight spray, curved spray, posy and 'L'-shaped spray.

Materials needed:
small mixed flowers preferably in shades of one colour or two colours. Pieces that could be used for a spray in shades of pink are: pink Hyacinth, pink Freesia, pink Carnations — feathered (see Chapter 10), 2 Carol Rose buds and one open Carol Rose. Grey foliage is attractive with pink flowers — leaves of Senecio greyii and Ruta could be used for this. When selecting flowers for a mixed spray try to include as many different shapes as possible
30 gauge (.32mm), 32 gauge (.28mm) and 36 gauge (.20mm) silver reel wire
gutta percha

The Hyacinth and Freesia are wired with 32 gauge (.28mm) silver reel wire with a double leg as in Chapter 11 (see head-dress and spray section). The feathered Carnation is wired with a double leg as described in Chapter 10. The three Roses are cut with just a small stem left and wired with 30 gauge (.32mm) silver, by pushing the wire through the seed-box and making a double leg mount. The Ruta has a

silver wire twisted from the bottom of the main stem to the top and is then mounted in a clump with 32 gauge (.28mm) silver wire. All pieces in the spray are covered with gutta percha.

Bind the sprays together with 36 gauge (.20mm) silver reel wire and make the shapes as already explained under straight sprays (p. 94); the same method is also used for curved sprays, clusters and 'L'-shaped sprays. Use the small pieces at the top of the spray and work to the larger pieces lower down towards the centre. Note that when doing sprays with mixed flowers it is best to have a large flower as the centre flower in the spray. Place this in as short as possible in the position that the tallest centre flower would be placed when doing a spray with one kind of flower. Flowers can be placed in higher around the largest flower to give variation of length. This applies to the various shaped corsages.

When mixed flowers are being used the flowers need to be 'grouped'. This ensures that some of each kind of flower is on either side of the spray; for example, the grouping of the flowers in the straight and curved sprays can be placed in at the top of the spray on one side and gradually brought through to the return end on the opposite side. I often feel that mixed sprays are made up of pieces which are too small — these do not last and the spray soon looks very untidy.

In the case of a posy spray the flowers can be brought through from one side to the other. This helps to distribute the flowers evenly and to make a well balanced spray. Finish these corsages by tapering the false stems to approximately 1in (2.5cm) and twisting the binding wire down to the bottom and cutting the wire away. Cover the false stem with gutta percha. For white sprays use white gutta percha, for coloured sprays use natural gutta percha.

13. HEAD~DRESSES

Flowers in the hair are always attractive and when well designed can add considerably to the overall picture. Everyone has their own idea on what they wish to wear so you may be asked to make all manner of shapes. In this book I have kept to the standard patterns, but these can be easily modified.

Flower head-dresses are worn by both brides and bridesmaids. There are various designs, some being more suitable for child bridesmaids, some for brides and adult bridesmaids. They can be made from fresh or artificial materials. If you are using artificial materials you can spread the work load over a longer period which sometimes helps.

Head-dresses are made from one type of flower, such as a tiara of Lily of the Valley or a half head-dress of white Hyacinth Bells, or they may be of small mixed flowers to match or contrast the dress and be of the same colourings as the bouquet of the bride or bridesmaid. They can also be made in two colours or colours going through a colour range, for example, blue, mauve and pink.

The wiring instructions for most of these flowers are given in Chapter 11 (see p. 79). Use buds half open and open flowers as this gives a lighter look to the head-dress.

When using mixed flowers in a head-dress choose different shaped flowers; this makes for a more interesting head-dress.

Child's Chunky Head-dress

This head-dress is for a child bridesmaid. It is one of the quickest head-dresses to make as it is fairly small. When it is worn it sits at the front of the head. Usually made of mixed flowers, the pieces for this head-dress need to be more chunky than for most head-dresses.

Flowers and leaves which could be used in the summer for this head-dress are mauve Stock (buds and flowers), blue Delphinium (buds and flowers),

Figure 13.1: Child's chunky head-dress, made up of Ivy, Hydrangea, Clematis seedpods, Hoya and baby Orchids

feathered pink Carnations, Ruta and grey-leafed Ivy. Use two 22 gauge (.71mm) × 14in (360mm) stub wires for the frame 32 gauge (.28mm) and 36 gauge (.20mm) silver reel wire. Cover with natural gutta percha for coloured flowers or white gutta percha for white flowers. You will need 1½ yards (1.5m) baby ribbon in the appropriate colour.

Make the frame by binding the two 22 gauge (.71mm) × 14in (360mm) wires together with 36 gauge (.20mm) silver wire and cover them with gutta percha. Make the frame into a circle, overlap about ½in (1.25cm) and bind firmly together with 36 gauge (.20mm) silver reel wire. Cover the binding with gutta percha.

Wire the Ivy leaves with 32 gauge (.28mm) silver. Wire the Ruta in clumps, pushing 32 gauge (.28mm) wire through and make a double leg mount.

Flowers are wired with 32 gauge (.28mm) silver

double leg as in the wiring of flowers for head-dresses and sprays.

The flowers are placed on the *top* of the frame. When attaching them to the frame binding wire is not required as the false legs are twisted round the frame instead. Always twist from immediately beneath the natural stem of the flower or leaf; make sure all the twists go in the same direction. After twisting the false legs round the frame several times, cut off the remaining part of the false leg, making sure it is cut from the top of the frame so there are no sharp wires underneath. The flowers sit flat at the top and a little over the sides and are placed very closely together, all going in the same direction. Group the different flowers from side to side. The width of the space in the centre of the head-dress when the flowers are on the frame is about 3in (7.5cm). The width of the flowers is 1–1½in (2.5–3.75cm). Leave a space of about 1in (2.5cm) between the beginning and the end of the flowers; this is for the ribbon. Two loops and four tails of ribbon are needed for the bow and are attached to the frame in the space left between the flowers. The tails hang down the back of the head.

Baby's All-round Head-dress

This head-dress is for a child bridesmaid; it sits well down on the head. It is usually made of mixed flowers and foliage.

Materials needed for this are small flowers and leaves. Pieces which could be used in the spring for this head-dress are Mimosa, 'Sol d'Or' Narcissus,

Figure 13.2: Working on a baby's all-round head-dress, made up of Tradescantia, Sedum, Geranium, Carnation petals, Heather and Statice

feathered yellow Carnations (see Chapter 10), straw Hyacinths, Ivy leaves and Pittosporum leaves. Four 22 gauge (.71mm) × 12in (310mm) stub wires are needed to form the frame, with 32 gauge (.28mm) and 36 gauge (.20mm) silver reel wire. You will need natural gutta percha for coloured head-dresses, and white for head-dresses made of white flowers.

First make the frame, overlapping two 22 gauge (.71mm) × 12in (310mm) wires about 2in (5cm) with the other two 22 gauge (.71cm) × 12in (310mm). Bind these wires together with 36 gauge (.20mm) silver wire, binding from the centre to the outside each time. Then cover with gutta percha.

The length of the head-dress will vary between 18–21in (45–52.5cm) according to the size of the child's head; the frame can be made smaller accordingly. Shape the frame to make it into a circle. Make a hook one end and a loop the other, each should be ½in (1.25cm) in length and bending outwards. The head-dress can be made with the hook and loop attached or open.

Next wire the leaves; each should be wired with 32 gauge (.28mm) silver wire with a stitch and single leg.

The flowers are wired with a 32 gauge (.28mm) silver wire, single leg. When the pieces have been prepared, attach the binding to the frame and bind the loop of the frame firmly into position. Bind each flower and leaf on its false leg just beneath the natural stem; the pieces go on at the *side* of the frame.

The first pieces slightly overlap the end of the loop. The flowers lie flat on the frame. The false legs are kept on the side of the frame. The width of the flowers on the frame is approximately 1–1½in (2.5–3.75cm). The flowers and leaves are grouped through from side to side to form a pattern. Continue to work round the frame in this way until you reach the hook. Cut the binding wire away. Cover with gutta percha from where the flowers and leaves finish.

Join the frame together and pull the flowers well down on the frame at the sides. There should be no gaps where the hooks meet.

This head-dress can also be made on ribbon instead of a wire frame. In this case, fold the ribbon round the false legs and bind with 36 gauge (.20mm) silver.

Adult's Half Head-dress

This head-dress may be worn by brides and also adult bridesmaids. It is worn across the top of the head. Usually mixed flowers and foliages go to make this head-dress, but flowers of one kind can also be used.

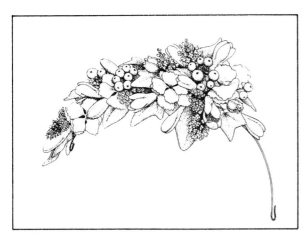

Figure 13.3: Adult's half head-dress in the making, including Ivy, Heather, Achillea, Hydrangea, Berries and Alstroemeria seed heads

Flowers and foliage which could, for example, be used in late spring or early summer are White Bells, Chincherinchee, feathered white Carnations and variegated Ivy. Two 22 gauge (.71mm) × 12in (310mm) stub wires, and 32 gauge (.28mm) and 36 gauge (.20mm) silver reel wire are needed. Use natural gutta percha for coloured head-dresses, and white gutta percha for white flowers.

Make the frame for the head-dress by binding together with 36 gauge (.20mm) silver wire two 22 gauge (.71mm) × 12in (310mm) and covering with gutta percha.

Measure and mark the centre of the frame. Bend it to a half hoop. Make a loop on either side bending it outwards.

Wire the leaves with 32 gauge (.28mm) silver reel wire, making a very neat stitch. Most of the leaves will have a single leg but a few are needed with a double leg; these you cover with gutta percha. The flowers are wired with 32 gauge (.28mm) silver as in the wiring of head-dresses and sprays. Again the majority will have a single, but some of each kind of flower need to be on double legs, then covered with gutta percha. About twenty flowers and leaves are needed with a double leg. Divide the single leg flowers into two sections; keep the double leg pieces separate.

Attach 36 gauge (.20mm) silver wire for binding to the loop at one side of the head-dress and bind the loop into position. With the same piece of wire attach the first flower, preferably a bud, but in any case a small flower, and let it overlap the frame very slightly. This should be a single leg piece as the double leg pieces are for the cluster in the centre of the head-dress. Place another flower or leaf which is a little shorter to one side and a third shorter still to the other side of the first flower. All the flowers with single legs should be bound beneath the natural stem.

Gradually become wider and build up slightly. The width is the same on either side. When approximately an inch (2.5cm) from the mark in the centre of the frame begin to use some of the double leg pieces. This enables you to get higher and also wide enough for the centre. When the binding wire is at the centre it should remain there until the centre cluster is completed. The only pieces at right angles to the frame are the two widest points at the centre, which are in a line with the mark. The width across the centre should be roughly 3in (7.5cm). All the flowers are placed at the top of the frame, as also should be the false legs. Do not leave these too long, but cut them away when necessary. Curve the flowers over the side slightly so that there will be no gap between the flowers and the hair. The tallest flower at the centre is about 1½in (3.75cm) high and in a line with the widest point. This needs to be built up too. Have good variation of length in the cluster. Make a return end. Use the double leg pieces for the cluster and also some single leg pieces to go in short.

After finishing the cluster taper the false legs away and bind them securely to the frame; cover this with gutta percha. Do the second side of the head-dress in exactly the same way working back to meet the return end; lift the return end flowers up for convenience. The false legs of the last pieces are placed in to go beneath the return end. Cut binding wire away. Replace any flowers which have been moved.

Remember the following important points. Mark the centre; allow fullness gradually, you don't want a strip of flowers with a sudden bump in the centre. Keep all wires on top of the frame and cut them out as you go. Don't have any sharp ends.

Back Spray Head-dress

This head-dress is for an adult bridesmaid. It is worn at the back of the head, as the name suggests. It is more suitable for a bridesmaid with long hair and preferably with hair turning up at the bottom, as the head-dress then sits well into the back of the head.

Generally made of mixed flowers, it is also attractive made from one kind of flower, such as small Rose buds and leaves.

The materials needed for this are small flowers and leaves. Pieces which could be used in the autumn are red Michaelmas Daisies, red Freesia, feathered red

Carnation petals, small red Roses (e.g. 'Garnette'), Andromeda and green Ivy. Two 22 gauge (.71mm) × 14in (360mm), 30 gauge (.32mm), 32 gauge (.28mm) and 36 gauge (.20mm) silver reel wire is required. You also need natural gutta percha for coloured flowers, and white gutta percha if using white flowers.

Begin by making the frame. Bind together the two 22 gauge (.71mm) × 14in (360mm) with 36 gauge (.20mm) silver binding wire. Cover with the gutta percha. Measure and mark the centre of the frame. Shape the frame and tip the ends downwards. Make a loop going outwards at either end. These can be bound into position when the flowers are being bound onto the frame.

Next, wire the leaves with 32 gauge (.28mm) silver double leg and cover them with gutta percha. Then wire the flowers with 32 gauge (.28mm) silver double leg and gutta them as described in the head-dress and spray notes in Chapter 11. With the exception of the Roses, these need to be wired on a slightly stronger wire if they are fairly heavy, so wire through the seed-box of the Rose with a 30 gauge (.32mm) silver wire and make a double leg mount and gutta. Before starting the head-dress divide the flowers into two parts; one pile should have a few more in for a cluster.

Take a length of 36 gauge (.20mm) binding wire, three wired pieces, some flowers and some leaves (making sure they are small pieces and preferably one bud) and make the three pieces into a spray. They should be of various lengths.

Attach the binding wire to these pieces and then attach the spray to the left hand side of the frame which is facing you at the loop of the frame. The pieces should overlap the frame approximately 1–1½in (2.5–6.25cm).

Place the other pieces onto the frame making sure they are not bound too closely to the head of the flower but extended out a little as these pieces have gutta percha on them. This gives the head-dress a looser look. Group the flowers from side to side. Gradually widen out and build up as the flowers and leaves are placed on the frame, getting slightly longer pieces on the inside edge than the outside. Travel with the binding wire all the time until the centre is reached. False legs must all go at the top of the frame; cut them away when necessary to as to make the head-dress lighter in weight. When at the centre mark, keep the binding here until the cluster is completed. The width at the cluster is in a line with the centre mark. The inside piece is roughly twice the length of the outside piece. This is because it makes the head-dress sit more comfortably on the head and tends to make it more secure. The depth of the centre flower in the cluster should be about 1in (2.5cm). Make a good return end to the cluster and bind tightly to the frame. Taper false legs of wires from the cluster and bind them down to the frame. Cover them with gutta percha.

If an open Rose is used in the centre this is placed down very low.

Work from the right hand side of the frame as for the left side, gradually getting wider and again building up to the centre. Work until you reach the cluster, lifting the return end up for convenience and making sure that when the flowers meet with the centre cluster they are the same width. The false legs from the last few flowers placed in from this side go under the return end. Bind firmly into position and cut the binding wire away. Replace return end pieces and make certain the flowers and leaves are arranged correctly and that some flowers come well down at the side of the frame.

Coronet

If chosen as a head-dress a coronet is generally only worn by the bride. It can be made in various patterns. It looks better if made from one kind of flower; for example, Lilly of the Valley, Hyacinth, Chincherinchee. The flowers can be used with their own foliage or need have no foliage at all, whichever is preferred.

The materials needed for this are 32 gauge (.28mm) and 36 gauge (.20mm) silver wire, two 22 gauge (.71mm) × 14in (360mm), white gutta percha or silver paper. If you are using coloured flowers, natural gutta percha can be used.

Bind the two 22 gauge (.71mm) × 14in (360mm) together with 36 gauge (.20mm) silver wire and gutta. Make them into a circle and overlap about ½in (1.25cm). Bind the frame together with 36 gauge (.20mm) reel wire and then cover with gutta percha. Mark even spots to indicate position of upright sprays.

The flowers are wired with 32 gauge (.28mm) or 36 gauge (.20mm) silver double leg depending on their size and covered with gutta percha. Make small sprays of flowers to stand up around the frame. Five or seven of these sprays are needed; bind them with 36 gauge (.20mm) silver wire. Smaller sprays can be made to go in between the longer sprays.

The flowers are placed along the top of the frame and at the sides. Bind them to the frame with 36 gauge (.20mm) silver wire. Cut the false legs away when necessary.

The sprays stand up straight on the top of the frame and the ones along the edges which fill in the sides lie flat.

Begin at the front of the coronet and work to the back, then begin at the front again and work to the back. When finishing, the false legs need to be placed in between the earlier pieces. Do see that your binding is firm to make the uprights stand rigidly.

If you are using Lily of the Valley for this head-dress the Valley needs to be kept as natural as possible, so the main stems should be wired up with 36 gauge (.20mm) silver wire. Then mount small pieces with 32 gauge (.28mm) silver double leg and cover with gutta percha. Some of the flowers can have their own foliage placed at the back of them. Mount these as for the flowers. This is explained in detail in wiring for head-dresses and sprays in Chapter 11.

For extra support when using very delicate materials little upright wires can be used on the main frame to help hold the sprays of flowers. Make up five sets of four flowers and five sets of two flowers — make your own design.

Divide frame into five. Allow ½in (1.25cm) overlap each end, 2.6in (7.5cm) between points.

Tiara Head-dress

This head-dress is usually worn by brides but, again, can be worn by bridesmaids. As with the Coronet, it is preferable to have one kind of flower; for example, Lily of the Valley, Hyacinth, Chincherinchee.

Materials needed for this are two 22 gauge (.71mm) × 10in (260mm) or 12in (310mm), 32 gauge (.28mm) and 36 gauge (.20mm) silver reel wire, white gutta percha if using white flowers, natural gutta percha if using coloured flowers or silver paper if preferred for either white or coloured flowers.

Make the frame by binding two 22 gauge (.71mm) × 10in (260mm) wires together with 36 gauge (.20mm) silver. Cover with gutta percha. Make up sets of flowers, double leg mounts and guttared:

1 with five flowers for centre
2 with four flowers
2 with three flowers
and two single

Start at the centre of the frame and bind in the main upright of flowers. Mark the frame 1in (2.5cm) from each end and from the centre divide and divide again.

Curve the frame round and make a loop going outwards on either end.

The pieces are wired as for a coronet and placed on the frame in a similar way. With a tiara it is better to graduate the height from high in the centre to shorter ones at the side. Begin in the centre and work to the sides each time. The flowers at the edge of the frame lie flat, each side facing the tallest flower in the centre.

When you reach the end of the frame, bend back the loop and let the false legs of the last few flowers go along the loop. Take the binding wire to the end, then cover with gutta percha. Do both sides of the tiara in this way.

Cluster Head-dress

This may be considered old-fashioned today, but when well made it can look most attractive. This head-dress is suitable for a bride and adult bridesmaid. It looks nicer made with only one kind of flower, but occasionally it is made with mixed flowers. It is worn across the top of the head, with a cluster coming on either side of the head.

Materials needed for this head-dress are one kind of small flower and a few small leaves. A flower which can be used from late winter to early spring is the Hyacinth. Pittosporum leaves can be used at this time of the year. You will also need two 22 gauge (.71mm) × 12in (310mm) stub wires, 32 gauge (.28mm) and 36 gauge (.20mm) silver reel wire. Natural gutta percha will be required for coloured head-dresses, or white gutta percha for white, or strips of silver paper for either coloured or white.

Make the frame of the head-dress by binding two 22 gauge (.71mm) × 12in (310mm) wires together with 36 gauge (.20mm) silver wire and then cover them with gutta percha. Shape the frame of the head-dress into a half loop, make a loop on either end and bind these down with 36 gauge (.20mm) silver wire.

Wire the leaves with a 32 gauge (.28mm) silver wire, stitch and single leg. The flowers are wired with 32 gauge (.28mm) silver wire, double leg and covered with gutta percha. It is nicer to make the cluster just from flowers, using no leaves, but if you do want to add leaves, then these should be wired with 32 gauge (.28mm) silver wire, stitch and double leg and covered with gutta percha.

Divide the flowers into two, making sure of an equal amount of buds in each. Make two small clusters, similar to a straight spray or corsage, but making them less pointed; the binding can be all in one place at the centre of the spray.

Taper the false legs of the stems and take the binding wires down, but do not cut the binding wire away.

Place a cluster on either side of the frame, the top

of each cluster overlapping the end of the frame by approximately one inch (2.5cm). Bind the false stem securely into position with the binding wire of each cluster. If the flowers are very heavy a 32 gauge (.28mm) wire may be needed to hold the cluster in place. Twist the binding wire up through the spray to hold it to the frame, and then down to the false stem again. Place the single leg leaves over the top of the frame, between the two clusters, just overlapping each other, binding them on the frame with 36 gauge (.20mm) silver wire under the natural stem of the leaf, and cutting their false legs away when necessary. The last leaf is placed and bound on back to front and turned back to form a return end. Cut the binding wire away.

Two And One Rose Head-dress

This head-dress is suitable for both brides and brides-maids; it is worn across the top of the head.

You will need one large, preferably open Rose, one medium or slightly open Rose and one small Rose, preferably a bud; also a selection of single Rose leaves and two small three-sprays of Rose leaves. To wire them you will require 22 gauge (.71mm) × 12in (310mm) stub wires, three 24 gauge (.56mm) × 7in (180mm) stub wires, 32 gauge (.28mm) and 36 gauge (.20mm) silver reel wires, and green, white or natural gutta percha, depending on the colour of the Roses.

The frame is made first of all. Bind together two 22 gauge (.71mm) × 12in (310mm) stub wires with 36 gauge (.20mm) silver wire. Cover these with gutta percha. Make a loop on either end and bind the loop down with 36 gauge (.20mm) silver wire. Shape the frame to a half loop.

Some of the leaves are wired with 32 gauge (.28mm) silver, a small stitch and double leg. The three-sprays are wired with 32 gauge (.28mm) silver, single stitch and double leg as explained in the Rose two-spray, and some small single leaves with 32 gauge (.28mm) silver, stitch and single leg.

The three Roses are all cut leaving a $\frac{1}{4}$in (6mm) of stem and a 24 gauge (.56mm) × 7in (180mm) wire is pushed up inside the stem. A 32 gauge (.28mm) silver wire is pushed through half way up the seedbox and is twisted round the stem and a little way down the stub wire. Cover with gutta percha from the twisted wire on the stem.

Two sprays need to be made for this head-dress: one containing two Roses, the small and medium ones, the other spray containing the one large Rose.

Make the two-spray by placing a leaf behind the smallest Rose, bind it into position with 36 gauge (.20mm) binding wire a little way down on the false leg. Place a three-spray of leaves to one side, the second Rose very slightly to one side and just beneath the first Rose; bind these with the 36 gauge (.20mm) binding. The binding wire can travel about $\frac{1}{2}$in (1.25cm), and then stay in one position just under the second Rose stem. Place a return end of leaves in to complete the spray. Taper the false legs to form a stem, take the binding wire down to the end and leave a piece of binding wire. The false stem should be about one inch (2.5cm).

To make the one-spray of Roses, with the largest Rose, place a three-spray of leaves behind the Rose and have a return end of leaves. The binding is in the same place just beneath the natural stem of the Rose. Finish the stem as for the two-spray of Roses.

The two-spray of Roses is placed to one side of the frame, with the top of the spray overlapping the frame by about an inch (2.5cm). Bind securely to the frame with the binding wire from the false stem, bind on the false stem and then up through the spray to the end of the frame, take the binding to the false stem again and cut away. Cover with gutta percha over the false stem.

The one-spray is placed three-quarters of the way up the frame and faces back to the two-spray. The spray is placed in such a way that it rests on the parting when worn. Bind to the frame on the false stem, cut the binding wire away and cover it with gutta percha.

Place the single leg leaves over the top of the frame, so they just overlap each other, the last leaf being placed and bound back to front and then placed back as a return end.

Another way to make this head-dress is to bind the pieces straight onto the frame rather than make the sprays for attaching later. Instead of leaves across the centre of the head you can bind the frame with ribbon.

Two And One Gardenia Head-dress

Perhaps it is silly to mention Gardenias because they are so difficult to obtain, but they do make a good head-dress — with modern growing methods who knows, they may be available again one day!

This is a head-dress for brides and bridesmaids; it is worn over the top of the head.

Materials used for this are three Gardenias, preferably one small, one medium and one larger, and a selection of Gardenia leaves. You will require two 22 gauge (.71mm) × 12in (310mm), 32 gauge (.28mm) and 36 gauge (.20mm) silver reel wire, and green or white gutta percha. Three pieces of cardboard are needed to back the Gardenias.

Wire the leaves first. Wire medium-sized leaves for backing the flowers with 32 gauge (.28mm) silver wire, stitch and double leg but do NOT cover them with gutta percha. The small leaves for over the top of the frame should be wired with 32 gauge (.28mm) silver, stitch and single leg, and some leaves with 32 gauge (.28mm) silver, stitch and double leg and these you do cover with gutta percha.

The Gardenias are wired as explained in Chapter 11, but using a 24 gauge (.56mm) × 7in (180mm) to make the head-dress lighter in weight. The two smallest Gardenias are used to make the two-spray, the largest to make the one-spray.

To make the two-spray, place the smallest flower first and then the medium one slightly to one side. Arrange the leaves through the spray, with the widest point at the second Gardenia. Make a return end of leaves. 36 gauge (.20mm) silver wire is used for binding and it travels about $\frac{1}{2}$in (1.25cm) and then remains in one place beneath the second flower. Cut the false legs to about one inch (2.5cm), and take the binding wire down to the bottom of the false stem.

The largest Gardenia has leaves placed attractively around it. Bind under the natural stem of the flower and keep the binding here.

The flowers and leaves are placed on the frame as for a two and one Rose head-dress.

14. BOUQUETS AND HANDSPRAYS

In the past, little consideration was given to the dress design, dress material or the figures of the brides and bridesmaids. The bride's bouquet was a gift from the groom and came as a surprise usually in the form of a large bouquet of Asparagus Fern with Carnations or Rose buds worked on a large ball of moss. According to the price, so the number of flowers used and the size of the bouquet varied, the highest-priced ones carrying ribbons and flowers right through to the tail of the bouquet.

Today, consideration is given to the dress material and design, and also to the figures of the ladies. Bouquets are much smaller, consequently very much lighter, and often contain very little foliage. They are of particular shapes and carefully chosen materials, with no unnecessary foliage and Fern introduced to hide the flowers and blur the effect of the chosen shape. There is no moss ball to hide these days!

Colour is another important consideration and much time is spent with the bride, her bridesmaids and often mother and future mother-in-law before a decision is reached. So often suggestions are forthcoming and a request for a little past history is made. How many times does a florist hear, 'I carried a little myrtle or orange blossom in my bouquet, dear. You have some in yours'! Usually a bride prefers an all-white bouquet.

Fresh flower head-dresses are also popular and should tie up with those used in the bouquet.

In the last few years, ideas have changed again and now many brides are happy to accept an artificial bouquet which they can keep as a memento of the day. So often I am asked how to preserve a bouquet but after it has been carried round and handled for a few hours there is not much point in trying to preserve it. The flowers should be in perfect condition if they are to be preserved, and processing should start straightaway before any sign of bruising appears.

The shapes and style of bouquets today have been much influenced by those made on the Continent and to my way of thinking many of them look like a collection of odd leaves with a few flowers added.

Once one has mastered the making up of a bouquet these 'collections' can be attempted if required, but for teaching purposes in the School we have kept to a few standard bouquet shapes which still look good and serve the purpose.

Only *whole* flowers should be used when making bouquets — the variations in flower size from a bud to a fully open bloom makes for a natural-looking bouquet. Remember the 'visual' balance and keep the larger flowers deep down. Mrs Spry always said feathered pieces should not be sprayed up — use these only in head-dress and corsage work.

There are various ways of making a bouquet. Some florists mount their materials and twist these mounts together (the outline on double mounts and the rest single legs) to form the bouquet handle. This is a firm way of working but the handle can become untidy. Others bind all the single leg mounts together and some will make up with a combination of both.

The following few points will help you.

Always bind in one place — don't overbind.

Place stems in from the correct angle — do not place on one side and bind in the stem on the other — in other words don't cross your wires through the bouquet.

Pull your outline flowers into position to get the balance at the beginning

Always work looking into a mirror.

Don't put your bouquet down on its face while making it; always stand it in a pot carefully, keeping it sprayed and covered with damp tissue.

Bouquets can always be made of just one flower, normally with its own foliage, but to help the student I have in each case made bouquets up of mixed flowers and foliages to help illustrate varieties to use and how one may group them in the bouquet.

Bouquet handle bow
To finish your bouquet handle use 1in (2.5cm) ribbon

of a chosen colour with a non-slip surface. Cut the handle to the width of your clenched fist and allow an extra 1in (2.5cm). If the wire handle is uneven, wrap around a little tissue paper to make it smooth and even. You will find the ribbon grips well on this.

Place 2in (5cm) of ribbon behind the handle, bring down and up the front of the handle, and secure with a spray pin at the bottom. Now bind as a finger bandage, catching in the width of the ribbon at the tip. Bind at an angle up to the top of the handle, making a loop and a slip knot at the top. Secure this with your bow. You will need about 1½yds (1.5m) of ribbon. Figure 14.4 shows a posy bouquet in the making.

Presentation Bouquet

As the name suggests this bouquet can be made to present to someone at a special occasion. It also makes a different-shaped bouquet for an adult bridesmaid and very occasionally this shape is carried by a bride.

The bouquet is 'egg' shaped, the more rounded part being at the top of the bouquet. The size can vary as to how many flowers are available or to the size of the person who will be carrying it.

Presentation bouquet on natural stems

Materials needed: a selection of mixed flowers and foliages. For example, the following could be used in the summer — six small stems of mauve Stock (side shoots), five pink Roses, one bunch of Pinks, one bunch of blue Scabious, two bunches of Nigella, variegated Ivy, Senecio greyii and Rose leaves. 22 gauge (.71mm) × 12in (310mm) and 22 gauge (.71mm) × 10in (260mm) wires will be used for mounting, 22 gauge (.71mm) and 24 gauge (.56mm) wires for wiring the flowers, 32 gauge (.28mm) silver wire, gutta percha and 1½ yards (1.5m) of 1½in (3.75cm) ribbon in an appropriate colour.

The single leaves are wired with a small stitch and a double leg covered with gutta percha and sprayed up. Some Ivy can be left in natural trails and wired as described in Chapter 11 for leaves. The Rose leaves are left in three-sprays.

All the flowers are wired as described in Chapter 11, using as light a wire as possible, for example 24 gauge (.56mm) on Pinks or a thick silver stub wire. The Stock may be sprayed up if the natural compound stems are too heavy.

Eight flowers are needed for the outline; it is better to have one or more of each kind of flower on the outline. Select the flowers, choosing the smaller blooms

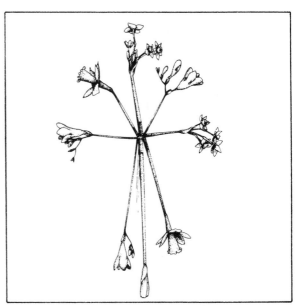

Figure 14.1: Presentation bouquet on natural stems
Stage one: Eight outline flowers in position — Narcissus
'Sol d'Or', Tulip, Daffodil, Freesia and Ivy

for the edge. Place them out on the table to get the shape and grouping. The first flower is the longest one in the top of the bouquet and the smallest one; the second flower at the top is slightly larger and is approximately a head shorter than the first flower. The third flower is again a little larger and a head shorter than the second flower. The fourth and fifth flowers are the widest point and are the same length as the second flower. The sixth flower is the longest flower in the tail of the bouquet and is one and a half times the length of the first flower — it needs to be a small one. The seventh flower is slightly larger and a head shorter than the sixth flower and, finally, the eighth flower is slightly larger and a head shorter than the seventh flower.

All the outline flowers are mounted with 22 gauge (.71mm) × 12in (310mm) double leg and the mount covered over with gutta percha. Take the first and second flower and place one of the false legs of the first flower through between the false legs of the second flower; twist the second false leg of the first flower round the other false legs about ½in (1.25cm) from the bottom of the natural stem.

The third flower has one of its false legs placed between the false legs of the first and second flower, and the other leg twisted around the rest of the false legs.

Attach the 32 gauge (.28mm) silver wire for binding from where the false legs have been twisted and

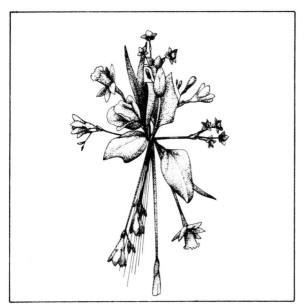

Figure 14.2: Presentation bouquet
Stage two: The centre foliage has been placed in deep

Figure 14.3: Presentation bouquet
Stage three: Front of the bouquet completed

the hole has been formed between the natural stems and the twisted wires. The rest of the flowers are put in position by placing one of the false legs through the hole and binding them into position where the binding wire has been attached and where it remains all the time. The bottom of the natural stems of the outline flowers form a circle. The sprayed up pieces do *not* go through the hole in the centre and are *not* mounted, but are placed in where they are required and bound into position. In this case it applies to the fifth and sixth flowers. The false legs of the flowers form the handle of the bouquet.

It is essential to keep the loops of the mounts at the back of the bouquet as this gives the flowers extra support. The remaining natural-stemmed flowers are mounted with 22 gauge (.71mm) × 10in (260mm) single leg and the mount covered over with gutta percha. Cut the flowers to the required length as they are needed. All the single leg mounts are placed through the hole of the bouquet, the natural stem going close to the hole to make the flowers firm.

Next place in the centre flower which is three-quarters the length of the first flower. This needs to be fairly small and pointed; a Rose bud is ideal. It leans towards the top of the bouquet. The rest of the flowers are placed in within the outline and are not taller than the centre flower. It is better to work from the outline to the centre, having plenty of variation of length and keeping the heavier flowers lower and nearer to the centre. Correctly group the flowers. Place the leaves

into position as you go along. Mount some of the smaller flowers in twos and threes. Make sure the bouquet is balanced with the weight falling towards the back. Never complete one section at a time. Spread the flowers evenly throughout the bouquet.

When all the flowers and leaves are in position, wire up three single leaves on double legs and twist the wires together, binding them at the back of the bouquet to neaten it.

Finish the handle — it should be cut off just a little wider than the width across the back of one's hand (4–4½, 10–11.25cm).

To make the presentation bouquet on extended legs, wire all the flowers having stem lengths from about 4in (10cm) to very short ones. Spray up the pipped flowers and leaves.

The outline flowers are the same proportions. The grouping is the same. Place all the flowers into position, beginning with the top three flowers and binding them into position at the required length. Then place the rest of the outline flowers into position, keeping the binding wire in *one position* all the time the bouquet is being made. There is no hole in the centre, but everything is placed in where it is required. Do not cross the false legs. The false legs form the handle. The rest of the bouquet is as for natural stems.

Posy Bouquet

This bouquet is made for brides and bridesmaids. The shape is round. The size can vary depending on how large or small the person is who is to carry it; the usual size for an adult is approximately 10in (25cm) in diameter.

Posy bouquet on natural stems

Materials needed for this are a selection of mixed flowers and foliages. For a spring posy bouquet use the following: five small cream Roses, two bunches of yellow Freesia (ten stems), three stems of white Hyacinth, one bunch (ten stems) of yellow 'Cheerfulness' Narcissus, variegated Ivy and Tradescantia. You will need 22 gauge (.71mm) × 12in (310mm) and 22 gauge (.71mm) × 10in (260mm) for mounting flowers, 22 gauge (.71mm) and 24 gauge (.56mm) wires for wiring the flowers, 32 gauge (.28mm) silver wire, gutta percha and 1½ yards (1.5m) of 1in (2.5cm) ribbon in an appropriate colour.

The Ivy leaves are wired with 32 gauge (.28mm) silver double legs and sprayed up. Some Ivy can be wired in trails and so can Tradescantia (see description of general wiring of leaves in Chapter 11).

The Roses, Freesia and 'Cheerfulness' are wired with the lightest wire possible to support them. The Hyacinths are pipped and sprayed up.

Seven flowers are needed for the outline and all should be the same length. It is better to introduce each kind of flower in the outline, choosing the smallest blooms. Place them on the table to make the outline design. All the outline flowers are mounted with 22 gauge (.71mm) × 12in (310mm) double leg and the mount is covered with gutta percha.

Take the first and second flower and place one of the false legs of the first flower through between the false legs of the second flower; twist the second leg of the first flower round the other false legs about ½in (1.25cm) from the end of the natural stem.

The seventh flower has one of its false legs placed between the false legs of the first and second flowers, and the other leg twisted round the rest of the false legs.

Attach the 32 gauge (.28mm) silver wire for binding from where the false legs have been twisted and a hole has been formed between the twisting of the false legs and the natural stems. The rest of the outline flowers are placed into position, putting one of the false legs through the hole and the other coming down the side. Bind them into position where the binding has already been attached, and where it remains all

Figure 14.4: Posy bouquet — stages of making up
Stage one: Outline of seven flowers — Nerine, Ivy, 'Bridal Pink' Rose and Carnation

Stage two: Filling in the centre

the time. The bottom of the natural stems form a circle.

The sprayed up pieces are *not* mounted and do *not* go through the hole, but are placed in where they are required and bound into position. In this case it applies to the third and sixth flowers. The false legs form the handle of the bouquet. It is important to keep the loops of the mounts at the back of the flower as this gives extra support. The remaining natural-stemmed

Stage three: More grouping and filling in, including Cobaea

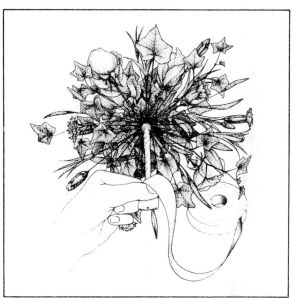

Stage five: Handle cut to desired length, bound with ribbon and secured at handle base

Stage four: Front of the posy completed

Stage six: Ribbon handle finished with a tie

flowers are mounted with 22 gauge (.71mm) × 10in (260mm) single leg and again the mount is covered with gutta percha. Cut the flowers to the required length as they are needed. All the single leg mounts are placed through the hole in the bouquet, with the end of the natural stem going close to the hole — this keeps the flowers close together and makes them firmer.

Place in the centre flower at this stage; this should be three-quarters the length of the outline flowers. It needs to be fairly small and also an 'important' flower, in this case a small Rose. It is placed in the centre and leans towards the top flower, and is the longest flower to build up to; nothing must be higher than the centre and nothing must be longer than the outline flowers. It is much better to work from the outline of the posy to

Stage seven: Finished handle completed with a bow

the centre, making sure of plenty of variation of length; the heaviest flowers must be nearest the centre and use buds to help to lighten. Group the flowers from one side to the other. Place the leaves attractively throughout the bouquet. If there are three larger leaves keep these near the centre to give 'body' to the bouquet.

Some flowers need to be mounted in twos or even threes. The balance of the bouquet is very important and the weight needs to go to the back. Distribute the flowers evenly through the posy. Never work in sections.

To finish the bouquet cut the handle to the required length, wire three leaves with 32 gauge (.28mm) silver on double leg, twist them together and bind them at the back of the bouquet to neaten it. The leaves are placed backwards, that is facing the person holding the bouquet.

Finish the handle as explained on p. 104.

To make a posy bouquet on 'extended legs', wire the flowers as explained in Chapter 11. Spray up the pipped flowers and leaves. Wire the trails of Ivy and Tradescantia as described in Chapter 11.

Take the seven outline flowers and bind them on the false legs to the required length. Keep the binding in one place. Place all the flowers in the position they are required, without a hole in the centre. The false legs form the handle. Do not cross the false legs; vary the lengths and the grouping of the flowers. The rest of the bouquet is made in the same way as for a natural-stemmed bouquet.

Loose Posy

This is a bouquet which is very suitable for child bridesmaids. It is round. The size varies depending on the age of the child but an average size is 6–7in (15–17.5cm).

Loose posy on natural stems

Materials needed for this are a selection of mixed flowers and leaves. An example of flowers which could be used in the late spring/early summer is as follows: five to seven orange Roses, three to five heads apricot Azalea, five to seven stems pale orange Ranunculus, one bunch Lachenalia, Rose leaves and Andromeda. You will also need 22 gauge (.71mm) × 10in (260mm) and 22 gauge (.71mm) × 7in (180mm) wire for mounting the flowers, 22 gauge (.71mm) and 24 gauge (.56mm) wire for wiring, 32 gauge (.28mm) silver wire, gutta percha, ½ yard (.5m) of 1in (2.5cm) ribbon and 2 yards (2m) of ½in (1.25cm) ribbon in an appropriate colour.

The leaves are wired with 32 gauge (.28mm) silver and guttared and are sprayed up as already described.

The Roses, Ranunculus and Lachenalia are wired as described in Chapter 11, using the lightest wire possible to give them support. The Azalea flowers are sprayed up.

Seven flowers are needed for the outline, and all must be the same length. It is more satisfactory to introduce each kind of flower in the outline, choosing the smallest blooms for this. Place them on the table to make the outline design.

Make up as for the posy bouquet but remember to place your stems so as the handle of this bouquet comes straight down under the flowers.

All the binding is in one place at the top of the handle. The end of the natural stems form a circle. The loops on the mounts on the flowers must be kept at the back of the stems to give them support when the outline is completed.

The remainder of the natural-stemmed flowers, with the exception of the centre flower, are cut to the required length when needed and mounted with 22 gauge (.71mm) × 7in (180mm) single leg. The mount is then covered with gutta percha.

The centre flower is carefully placed; this flower should be slightly longer than the outline flowers, and it is mounted on a 22 gauge (.71mm) × 10in (260mm) with a double leg. It is a fairly pointed flower and stands up straight in the centre of the bouquet.

When placing the other flowers and leaves in the posy they should not be longer than the outline or taller than the centre flower. Work from the outline to the centre, gradually building up to the centre; do not forget the larger, shorter flowers should be nearer to the centre and use plenty of buds. Have many variations of length, group the flowers from side to side, merging each group slightly into the other. Arrange the leaves through the posy, keeping the Rose leaves with the Roses. Never bind on the natural stems of the flowers but always on the false legs. Some small flowers can be mounted in twos and even threes. Have the flowers evenly spaced throughout the posy.

Wire approximately seven leaves on double legs and bind these leaves under the posy to neaten it, making sure the right side of the leaf is showing.

Cut the handle to the required length and finish as explained on p. 104.

To make a loose posy on extended legs, wire the flowers as explained in Chapter 11, under extended legs. Spray up the pipped flowers and leaves. None of the flower stems must be more than $2\frac{1}{2}$in (6.25cm) and the lengths should be varied down to very short stems.

Take seven outline flowers and bind them together on the false legs at the required length. Bend them at right angles to the false legs which form the handle. Place the centre flower in the centre; this should be slightly longer than the outline flowers.

The rest of the flowers and leaves are placed in the same position as for a natural-stemmed loose posy. Binding is in one place all the time. Do not cross false legs. The posy is finished as a natural-stemmed posy.

Crescent Bouquet

This is a popular bouquet and appears in slightly varying shapes under the same name.

Crescent bouquet on natural stems
Materials needed for this bouquet are a selection of mixed flowers and foliages. It can also look attractive made from one type of flower, for example Roses. Flowers which can be used in the winter are one bunch of red Ranunculus, three or five stems of red Nerine, three red Gerbera, three 'Garnette' Roses, Andromeda foliage, red Croton leaves and Rose leaves. You will need 22 gauge (.71mm) × 12in (310mm) and 22 gauge (.71mm) × 10in (260mm) wire for mounting the flowers, 22 gauge (.71mm) and 24 gauge (.56mm) wire for wiring, 32 gauge (.28mm) silver wire, gutta percha and $1\frac{1}{2}$ yards (1.5m) of $1\frac{1}{2}$in (3.75cm) ribbon in an appropriate colour.

The leaves are sprayed up with 32 gauge (.28mm) silver wire on double leg mounts and guttared. If the Croton leaves are fairly large they can be put singly on the wire. The leaves are wired as for Carnation grass (see p. 74).

The Ranunculus, Gerbera and Roses are wired using the lightest wire possible to support them. The Nerine are sprayed up in the same way as for Stephanotis (see p. 81).

Seven flowers or leaves are needed for the outline. It is better to have one or more of each kind introduced in the outline; this determines the pattern or grouping in the bouquet. Select the flowers, choosing the smaller blooms for the outline and placing them on the table to get the shape. For this bouquet decide on the width and place these flowers in first. If possible have sprayed up pieces on the outside edges, in this case on one side Nerine and on the other side Andromeda; both of these should be the same length. A flower going above these flowers on either side should be slightly shorter than the widest ones on either side; put a Nerine above the Andromeda and an Andromeda above the Nerine. The flower at the top of the bouquet is between a half and three-quarters the length of the widest flower. A Rose can be used in this particular bouquet. A flower nearly a head shorter goes on one side of this, then one on the opposite side a head shorter still. A Ranunculus and a Gerbera can go on either side.

Mount all the natural-stemmed flowers with 22 gauge (.71mm) × 12in (310mm) double leg and cover the mount with gutta percha.

Take the first and second flower and place one false leg of the first flower through between the false legs of the second flower; twist the second leg of the first flower round the other false legs about a $\frac{1}{4}$in (.6cm) from the end of the natural stems.

The third flower has a false leg placed between the false legs of the first and second flower and the other leg is twisted around the rest of the false legs.

Attach the 32 gauge (.28mm) binding wire from where the false legs have been twisted; a hole has been formed between the natural stems and the twisted false legs. As the other outline pieces are sprayed up place them into position at the sides. If they were natural-stem mounted on false legs, however, each false leg would then be placed in through the centre hole with the second leg going down the side and bound into position. The side flowers, whether sprayed up or on natural stems are gently curved all the way along the wire to get the required shape. It is important to keep the loops of the flowers at the back of the stem to give it support.

The remaining natural-stemmed flowers are cut to the required lengths as needed and mounted on 22 gauge (.71mm) × 10in (260mm) with a single leg and the mounts are covered with gutta percha. All the single legs are placed through the hole of the bouquet, the natural stem going close to the hole to make the flowers very firm. Once the outline is wired in, pull back the top flowers to get the bouquet to balance well in the hand.

Place in the centre flower, which is three-quarters the length of the first flower; this should stand in a fairly upright position. Choose a fairly small flower for this; a Rose bud is suitable with this selection of flowers. The rest of the flowers are placed within the outline and not any higher than the centre flower. It is more satisfactory to work from the outline to the centre of the bouquet, having plenty of variation of length and keeping the heavier flowers lower nearer the centre, especially in the case of the Gerbera. Group the flowers, place the leaves attractively through the flowers with the Crotons nearer the centre. Place the Rose leaves with the Roses. Mount some flowers in twos. Spread the flowers evenly through the bouquet. Have flowers placed along the bottom edge of the bouquet in a broken line with a spray of leaves well over the handle. Make sure the bouquet is balanced, leaning slightly backwards.

Wire three leaves with single stitch and double leg and twist them together; bind them at the back of the bouquet. Finish as explained on pp. 104 and 108.

To make a crescent bouquet on extended legs, wire all the flowers and spray up the pipped flowers and leaves. The outline flowers should be in the same proportions as for natural stems; the grouping is also the same. No hole in the centre is required, but the false legs are placed in position and bound with 32 gauge (.28mm) silver reel wire. Keep the binding all in one place. Do not cross the false legs. The false legs form the handle. The rest of the bouquet is made in the same way as for a natural-stemmed crescent.

Remember the balance is so important — in so many cases the bouquet appears to be falling forward on its face, so do pull back those first few flowers; then you will have room to set down some more flowers deep into the bouquet.

You can make the bouquet in two halves and join these together, but I think you will find the method I have described here an easier way of arriving at a crescent bouquet.

Straight Handspray Or Shower

This is probably the most popular bride's bouquet. Adult bridesmaids also carry them and if there is more than one bridesmaid, matching pairs can be made, with the grouping going in the opposite way.

The handspray is fairly long and thin. The size varies according to the size of the person carrying it and, to a certain extent, the materials used.

The materials needed are a selection of mixed flowers. A suitable collection which could be used in the summer are Lily of the Valley (ten to twelve stems), Bridal Gladioli (seven stems), eighteen pips of Stephanotis, three Eucharis Lilies, Peperomia, variegated Ivy and three Hosta leaves. You will need 30 gauge (.32mm), 32 gauge (.28mm) and 36 gauge (.20mm) silver reel wire, 22 gauge (.71mm) × 14in (360mm) and 24 gauge (.56mm) × 7in (180mm) wire, white gutta percha and 1½ yards (1.5m) of 1½in (3.75cm) ribbon in an appropriate colour.

The single leaves, with the exception of the Hosta, are wired with a small stitch and double leg; they are guttared and sprayed up in threes and fives. The trails of Ivy can be used with 32 gauge (.28mm) wire down the stem and 22 gauge (.71mm) × 14in (360mm) for the false leg.

The Hosta can be wired with 32 gauge (.28mm) silver, with a supporting loop behind the leaf, and having ½in (1.25cm) of stem on the leaf. Then a 22 gauge (.71mm) × 7in (180mm) wire is pushed up inside the stem and the remainder of the wire from the single stitch twisted down the stub wire, and then covered with gutta percha.

Figure 14.5: Straight handspray (shower) viewed from the side

The Lily of the Valley is wired in single stems normally, but it can be extended in twos with or without a leaf at the back. Forced Valley foliage is a good colour and adds interest to the bouquet. Wire each flower as suggested in Chapter 11.

Cover all the false legs with gutta percha. The lengths of the flowers should vary from about 5in (12.5cm) to very short ones, the shorter ones being the larger flowers.

To begin the handspray, attach a piece of 36 gauge (.20mm) silver wire at about 7in (17.5cm) from the top of the longest flower; this wire keeps the tail of the handspray more flexible. When this wire breaks, attach a 32 gauge (.28mm) silver wire. The tail of the handspray needs to be very thin and pointed at the beginning, gradually getting wider towards the centre. With this selection of flowers you could begin with a piece of Bridal Gladioli and then a five-spray of Stephanotis on one side and a piece of Lily of the Valley on the other, each shorter in length than the last.

Group the flowers through so that different weight flowers are well balanced; as there are five different kinds of flowers, I would suggest that the Bridal Gladioli and the Stephanotis go through one way and the Freesia and Lily of the Valley the other way. The Eucharis Lilies go towards the centre to give 'body' to the middle; this can be helped by placing the Hosta leaves in the centre of the handspray too. The Ivy leaves should be placed with the Stephanotis and Gladioli, the Peperomia leaves with the Valley and Freesia.

Gradually make the handspray wider until it is about 9in (22.5cm) long in the tail for an average-sized spray. Do not make it too wide; it is far more elegant if kept reasonably thin. Travel with the binding until the centre is reached. When at the centre the grouping crosses to the opposite sides at the widest points. Build the smaller flowers up higher; the spray gradually gets higher to the centre. Place the larger flowers in lower to give depth. Introduce one Eucharis Lily in the tail.

All the false legs must reach the centre. When at the widest point the binding wire stays in one position. At this stage the handle of the handspray is bent back to come in line with the tail of the handspray. The bend must be at the binding wire. The return end of the handspray is half the length of the tail — it is better longer rather than shorter. The shape of the return end is rounded. Continue to group the flowers such as the Lily of the Valley and keep the larger flowers, such as Eucharis Lilies in lower. Do not have any flowers in straight lines but zig zag them slightly.

Again, balance is very important and the top of the bouquet should lean slightly back; the tail of the bouquet will hang down parallel to the body if well made. If too heavily wired this will stick out and look very rigid. There should be lots of movement in the tail if the bouquet is well made and lightly wired.

The handle should sit comfortably in the hand; it should be about $4\frac{1}{2}$in (11–25cm) long and nicely tapered.

Curved Handspray Or Shower

The curved handspray is less formal than the straight one. It may be carried by a bride or adult bridesmaid. If bridesmaids are carrying them they can be made in pairs, one curving left to right, the other right to left — see then that they are photographed properly.

If carried by a bride, the spray should curve from left to right; this looks better and is easier to hold when she comes out of the church with her bridegroom. The curved handspray can be fairly long — the size of it depends on the materials used and the height of the bride.

If the bride and bridesmaids are to carry handsprays, see that the bride's is a little larger and made up of more important flowers. I think that a selection of mixed flowers and leaves make a more interesting bouquet but it can be of just one type of flower.

A suitable collection which could be used for this is: three Cymbidium Orchids in cream, two stems of cream Singapore Orchids, ten stems of cream Freesia, four stems of straw Hyacinth, cream Sedum foliage, cream variegated Ivy and three fairly large Scindapsus leaves. You will need 30 gauge (.28mm), 32 gauge (.30mm) and 36 gauge (.20mm) silver reel wire, 24 gauge (.56mm) × 7in (180mm) and 22 gauge (.71mm) × 14in (360mm) wire, natural gutta percha and $1\frac{1}{2}$ yards (1.5m) of $1\frac{1}{2}$in (3.75cm) of ribbon in an appropriate colour.

The single leaves of the Ivy are wired on double legs and guttared. Spray up in threes and fives. The trails of Ivy and Sedum can be wired with 32 gauge (.28mm) wire down the stem and 22 gauge (.71mm) × 14in (360mm) for the false leg.

The three Scindapsus are wired with 32 gauge (.28mm) making a loop and stitch at the back of the leaf. Leave $\frac{1}{2}$in (1.25cm) of stem on the leaf into which the stub wire is pushed. Bind together with the silver wire from the back of the leaf and then cover with gutta percha. The Orchids and Freesia are wired (see Chapter 11). The Hyacinth pips are sprayed up in threes and fives. Gutta all the false legs, the lengths of the flowers being from 5in (12.5cm) to very short ones; the shorter flowers should be the larger ones.

To begin the handspray attach a piece of 36 gauge (.20mm) silver wire at about 7in (17.5cm) from the top of the longest flower; this wire keeps the tail more flexible. When the wire breaks join a piece of 32 gauge (.28mm) silver.

The tail needs to be pointed and the handspray should gradually widen as you reach the centre, but to get the curve, build up on one side much more than the other. Obviously this depends on which side the curve is required. On the short side only very short flowers are placed.

As well as building out at the sides, the flowers and leaves need to be built up to the centre. These, if possible, should be the lighter flowers and leaves to gradually lift the bouquet. Short, larger flowers need to be placed in low to give depth.

For this particular handspray a five-spray of Hyacinth pips could be placed in at the tail and these could build up on the longer side. The Ivy could go through with this. To balance the bouquet well, place the Freesia and Sedum on the other side.

The three Cymbidium Orchids, together with the Singapore Orchids and the three Scindapsus, should be kept near the centre. The longest flower at the widest point could be a small piece of Freesia as the grouping of the flowers crosses over at this stage. Place an Orchid in as you reach the centre of the bouquet and also a Scindapsus leaf.

Travel with the binding wire until the tail is about 9in (22.5cm) for the average-sized handspray, then keep the binding in one position. The widest point of the spray is where the binding wire remains.

All the false legs must reach the centre and at this stage the return end is placed into position. The length should be half the tail of the handspray — again, it is better if slightly longer than half rather than under.

Place the largest piece — it is a good idea to have the same kind of piece you began with in the tail, for example Hyacinth — and bend it back over the handle towards the shorter side to form a curve.

Place in other pieces to meet with the widest point on either side making sure the inside edge of the curve is very short, to keep the shape.

Build the return end up to meet the centre. Put the larger flowers in shorter for depth; this includes the Orchids and Scindapsus leaves. Make sure the Orchids are not in a straight line; the centre one should lean a little to the top.

Zigzag all the flowers through to give interest but make sure they are grouped from one side to the opposite side.

The handle should sit comfortably in the hand. Finish as explained on p. 104.

Muff Spray

In the winter bridesmaids may carry muffs instead of bouquets and these may have sprays of flowers attached to them. The shape of the spray can vary. It can be a straight, curved or cluster spray, or in the form of a crescent spray.

Here are the instructions for making a crescent spray for attaching to the muff.

The materials needed for this are a selection of mixed flowers and foliages. A collection suitable for the winter would be three Christmas Roses (Helleborus niger), yellow Holly Berries, white Freesia, variegated Holly leaves and variegated Ivy leaves. You will also need 30 gauge (.32mm), 32 gauge (.28mm) and 36 gauge (.20mm) silver reel wire and natural gutta percha.

The flowers are mounted as for a spray, using 30 gauge (.32mm) or 32 gauge (.28mm) silver depending on the size and weight of the flower, with a double leg and covered with gutta percha. Mount the berries in clumps with 30 gauge (.32mm) silver double leg and gutta. The leaves are wired with 32 gauge (.28mm) silver on double legs and guttared. The smaller leaves of both the Ivy and Holly can be sprayed up but do *not* put them on a 22 gauge (.71mm) × 14in (360mm), just have them on their own false legs.

Take a small flower or leaf for either side of the spray, a spray of Freesia buds on one side and a small spray of Holly leaves on the opposite side. Bind with 36 gauge (.20mm) silver wire. Do not make the spray as wide as the muff, but leave about an inch (2.5cm) on either side. Place a slightly shorter flower or leaf on either side just above the first pieces.

A Freesia can be over the Holly leaf and a spray of Holly leaves over the Freesia buds.

The longest flower in the centre at the top is between half and three-quarters the length of the longest flowers at the side; this can be a Christmas Rose bud. A flower or bud should be placed on either side of it, each needing to be a fraction shorter than the previous flower. This can be a Freesia on one side and a clump of Holly Berries on the other.

The centre flower in the middle of the spray is three-quarters the length of the bouquet flower at the top.

Group the flowers, Berries and leaves through the bouquet, gradually filling in the outline but not making it too heavy. Have a broken line at the bottom of the spray with a leaf well down over the false stem. Build the flowers higher to the centre flower with plenty of variation of length. Finish by tapering the false legs to about one inch (2.5cm). Take the binding wire down to the end and cut it away. Cover with gutta percha.

The spray is stitched to the muff.

Flower Ball

A flower ball is carried by a child bridesmaid. It is a very popular and easy way for children to carry flowers; the flower ball is usually tied to the child's wrist so it cannot be dropped. It is usually made with mixed, fairly chunky flowers.

Figure 14.6: Flower ball

Materials needed for this are a selection of small mixed flowers. A suitable collection which could be used in the autumn are small red Dahlia buds, red button Asters, 'Garnette' Roses, Hydrangea which has turned red, the autumn-coloured leaves of the Cotoneaster and Ivy leaves. You will need 20 gauge (.90mm) × 10in (260mm) wire, 32 gauge (.28mm) silver wire and 24 gauge (.56mm) × 7in (180mm) or thick silver stub wire, 2 yards (2m) of baby ribbon in an appropriate colour, and a small piece of tissue paper.

Take the 20 gauge (.90mm) × 10in (260mm) wire and gutta in the centre of it, then bend it over to form a hairpin.

Make a ball of moss and bind it into shape with 32 gauge (.28mm) wire. It needs to be roughly the size of a golf ball and must be moist. Push the 20 gauge (.90mm) × 10in (260mm) hairpin through the centre of the ball of moss so the ends come through the bottom of it. Bend these back into the moss ball, and leave a loop of the wire at the top of the moss ball. Cover the ball with tissue paper pinned on with 24 gauge (.56mm) × 7in (180mm) hairpins against the loop; this keeps the flowers clean from the moss.

Wire the leaves with 32 gauge (.28mm) silver and do not leave legs on the mount from the stitch, but mount with 24 gauge (.56mm) × 7in (180mm) or a thick stub wire with a double leg mount.

The flowers are mounted on 24 gauge (.56mm) × 7in (180mm) or a thick stub wire with a short double leg mount. The Hydrangea can be bound tightly together first with 32 gauge (.28mm) silver wire and then mounted.

When all the wiring is completed push the mounts of the flowers and leaves into the moss, keeping the flowers and leaves close together but fairly mixed. You can also make patterns if you prefer.

Begin placing the pieces in at the bottom and work to the top. When the moss ball is completely covered with flowers take some of the ribbon and make two bows each with two loops and two fairly long tails. Mount these on 24 gauge (.56mm) × 7in (180mm), double leg and place one on either side of the loop. Thread a piece of ribbon through the loop and tie, leave fairly long ends to tie round the child's wrist. If you prefer, a bow can be tied at the end of this piece of ribbon so that it can be slipped over the child's wrist.

The size of the flower ball when finished is approximately the size of a large round orange.

Prayer Book Spray

A prayer book spray makes a change from a bouquet. Some brides like to carry a white prayer book and the addition of flowers makes it more attractive (see Plate 24). The flowers are attached to ribbon which acts as a book marker for the marriage service. Occasionally adult bridesmaids will also carry prayer books with a spray on them.

Prayer book sprays for brides are usually made with white flowers either in mixed flowers or one kind of flower, for example Orchids or Roses. The flowers are placed in various ways on the book. They can go diagonally across it or straight across, and smaller sprays can be placed on the tails of the ribbon.

The materials needed for this spray are a selection of small mixed interesting flowers. A collection which could be used in late spring is Eucharis Lily, white Freesia, Lily of the Valley, white Hyacinth, Tradescantia and variegated Ivy. You will need 30 gauge (.32mm), 32 gauge (.28mm) and 36 gauge (.20mm) silver reel wire, gutta percha and 1½–2 yards (1.5–2m) of white satin ribbon 1½–2in (3.75–5cm) wide, depending on how large the book is.

Attach the ribbon to the prayer book; it should go through marking the place at the marriage service and then over the top of the book, leaving the tails of ribbon at different lengths. Stitch the ribbon together with a neat running thread where it meets the edge of the book. This will hold it firmly and make it easy to attach.

The flowers are wired with a double leg and guttared as for the wiring of flowers for head-dresses and sprays using 32 gauge (.28mm) silver wire on most flowers. On heavier ones you will need 30 gauge (.32mm) silver.

The leaves are wired with a small stitch and double leg, then covered with gutta percha. Use 32 gauge (.28mm) silver wire for the Ivy leaves and 36 gauge (.20mm) for the Tradescantia, mounting the tip ends of the Tradescantia with 32 gauge (.28mm) silver and then covering them with gutta percha.

Make a spray for the top of the prayer book and bind it with 36 gauge (.20mm) silver; it is made as for a straight mixed spray (see p. 94) but is a little longer. It should be long enough to enable the end of the spray to be bent over the end of the book.

One or two smaller sprays can be made to go on the tails of ribbon. These can be made as miniature clusters or curved sprays. If making two sprays one could curve one way and the other the opposite way, one being slightly smaller than the other. All the sprays are stitched into position with a cotton thread.

Victorian Posy

A Victorian posy can be of two kinds:

1   When the natural flower stems are bound together around a central bud making rings of colour. These stems are held in position with a collar or posy frill and finished with a bow. Rather bulky, this can be sent as a posy to stand in a vase as an old-fashioned type of decoration. Bunches are often tied like this on the Continent. The bouquet is made by holding in the hand and turning with one hand, placing the flowers in with the other. At the end the stems are all tied together.

2   The wired Victorian posy can be used in wedding work. All flowers are on false stems and backed by foliage or a posy frill. This posy is usually carried by child bridesmaids, or occasionally by adults.

A wired Victorian posy

The size varies according to the age of the child. If carried by an adult it would be about 9–10in (22.5–25cm) across, although it is always better to keep it reasonably small. A posy frill can be used around the edge; these can be bought in various sizes. It is more natural looking, however, to have an edging of leaves instead of the frill.

Materials needed for the Victorian posy are a pointed flower and a selection of small flowers and leaves. A suitable collection which could be used in the late summer are a pink Rose bud, six stems of mauve Stock, six stems of Michaelmas Daisies, four feathered pink Carnations and Eucalpytus leaves all of the same size. You will also need 30 gauge (.32mm) and 32 gauge (.28mm) silver wire, 24 gauge (.56mm) × 7in (180mm) stub wire, gutta percha, ½ yard (.5m) of 1in (2.5cm) ribbon and 2 yards (2m) of ½in (1.25cm) ribbon in an appropriate colour.

First decide in which rows the flowers are to be placed. Try to keep the buds nearer to the centre and gradually work to larger flowers towards the edge. In this case the first row is Michaelmas Daisy buds, the second row Stock buds, the third row Michaelmas Daisy flowers, the fourth row Stock flowers, the fifth row feathered Carnations and the sixth row Eucalyptus leaves.

The flowers are wired as for head-dresses. They have a lighter wire on the inside, gradually working to thicker wires towards the outside edge. The first two rows can be wired with 32 gauge (.28mm) wire making a double leg mount and the false legs of two flowers are twisted together.

The rest of the flowers can be wired on 30 gauge (.32mm) silver, double leg and again the false legs can be twisted together. The feathered Carnations are done in this way with the 30 gauge (.32mm) wire as explained in Chaper 11. The leaves are wired with 32 gauge (.28mm) silver on double leg and some of the false legs of two leaves twisted together, but leaving seven or eight as single leaves. The ones which have been twisted together are mounted on the false legs with 24 gauge (.56mm) × 7in (180mm) single leg.

If the flowers need more support towards the outside edge these too can be mounted after the two have been twisted together with 24 gauge (.56mm) × 7in (180mm).

The Rose bud is cut, leaving a ¼in (.6cm) of stem, and is mounted on a 24 gauge (.56mm) × 7in (180mm) single leg. Cover the mount and a little way down the stub wire with gutta percha.

When all the flowers and leaves have been wired, join a length of 32 gauge (.28mm) silver wire under the small stem of the Rose. Place the row of Michaelmas Daisy buds around this Rose so that the Rose shows about ½in (1.25cm) above the buds, keeping them as close as possible to the Rose, with the buds touching each other and facing upwards. Bind the buds into position as they are placed in.

Keeping the same piece of binding wire and also keeping it in the one place, put in the second row — in this case the Stock buds. Again, facing them upwards, they go close to the first row and on roughly the same level.

Continue to place in the third and fourth rows in this way; they can slope very slightly downwards, but this must not be too noticeable and the binding must still be kept in the same place. The fifth row, the feathered Carnations, are placed in as an edging, with about ½in (1.25cm) of the Carnation showing beyond the flowers of the previous row. If you are using a posy frill it can be placed on at this stage. Choose the size so that an inch of it shows beyond the flowers.

If using the leaves place them around the last row of flowers so the tips of the leaves show by ½–¾in (1.25–1.85cm).

Neaten the back by placing the seven or eight single leaves to cover the wires; place them so that the right side of the leaf is seen.

Cut the handle to the required length and finish as explained on p. 104.

Bridesmaid's Basket

The bridesmaid's basket is usually carried by child bridesmaids rather than adults. A simple basket can be bought; it needs to be a small, attractive shape with a fairly high handle. Pretty mixed flowers should be used to give a pleasing effect and pick up the overall colour scheme. Some brides prefer a basket of one type of flower and colour which may be more sophisticated.

The materials needed for this are a selection of fairly small mixed flowers and leaves. A suitable collection that could be used in the autumn would be two or three side stems of fairly small apricot Stock, three pale orange Dahlia buds or very small flowers, one or two stems of 'Sybil' spray Chrysanthemums,

three to five pale orange Roses, three orange Croton leaves which need to be small and Andromeda foliage. You also need a small basket with a handle, Sphagnum moss, white tissue paper, polythene or waxed paper, 22 gauge (.71mm) and 24 gauge (.56mm) stub wire, 30 gauge (.32mm) and 32 gauge (.28mm) silver reel wire, gutta percha and 1 yard (1m) of 1in (2.5cm) ribbon in an appropriate colour.

First line the basket with either polythene or waxed paper to keep the basket dry. Next fill the basket with moss or oasis. (When using oasis, natural stems can replace the wired mounts; these are just pushed into the damp surface as one would do when arranging flowers — simple and quick. The disadvantage is that wet oasis in the basket is heavy to carry and with small children this may become a burden after the novelty has worn off.)

The basket should be filled to about ½in (1.25cm) from the top and packed in fairly tightly. Make sure the moss is damp. The moss is held into position by threading 32 gauge (.28mm) wire backwards and forwards, first widthways and then lengthways going through the wickerwork of the basket at the sides each time.

Cover the top of the moss with tissue paper. Cut to the correct size and shape and pin this into position with hairpins made from 24 gauge (.56mm) × 3½in (90mm) wires. This tissue paper keeps the flowers clean from the moss.

Take some of the single Andromeda leaves, all roughly the same size and pin them as an edging round the basket, using 24 gauge (.56mm) × 3½in (90mm) hairpins. They should overlap the basket by about 1in (2.5cm).

Figure 14.7: Bridesmaid's basket, made up of Heather, spray Carnations, Freesia, Roses and mixed foliage

Wire the Roses, Chrysanthemums and Dahlias as explained in Chapter 11, using the lightest wire possible to support them. The Stock is sprayed up. The Andromeda sprays need a 32 gauge (.28mm) wire twisted up the main stem. The Croton leaves will need a 30 gauge (.32mm) or 32 gauge (.28mm) wire depending on the weight of the leaves. Make a stitch and twist the wire round the stem, then cut both wires level with the natural stem.

Rose leaves can be wired with a 32 gauge (.28mm) silver, stitch; they should be in three-sprays. All the flowers and leaves on natural stems are cut to the required length and mounted with 22 gauge (.71mm) × 7in (180mm) double leg. Cover the mounts with gutta percha but not the double legs.

Decide on the grouping and put the outline flowers into position. There should be three either end, one each side for width, with the tallest one in the centre. These outline flowers should be small ones. The sprayed up pieces are not mounted, but pushed into the moss as they are already on wires. In the case of natural-stemmed flowers and leaves these should be pushed well down to enable the bottom of the stem to take some moisture from the moss.

The longest flowers at the side can be a Stock on one side and a bud of Chrysanthemum on the other. These are placed two-thirds of the way back in the basket. Have a flower on either side of the longest flowers, each a head shorter than the previous one. Add to one side of the Stock another piece of Stock and on the other side of it a Chrysanthemum bud. On the opposite side where the Chrysanthemum bud has been placed again put a flower on either side of it, in this case another Chrysanthemum bud and a piece of sprayed up Stock. The widest flowers can both be Dahlia buds, the front one coming well over the edge but the back one very short. Each comes at a different side of the handle.

The centre flower again goes two-thirds of the way back and can be a small Rose bud. It comes about 2in (5cm) down from the handle.

The rest of the flowers come within these outline points. Group the flowers through: the Roses are placed in fairly near the centre, grouping through with the spray Chrysanthemums. Do not place them in a straight line. The outside pieces are gently curved over the sides of the basket.

Two or more small flowers can be mounted together. The three Croton leaves need to be placed near to the centre. Take the foliage through attractively, keeping the Rose leaves with the Roses.

Gradually build up to the centre flower. The flowers should be placed in very firmly so that there is no likelihood of their falling out, even with rough handling by the bridesmaid!

A bow can be made with the ribbon and placed on the handle at the front of the basket. Do not have the ends of the bow too long.

15.FUNERAL WORK

The choice of a mourning wreath is one which should be given deliberation. In addition to being a floral message of memory and a token of sympathy, it can express the individuality of the sender. Sometimes it is made of flowers which were particular favourites of the deceased; for example, a true gardener should be sent flowers typical of a garden and not commercial florist materials.

It is important that the colouring and the choice, if left to the florist, are in keeping with the occasion. Strong colours, for example mixed reds or oranges, might be suitable for a man, whereas mauve, pinks and pastel colours are more fitting for a woman. In the case of a child, use *small* and *simple* flowers.

Customers coming into the shop usually fit into one of two categories. Either they are too distressed to be able to say what they really require and in this case the assistant can help with careful suggestions which are in good taste, or they have clearly in their mind just what they want. However distasteful the requirements may be to the workroom, they must be followed implicitly.

Today the obituary notices often read 'no flowers by request', but there is no reason why flowers should not be sent in the form of a lovely arrangement to the home of closest members of the deceased's family. In many cases, the message reads 'flowers suitable for a hospital'. Again, why not send an arrangement which would be far nicer and save so much trouble at the hospital? How many hospitals really want those terrible bunches so often encased in a wet cellophane bag and damaged or wilted to such an extent that they are really not worth spending time on arranging for the entrance hall or ward? My own view on this is to send flowers (preferably arranged) straight to an old people's home where they will be welcomed with open arms. There, time is on their side and something to give an interest and some colour is much appreciated. Many hospitals have more flowers than they can really cope with, or do not have suitable containers in which to make the arrangement.

Funeral work can be divided into two groups:

1 *Loose work* where the flowers and stems stand away from the frame or base which is lightly greened. The flowers are of different lengths and the spaces between are filled with interesting foliages. It is important that the flowers come down to the sides of the frame and lie flat on the table — so often you may see the flowers standing upright in rows and nothing along the side. The shape of the frame must be carefully followed. With a cross, attention must be paid to proportion of the frame, and it must have square ends.

Many flowers are suitable for loose work providing they will stand up to wiring and fairly heavy handling.

2 *Foundation work* (this is not necessarily for funerals) With this type of floristry the flowers are brought right down onto the frame with the minimum of stem left on the flower head. Usually this is more expensive work requiring many more flowers. The frame can have an edging but in most cases looks more clean cut without. The frames for foundation work require firm mossing and must be a perfect shape. Before placing any flowers on the frame, the moss must be covered with a layer of tissue paper. This will help to keep the flower heads clean and mask any of the moss that might show.

Foundation work will also be used when making badges, coats of arms, and signs in flowers. Another brilliant form of this work is done in Holland, for example, with the flower mosaics and pictures displayed along the roadsides during flower festivals. In this case the flowers are not wired, but carefully placed in damp sand on a slightly raised framework. Similar work is done in England for the Well dressing ceremonies in Derbyshire — here petals are used on damp clay.

Many flowers can be used in foundation work, but probably the best results are obtained from the following: Stocks, Hydrangeas, Violets, Hyacinth 'bells' or 'pips'. For the cheaper work small Daffodils, Polyanthus, Esther Reads, Dahlias (small pompom), Scabious and Chrysanthemums can be used.

Mixed foliage used in funeral work can be most effective. Another foundation which is seldom used, but is most effective, is Reindeer Moss. This, however, is very expensive today and not readily obtainable.

When making a design in flowers you will achieve a much more even effect by using many of the same flowers in different colours. For example, red, yellow and white Carnation petals will give you a better effect than red Carnations, yellow Chrysanthemums and white Hyacinth bells.

The smaller the flower the more compact the base will be, but do remember, smaller flowers mean extra cost both in time and wires.

Work your design like a tapestry. Draw out the plan on the tissue paper covering the frame, which should be firm but contain less moss than when making a loose design. Fill in the small sections first, then do the bulky areas last.

Quite frankly, I hate having to do some of the funeral designs such as vacant chairs. My choice would be from the spray on a board, posy pad, simple wreath or coffin cross if I could not send an arrangement. There are many who love these special designs, however, and when they are ordered they certainly are a challenge for the florist. If you have to do them, do them well.

Through my work with flowers over the years I have been privileged to visit many countries and to see some of their wonderful wild flowers. Perhaps Switzerland comes top for these and I can think of nothing more beautiful than the Alpines that I try to see growing wild each time I visit. On these occasions I long to collect the Gentians, Edelweiss, Alpenrose, Trollius, Violas, white Daisies and many other flowers to make a wreath in the style which Mrs Spry used to like — a circle of flower heads massed together to make a tapestry of colour.

Anyone visiting the little chapel beside a small lake just above Zermatt cannot fail to be moved on seeing a most perfect painting above the altar. It is that of a young climber together with ropes and ice axe handing over a beautifully simple cluster wreath of Alpine flowers to an angel with arms outstretched to receive it — a most perfect picture and so simple, yet so unexpected up in the mountains.

I often visit graveyards just to look at the work produced in different countries. I cannot bring myself to accept the wreaths made of plastic flowers and leaves that are so often to be seen in Switzerland when over the cemetery wall are a wealth of wild flowers and foliages!

In Japan one hires a wreath for the occasion. It stands on a tripod covered in black ribbons for the service and then is returned to the flower shop. It may next be used for a happier occasion, say the opening of a new business, when it again stands on a tripod but this time it is decked out in bright colours!

Frames For Funeral Work

Wreath

This is a round wire frame available in various sizes from 10in (25cm) diameter. The really large frames may be fitted with tripod legs so that they are stood up rather than laid on the ground. Various systems of flower work can be added to the moss frame, for example a bunch spray, crescent spray, loose work, foundation, grouped and clumps.

Cross

These are purchased in various sizes. An extra large cross is known as a coffin cross and this is very suitable as a 'family' tribute. Cross frames are used for 'loose' and foundation work. Sprays of flowers can be added to the cross, with the longest flower three-quarters down the foot. The most suitable are a slanting spray or a foot spray.

Chaplet

These come in various sizes, and can have a crescent, bunch or 'anchor' spray attached across the base. The larger ones will be fitted with tripod legs.

A 'cycas' chaplet has only one wire to the top of the frame to which the real or plastic cycas fronds are secured. The base is a double area for mossing.

Cushion

Available in various sizes, these are pointed at the corners. They have a lid and a base with small feet. The frame is square.

You may occasionally see a round cushion frame, but these can be made easily enough by covering a wreath frame with wire netting on both sides.

Pillow

Again, available in various sizes these are pointed at

the corners. The frame is rectangular and has a base with a lid.

Heart (Open)
Available in various sizes.

Figure 15.1: Cushion heart — foundation of flowers with foliage edge

Heart (Cushion)
These can be purchased in various sizes with a base and lid as for pillows and cushions. The base is flat with no feet, the lid raised to give fullness.

All these frames can be purchased in oasis today and many florists will use them rather than the old wire frames which require time to prepare and use so much moss. I still feel myself that the better result is

Figure 15.2: Outline of foliage for a cross. Note square ends

Figure 15.3: Cross with spray. Mixed foliage base and spray of Tulips, Tulip foliage, Ivy and Berries

Figure 15.4: Foundation work of Chrysanthemum on a cross. Note the paper beneath the flowers

obtained with a mossed frame but the cost of making some of these tributes can be high, both in materials and time. Remember also that oasis bases hold water enabling the flowerwork to be started earlier with long-lasting qualities. Gone are the days when the florist worked all hours and through the weekend for an early Monday morning funeral.

Loose work can only be done on the simple designs, such as a wreath, cross, chaplet and open heart. All the fancy shapes have to be done in foundation or based work.

Mossing

This is a most important part in the making of a floral tribute. It is the foundation on which the flowerwork is built. If not firm enough, the mounts will fall out while in transit.

Round wreath

Tease the moss and remove any foreign bodies. Tie the string (attached to a bobbin) in a knot on the inside of the frame. Bring the bobbin underneath the frame. Mould the moss to shape in your hands and place on the outside of the frame. Secure by stringing over and under the frame evenly at ¾–1in (1.85–2.5cm) spacings. Work clockwise keeping the moss firm and the bobbin of string close to the frame to prevent the string breaking. Tuck the new end of moss under the previous bound one. Continue around the frame until the final handful of moss. This must be a double handful if a spray of flowers is to be added to the frame. Fasten off the string neatly on the underside of the frame. Clean away surplus moss and trim frame.

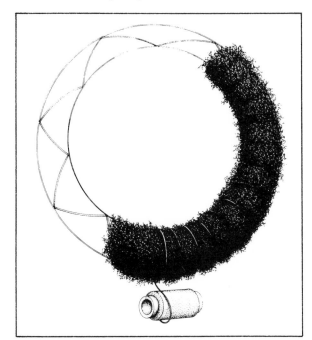

Figure 15.5: Mossing a wreath frame

Chaplet

Commence mossing at the tip of the chaplet. Join the mossing string onto the inside of the frame, and bring the bobbin underneath the frame. Place the first handful of moss well over the end of the frame. Take the string two or three times around the complete tip of the frame. Continue mossing firmly and neatly at ¾–1in (1.85–2.5cm) intervals.

Follow the line and shape of the chaplet. If a spray is to be added, ensure that the double handfuls forming a 'bump' are correctly placed. For the anchor spray the bump should be placed at the centre bottom of the frame. For the crescent spray the bump should be placed at the left hand curve. For the bunch spray the bump should be placed on the left hand side at the point where the frame starts to straighten.

Complete the mossing to where you commenced and fasten the string off neatly underneath the frame. Remove any surplus moss from the frame and trim neatly, paying special attention to the 'tip' which should be firmly pointed with no wire frame protruding.

The cross

Commence mossing at the foot of the frame. Attach the string on the far side of the frame and bring the bobbin underneath the frame. Take the moss over all the ends of the frame to ensure that when finished all ends are square and no part of the frame protrudes. Place well-teased moulded handfuls of moss onto the frame and string evenly at ¾–1in (1.85–2.5cm) intervals, each subsequent handful tucked in neatly to the preceding one. Moss to the centre of the frame, then wind the string along to the end of one arm and moss in a similar manner towards the centre. Moss the other arm and top of the cross in the same way.

If a spray of flowers is to be added, make a 'bump' in the appropriate position — at the centre for the straight and diagonal sprays, and a hand's width up from the foot of the cross for a foot spray. To finish mossing take the string diagonally twice across the centre of the cross and fasten off neatly at the back of the frame.

Trim the frame well so that all ends are square and surplus moss removed.

Open heart

Moss this as for the Chaplet (see above).

When mossing no surplus moss should be caught into the underside of the frame. This is untidy and adds extra weight to the work. Some moss may be very dry and will need some damping down, but take care not to make it too wet as again the frame will become unnecessarily heavy.

Closed frames

These include Hearts, Pillows and Cushions, and Open Books.

Oiled or waxed paper or a piece of polythene is used to line the base and brought up the sides of the frame. Tease the moss and pack it well into the corners first, then work towards the centre. The base must be tightly packed with moss with a slight incline at the centre. Place the lid onto the frame and, with a packing needle threaded with mossing string, 'sew' the frame together. As these frames are usually finished in foundation or block work the top of the frames are covered in tissue paper.

Vacant chair

Moss the front and back legs, back and seat. Back the frame with laurel leaves or waxed paper. Cover the 'fronts' with tissue paper.

Gates of heaven

The cross and gates which are ajar are usually painted black or gold. Moss the base and arch and back with laurel leaves or waxed paper. Cover the 'fronts' with tissue paper.

Figure 15.6: Gates of heaven

Broken pillar

Moss the pillar and base. Back the base with laurel leaves or waxed paper. Cover with tissue paper.

BACKING THE FRAME. When using laurel leaves for backing a frame cut the stalk end away. Using hairpins made from half lengths of 22 gauge (.71mm) × 7in (180mm) wire, pin the leaf across the underside of the frame, with one pin above the outer

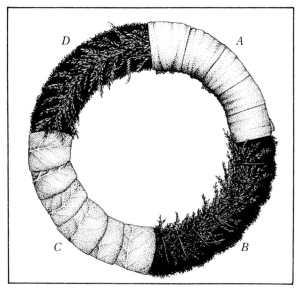

Figure 15.7: Different forms of backing a wreath
A. Wreathwrap (polythene bandage)
B. Cupressus bound on
C. Laurel
D. Pinned Cupressus

frame and the other pin above the inner frame. Pin strips of polythene or waxed paper in a similar manner.

Preparing Greening For Wreathwork

When using foliage to cover the moss on a funeral design it is advisable to use a mixture of at least three varieties. The foliage needs to be of a fairly long-lasting nature; for example, Cupressus, Cumberland Pine (Hemlock), Box, Eucalyptus, Andromeda, etc. It is also advisable to choose a selection of various-

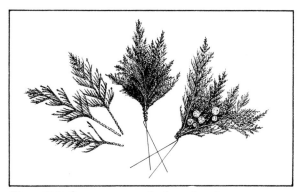

Figure 15.8: Cupressus mounts for funeral work

shaped leaves including some of the single leaf type which can be mounted in twos, such as Portuguese Laurel, the Cupressus type, the small leaves of the Box and the leaves of Mahonia aquifolium.

The various pieces need to be mounted on a 22 gauge (.71mm) × 7in (180mm) wire. The pieces such as Cupressus should be made up of two or three small pieces, the slightly longer piece in the centre with slightly shorter ones on either side.

The stems should be the same length at the end and should be cleaned of foliage at the base. Mount with 22 gauge (.71mm) × 7in (180mm) double leg.

Usually three sizes of greenwork are needed, these sizes vary according to the size of the frame. For a small frame they need to be much smaller.

With Berberis keep the leaves in sprays of three and mount one or two together. Pierce the 22 gauge (.71mm) × 7in (180mm) through the three leaves and mount on a double leg.

Again the three sizes of greenwork are needed for each wreath. If the leaves are very large they can be taken off and two used together. This is done by placing the two together and mounting on a double leg mount. Any other single leaves, such as Laurel, Gaultheria, Eucalyptus, etc. are done in this way.

Leaves such as Box are cut to small sprays and two or three pieces mounted together with a 22 gauge (.71mm) × 7in (180mm) double leg.

Natural Funeral Bunch

These are often requested because they can go straight to a hospital or an old people's home after the service. No wires are used and the bunch should be a facing arrangement made in the hand; it can then be placed directly into a vase (see Plate 27). Sometimes you will find florists wire their flowers before tying the bunch — this should then be called a Funeral Sheaf. Hospitals will not accept flowers which have been wired.

Funeral bunches can be made in any size, but usually you would use at least three or four dozen flowers. An example of a spring bunch would be:

3/5 stems of eucalyptus
10 'Paper White' Narcissi
10 cream-coloured Daffodils
5 pink Tulips
2–3 bunches of Freesia
a couple of small green Helleborus foetidus

How to make a natural funeral bunch

Select a well-shaped piece of foliage for the back, trimming off any basal shoots to make a piece of clear stem to hold. Attach a reel of green string to this; take the largest and most pointed flower and bind once on to the stem of foliage. Now place the flowers in twos and threes and pieces of foliage as required, binding round once for each piece always in the same place and in the same direction, going under the stems and not over the flower heads. Bind firmly, but not too tightly or you may fracture the stem.

It is usual to hold the bunch in the left hand, placing each stem in position and binding with the right hand. Bind from the right hand side over to the left and under the stalks. Place your left hand thumb over the string to keep it from slipping. By doing it this way you get a firm pull on the back of the stems and use the minimum amount of string. Never go over the heads of the flowers with the string — you damage the flowers this way. Work always with the reel going over the base of the stems. Make the bunch quite pointed and try to use any natural curving material for the sides. These stems are crossed over slightly to give a slight spread to the base of the bunch.

Group your flower shapes and colour carefully so as to get full value from each stem. Widen the bunch towards the base and allow fullness to the centre so that the flowers come forward over the hand when just holding on the binding. This prevents a very flat-looking bunch. When finished cover the binding string with a plaited raffia or ribbon which is just wrapped round and pinned on to the stems at the back. Some florists will finish off with a bow. Trim the stems if they are very uneven.

Many find this type of bunch difficult to do. It is most important to get it flat in the hand and not twisted, also to see that you place enough flowers over the wrist on the left hand side. Hold the materials between the thumb and first two fingers of the left hand. Keep the hand open in order that the stems may radiate from the binding.

Sheaf On A Board

This is a funeral design which gives a good display for a fairly small outlay. It can appear as a natural bunch with a return end of stalks or have a rounded end of flowers, in which case a few more flowers are needed.

The whole design is worked on a mossed board approximately 4in × 8in (10cm × 20cm) or an oasis tray. The moss is teased out, damped, then tied firmly with mossing string, giving a fairly thick firm pad for holding the wire mounts. The string should go round the board at ½in (1.25cm) intervals, finishing off with two or three times across the length of the pad. Keep the board clear of moss on the underside. Finish off the back of the board with a cover of oiled paper or laurel leaves. Trim off surplus moss as for wreathwork. Cover the moss with pinned laurel or small mounts of Cupressus. Make a neat edge and keep the corners square.

Commence by placing a good framework of backing foliage. This is mounted on 20 gauge (.90mm) × 10in (260mm) or 12in (310mm) double legs, and placed firmly between the board and the moss. It must be firm because it is on this framework that the design is made.

The flowers are mounted on 20 gauge (.90mm) × 10in (260mm) double legs. Divide out the materials, planning groups and flower shapes, leaving something important for the centre of the sheaf.

Place the first flower well into the end of the board and work down to the centre flower, gradually increasing the width, so that at the widest point the flowers are about 2–3in (5–7.5cm) from the moss pad. The centre flower is about two-thirds of the way down the length of the sheaf. Allow plenty of 'in and out' with the flowers, and fill in carefully with foliage as you work down the pad.

Support the centre flower with one or two well-placed flowers at different heights at the side. After completing this part, commence the return end. If using stalks see that these start at the end of the moss pad going well in between the moss and board — so many people pick up the sheaf by these stalks. Flowers should also start from this place if used in the return and work back to the centre flower, keeping this end more round in shape. There is nothing to stop you and, in fact, it is better to put some flowers in, in twos and threes.

The main points to watch are proportion, shape and good colour grouping, working through to a clean clear-cut centre.

If using oasis, I usually find half to three-quarters of a block will be enough. Cover with a layer of wire netting and secure with oasis tape or string. The flowers need not be wired, just set them into the base in exactly the same way as when using a moss pad. The advantage of using oasis is that an early start can be made to a big order because the flowers last well. If you are using a whole block, the weight factor is considerable and care should be taken when lifting the spray off the ground.

A *posy pad* is made in the same way, but must be round. Either use a moss pad or a small round oasis tray. These were first designed by Constance Spry in the 1920s and made up of early mixed spring flowers from choice, using such material as Hellebore, Roman Hyacinths, Freesias, Grape Hyacinths, Snowdrops, Violets and any interesting small pieces with Eucalyptus and Rosemary for foliage. They were charming and simple. Now they are made all the time and more mundane flowers used which to my way of thinking are not so attractive. Always try to keep to small and simple flowers for this design.

Loose Wreath

This is the name given to the funeral design where the flowers stand up away from the frame. The frame is mossed and has a good green edging of mixed foliage or Cupressus. The top of the frame can have the foliage in larger pieces mounted or pinned on the frame — the moss should not show.

This type of wreath is found mostly in the provinces and country districts; it is a less expensive and fairly quick tribute to make. Depending on size, so the number of flowers vary, but they appear in circles on the frame when looked at from above. A loose wreath can be made using all the same kind of flower or different types, depending on the effect required. All flowers are wired internally where possible, then mounted on 20 gauge (.90mm) × 7in (180mm) wires.

The tallest row of flowers are placed first, standing off the frame about 4–5in (10–12.5cm) high (again depending on the size of the frame). There must be an uneven number to give the round effect — five, seven, nine. If four were used, for instance, it would look square straightaway. It is most important that these be evenly spaced and of the same height, otherwise the shape can easily be thrown out.

The second row of flowers are short and placed between the first row. The third row of flowers are slightly shorter than the first row and go on the outside of the frame following the line of the foliage but overlapping it slightly at an angle. Keep these evenly spaced. The flowers on the fourth or inside row are a little shorter than the third row; they should go in at an angle following the foliage, facing towards the centre slightly. For the fifth row, the stems are half way between the first and second row in length, and are evenly spaced between the outside and centre rows. The sixth row is the same length as for the fifth and these are evenly spaced between inside and centre flowers. Any other rows necessary to fill in are placed in rings allowing 'in and out' between each flower. Fill in with pieces of foliage similar to that used for greening or that of the flowers used.

When grouped flowers are wanted, try to work to a pattern on the frame using five or seven types of flowers.

For clusters, the frame is greened as for loose work. Have an uneven number of clusters — five or seven and so on. All flowers cluster around a centre one at different lengths. These can be most attractive designs, but care must be taken to choose suitable flowers. A lovely effect can be obtained by having a bun moss foundation with clusters of small spring flowers worked onto it. This would be very suitable for a child. Mixed clusters of foliages are also most effective.

All loose work is done in the same way when working on a heart or chaplet frame; great care must be given to keeping the shape of the frame.

Laurel

This is an important foliage for green foundation work and when done well can make a very neat and attractive background. It is especially suitable for use in designs in connection with service funerals and perhaps looks best as a chaplet foundation.

Pinned Laurel

This is the quickest and easiest form of laurel to use. The branches are carefully stripped of foliage, and any badly marked or misshapen leaves discarded. The rest are graded out into three sizes: large, medium and small. These leaves are then cleaned with soft tissue paper, and wiped over with a thin oil and polished. When carefully done, this makes the leaves supple and shiny. The foliage is pinned with pieces of 22 gauge (.71mm) × 3½in (90mm) stub wire, made into hairpins.

Remove the bottom third of each leaf. Use one or two pins to each leaf shape. The 'bump' is on the left hand side on the outside edge when completed, with the leaves at a two o'clock angle to the frame. Each leaf is pinned on at an angle through the mid-rib about half way up so that it just touches the table on the edge. The second pin is at the base of the leaf. Start placing your leaves from the bump. Use the medium-sized leaves.

Place the second leaf with its edge just touching the mid-rib of the last — complete the frame, looking at the back at every four to six leaves to see that the effect is correct and the shape is maintained. The second row goes on the inside and is of small leaves. The third row goes on top of the first row towards the centre of the frame.

Usually for the medium-sized frame, five rows of leaves are necessary. For larger frames more will be needed. All pins should be placed through the leaf, so that they do not show when it is completed. Overlap the leaves to form a 'fish-scale' effect. Complete the outer and inner edges but do not cover the bump with pinned laurel. The bump may be covered with two or three leaves criss-crossed at the end.

Pleated Laurel

Use perfect medium-sized leaves; clean them with soft tissue. Place the ends together and shorten them at the

Figure 15.9: Pinned Laurel

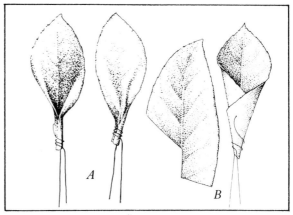

Figure 15.10: Laurel leaves in different forms
A. Pleated   B. Curled

ends by about half. Fold gently inwards down the centre vein with the sides back down making a letter 'M'. DO NOT CREASE LEAVES. Double leg mount with a 22 gauge (.71mm) × 10in (280mm) wire. The leaves are placed onto the frame as with pinned laurel.

When greening a chaplet with pleated laurel the leaves must be graduated, the smaller leaves used at the top becoming larger as the frame widens. Always green into the bump wherever it may be on the frame. Finish by pinning one or two leaves over the bump.

Curled Laurel

Use perfect medium-sized leaves; clean them with a soft tissue. Cut away about a third of the leaf. Cut straight across the leaf. Then cut up parallel with the mid-rib on the right hand side for about the same distance (1in, 2.5cm). Cut over the vein and across the vein at about 45 degrees. By removing part of the mid-rib you make the leaf easier to handle as it is not so thick.

Place the index finger of your left hand down the vein on the upper side of the leaf. Bring the diagonal cut edge over holding it with your finger and thumb and then wrap the bottom piece around the base to form a cone. Hold it in place with your thumb and index finger and double leg mount with a 22 gauge (.71mm) × 10in (180mm) wire. The wire should pass through the cone in a diagonal manner. When greening a frame with curled laurel the 'cones' interlock and the outside of the cones should not be visible. A small cross takes at least 150 pieces of curled laurel. Always work into the 'bump', which should be covered with two or three criss-crossed leaves. Care must also be taken to keep the ends of the cross square. Insert three small curled leaves on each end to keep ends square, then insert more leaves down the sides as with greening. Fill in the top with slightly larger cones.

Figure 15.11: Outline of crescent spray on a Laurel base

Figure 15.12: Completed crescent spray on Laurel — includes Chrysanthemum and Physostegia

---

Designs On Frames

Points to remember when making designs on fancy frames

1 Moss firmly but keep the frame reasonably thin.
2 Trim well and keep a perfect shape — the addition of flowers will take from the shape rather than add to it.
3 Use as many of one type of flowers as you can, making use of different colours rather than different types of flowers.

4 Cover your work with tissue paper before starting the pinning of the flowers. It keeps the flowers clean, and the moss base will not show through if the petals are not quite evenly placed.
5 Work your foundation pieces from the outside edge to the point where your spray rests on the frame.
6 Draw any fancy pattern on the paper and fill in difficult pieces first, then work the main body of flowers last. For instance, if you are making a Union Jack draw to scale first.

7 Always try to keep the design as simple as possible — the effect will be better. If you try to be too clever, the whole effect can be lost.

8 Remember many designs done in foundation will stand up so see that the back is well finished off. Any spray mounts must be tucked back into the moss should they appear at the back. This is important with any wreathwork.

Flowers which can be pinned onto the frame:

Border Carnations
Cornflower
Daffodils — small flowers
Esther Reed
Marigolds
Narcissi — 'Sol d'Or', 'Paper White', 'Buxton', etc.
Scabious
Small Aster (doubles)
Small Chrysanthemums — double varieties
Zinnia

When using the above remember:
Pins should be made from 24 gauge (.56mm) wire.
Remove stalks to a very short stub.
Pierce through and pinch wire together.
No need to twist wire.

For bunching together to form flat-backed pieces:

Hydrangea
Lilac
Polyanthus
Primroses
Small Narcissi
Violets
Wallflower

When using the above remember:
Bind 4–5 flowers together with 36 gauge (.20mm) wire. Pin onto frame with 22 gauge (.71mm) or 24 gauge (.56mm) wire hairpin.

Lichen or Reindeer Moss is pinned on with 24 gauge (.56mm) pins. *Bun Moss*, which often requires trimming at the back before placing on the frame, is secured with 22 gauge (.71mm) hairpins.

Cushions and pillows

These are usually used for the more expensive floral tributes. The main body of the work is completed in a foundation of flowers and on this is placed a spray. Cushions and pillows can be made on mossed wire bases or oasis frames.

The wire frames for these designs are made in two pieces: a base with legs, and a lid. For a small cushion, two lids can be used — this will give a less heavy appearance to the frame.

Commence the work by lining the base with oiled paper or plastic sheeting, allowing a little to come up the sides and making sure this lining keeps the shape of the frame. Fill with moss, pressing well into the sides and corners. When using a large frame, straw or shavings can be used in the centre of the base to make the frame lighter. The finished shape should allow a slightly raised centre. Fix on the lid, securing the corners and centre sides with 22 gauge (.71mm) × 7in (180mm) wires twisted and pushed back into the moss, or sew up with a packing needle and string. Trim out the paper. Bind the corners with string. Before commencing the foundation, decide whether an edging of foliage is necessary — this can be of Cupressus, Ivy, Heather, Eucalyptus — mounted on 22 gauge (.71mm) × 7in (180mm) and inserted just at the top of the frame and bent over.

If a foundation of bun moss or lichen moss is required this should be pinned on now, getting a very even depth to it. When pinning use 22 gauge (.71mm) × 7in (180mm) cut in half to make hairpins. The bun moss may need to be trimmed on the back before it can be used because it is often far too thick. Commence at the corners and work into the place for the spray which is usually on the left hand top corner of the frame.

If you are using a flower foundation, first cover the frame with tissue paper. This helps to keep the flowers clean, and also does not allow the dark base of moss to show through if any gaps appear between the flowers. Most of the flowers can be wired with 28 gauge (.38mm) or 30 gauge (.32mm). These can be as pins or double leg mounts.

Always work your foundation *from the corners* to the place where the spray of flowers will be fixed, usually in the top left hand quarter. By doing so, should you run out of pieces, those last few oddments will be under the spray and not seen in an important area. Get your pieces on evenly and see that those at the edges and corners are firmly secured. These areas get handled the most and the mounts must not fall out with rough handling.

Now let me just mention some of the 'traditional' funeral designs which still seem to be popular in the more densely populated areas of this country. They have been seen at funerals for many many years and are still asked for today.

Gates of heaven or gates ajar

These frames are readily available in the market and today you find the 'golden gates' made so that they are always open. I find it better to spray the gates with a gold aerosol paint and not to try and cover them with flowers. Keep the frame simply covered with small flowers and allow a small spray of flowers up the left side of the arch and across the front of the base of the frame. Neatly cover the back.

Vacant chair

These today are in two forms (antique and modern), but the upright Windsor chair is still the most popular. The bar across the back readily holds the name of the deceased.

Again it is important to use small neat flowers to keep the shape. The cross bars holding the legs can be treated with a spray paint. A spray of flowers across the seat is all that is required. Names go across the bar at the back — use dull black paint rather than those silver glittered letters. Be sure to see that all these designs are neatly finished at the back.

Names, musical instruments, toys, all of which may be purchased through the market sundriesman, come into use from time to time and all are treated in the same way. Moss carefully to get the correct shape, then simply cover by pinning or mounting flowers all over the frame — the spray of flowers, if required, may give just a change to the frame contours but they must not detract from the shape.

These frames, however much one may dislike them, are a real challenge to one's ability as a florist and to look good they must really be done well. The costing of them takes a lot of working out because the amount of time and materials used are often consider-able. To me what is so sad is that so often the people choosing this type of tribute are the ones who can least afford it. Tradition dies hard and in some areas a funeral is not complete without the vacant chair, etc. And again, who are we to turn away trade? If a customer chooses this type of work, tackle it whole-heartedly and make a real show of expert floristry.

PART THREE

THE
WORK
OF
A
FLORIST

16. RUNNING A FLOWER SHOP

Shop Display

This is an extremely important subject — flowers that are not well displayed can be lost to the public eye. The type of flowers that you can sell in one place — for instance, the West End of London — will differ greatly from those in a small market town. You will find differences in requirements from county to county and from North to South. But there has been a levelling out of ideas and flower requirements as training in floristry has widened throughout the country.

It is almost true to say that everyone loves flowers and to a great extent, if well displayed, flowers sell themselves, but with the present economic climate flowers tend to be considered a luxury, so more effort is needed to sell them.

A good sales person must be enthusiastic and know the job inside out. It is important that the quality and price are right. In other words, service has to go with the price these days. It takes a long time to acquire a good reputation, and not very long to acquire a bad one. Once you have a bad name, it stays with you for a long while.

It often happens that a customer will get to know a certain assistant and always asks for the same person on telephoning or visiting the shop. This is fine, but there will be occasions when he or she is not available and others must cope. It is always a good policy to discuss customers (in the nicest way!) between the staff and make notes of likes and dislikes, money spent, etc. to cover these occasions. Once a person has your confidence they expect the work to be carried out without further discussion, and hate continually to be asked questions which they feel are unnecessary.

There are customers, especially men, who leave everything to their pet assistant which is fine but, without another person covering for her, this can occasionally cause trouble.

A new customer can sometimes mean hard work, and I always feel rather like a ballet dancer on stage moving gracefully round the shop, with arms outstretched, carefully gathering this and that to create a beautiful bunch in one's hand. Always carefully place the flowers and foliages (remember you can always 'sell up' at a greater profit to yourself with a stem or two of good backing material) with the most important flowers at the centre for a focal point. Discuss the colourings as you build up the bouquet, bearing in mind the room in which the flowers will be placed. Name the flowers you are using, and give any interesting tips about them. Really be enthusiastic in your approach and make something with the use of your hands. As you go, price the bunch and when you consider you have a nice collection say, 'That will be ... but to make it really effective you should have a few extra Freesia'. Suggest gift packing to finish the sale well. It is hoped by now that the customer is pleased with the service and he will submit his name, etc., and ask for yours — another customer to your list.

Let us just discuss points of importance with regard to running a flower shop and some of the things that I would look for in taking over another shop. These are observations I have made over the years, and I feel that they may help you to decide when looking at premises.

So much will depend on whether you are building a new shop or taking over an established or old property, and also the trade for which you are looking. Let us presume it will be a true flower and floristry business, and not just for the sale of cut flowers, which can be carried out from any lock-up shop.

From choice, I would take a corner premises because there is usually more light and larger window space. You can then easily divide the shop into flower sales one side and make-up, sundries, etc. in the other section. If you cannot obtain a corner, a large-fronted shop with the door on one side or dividing the area equally is best. Try to avoid a little shop window one side, then a door and the rest a big glass area; the small section is so difficult to dress attractively. If it is facing a sunny quarter — in Britain this is not often a great problem — do have blinds fitted, and these can be used to shelter from the rain. Encourage people to stop and look — after a time they will come in. Georgian-style windows look attractive, but really for ease of display the large plate glass (well insured) window is the best.

I always think that you should have an entrance at the back of the shop — this allows for market deliveries, stock, etc. to move freely into the building without disturbing the customers. Also all orders can be taken out to the van this way. A little extra storage space outside at the back will also be useful for foliages, moss, soil and the many other materials so important to the business yet a nuisance in the workroom itself.

Having found the right premises let us go inside. Here straightaway I would suggest the less fixtures the better, so that you can change the interior around to suit the occasion. What you do want to do from the word go is to attract people, and this you will do with interesting shop displays.

If it is an old building the ceiling may be very high. This can either be brought down lower with a false ceiling, whereby you can hide the light fittings above it, or painted a dark colour — such as blue or black — which, in turn, brings the eye down to the flower level.

Lighting is extremely important and money spent on spots, individual switches for each point, time switches and, maybe, hidden tubes behind the ceiling cornice to give just a glow of light to the shop, will be well worthwhile. We all know what clever lighting can do to a theatrical set and how the whole stage can change. This is what we may want to do within the shop.

At times the evening display may be covered by just one light, but it will still draw the crowds to look at it, the rest of the shop being in darkness.

Using mirrors on the wall again makes a big difference to the shop, and one wall of mirrors can multiply the shop area. However, it does show up the faults too, so be careful. One point to remember is that it does make the shop appear to hold far more flowers.

The floor is another important area, and this can spoil the whole effect if not well done. Stone or terrazzo is ideal — it is cool, easy to clean and has a non-slip surface. Heavy duty lino needs to be sealed to stop water getting underneath, and must be in a colouring which does not show the dirt. I remember once we had a shop with the typical black and white squares of a Dutch interior. It was charming for the first half hour, then quite impossible for the rest of the day. Have a deep skirting with curves to all corners because this is easier to keep clean. One type of floor to avoid is wood block; these look nice but are not serviceable where

water is likely to be spilt. The water soaks in and the blocks swell causing uneven surfaces.

The window area itself should just be a raised floor to bring the materials within it up a little and stop customers walking into it, and — it can happen — walking through the glass. A large pedestal or attractive table will be ideal to stand arrangements on, and one or two stands can raise items to different levels. Avoid a tiered effect with vase after vase filling the window. The wall colouring within the shop should be white, pale grey or green, and in a washable paint. Wallpaper, although most effective, is very soon damaged by water and can be an expensive item to maintain. I would suggest each window has a pair of curtains to it which can be pulled behind the window contents so that you can isolate the shop interior at times. These should run from floor to ceiling and in the daytime be pulled to either side of the window area, framing the window from inside the shop, and folding back onto the pillars beside the window. A number of different colourings will be helpful with the displays at weekends. The use of water trickling down the window to keep the atmosphere moist and the window clear is not necessary in Britain, and is an added expense. It can be a hazard when the little drain from the window base gets blocked! In a hot climate it is ideal, and certainly worth considering. Where unnecessary, however, it distracts the eye when trying to get a clear picture of the shop's contents, and if vases are priced makes it impossible to read the tickets.

Try to keep one area for cut flowers, one for all the flowering and foliage plants, and one for sundries. Keep your colours in groups in the cut-flower section, so that when picking out it is easy to gather the creams, apricots and peach colours to make a bunch for your customer. There is much controversy about whether prices should be displayed, and in the very exclusive shops it is never mentioned. I feel that this is wrong — everything should be neatly priced and the window should carry a whole range of items for sale right through the price scale. Once you have a customer in the shop you can then strike the correct deal. If there are no prices, ten chances to one, most customers will not even enter because they will feel it out of their range.

The shop window, with luck, will not stay intact for long because sales will be taking place all the time. It is important to have more made-up work ready to take the place of items sold. Never leave a vase of flowers with just one bunch left in it, or put a lot of oddments into one vase — this makes for an 'end of range' appearance. These flowers should be taken straight to the workroom where they can be used up in turn. Keep your display vases well stocked all the time, and always pick up the odd leaf that has fallen, and see that the place is tidy. Do keep stock moving in the correct order, so as to eliminate waste.

All display vases should be of the same pattern but, of course, of different sizes. They should be in a good shape that displays flowers well, and a neutral colour; pale grey, white or celadon green are excellent. They should be well balanced, not too heavy to carry when full, and be easy to keep clean. These, may I say, are not easy to find, and it would pay to ask a potter to make them for you. Have a few really large ones for the Gladioli, Delphiniums, etc., down to flat shallow bowls for Violets, Snowdrops and Primroses.

If the vases and bowls are attractive you will find also that you can sell them to customers, which is another outlet. Go in for mixed bunches, half bunches and sell some flowers on individual stems instead of in the normal bunch. This will help trade because the customers will choose exactly what they want.

I believe that one should always be close at hand to help. That does not mean that you should jump out at the customer as soon as they open the door. How often have you walked into a shop, looked round, and had difficulty in getting served? This is not encouraging trade. One should go forward with a greeting, offer help, and make suggestions of what is available saying, 'Please do have a good look round.'

Again, neat pricing is a great help. Labels must be clear and apply to the correct article, otherwise you can be in trouble.

At one stage we did try having a workroom in the shop, but this had its problems. Customers tended to get in the way, were even known to stand over the work going on and make suggestions about more flowers in some places. Quite frankly it did not work! It could be that one person works in a corner of the shop doing small wiring-up jobs, but ready to come forward to any person entering the shop.

You will notice I have said nothing yet about any furniture in the shop. You will need a desk and chairs and all the writing equipment, clean blotting pad and a pen that works. Cheap pens mean bad writing, and in the end you will find that what you save on one you will lose on the number of cards thrown away.

I would strongly advise the making of a wedding book with good photographs of *your own work* to show to customers, also any other work which you may have done which will be of interest.

Display benches and shelves should all be movable so that the shop interior can be changed all the time. Do not attach the wrapping paper to the walls. A

Figure 16.1: Equipment needed on the work bench

wrapping trolley is ideal — it should have everything applicable to wrapping on it. It should be on wheels so it can be moved anywhere in the shop, with paper rolls on each end. Cellophane, wetwrap and tissue, cellophane boxes, ribbons, care cards, etc. should all be to hand. The top should be in formica, with trays underneath which pull out from either side. See that some form of trap is there to stop water from the stems running into the trays. A small till can be incorporated. Stapling gun and Sellotape machine should also be available along with a spare pair of scissors.

Displays should always be topical or advertising coming events such as Valentine's Day, Mothering Sunday, Easter, and always say it in or with flowers. 'An empty window declares the sadness of a missed opportunity' was a statement made by George Foss

Figure 16.2: Valentine heart

when writing many years ago, but how right he was. Never miss an opportunity to put your work before the public. Give the customer as much choice as you can in the matter of gifts for all occasions.

Every weekend there should be a display — always something lasting, so in really hot weather play safe and use china, glass and maybe artificial flowers.

There are mixed feelings about displaying funeral flowers. I believe that there should always be on view one or two items suitable for a funeral. Today with many changes taking place, a posy pad and a spray on a board (both done in oasis) do not look so funereal, but at the same time I feel frames done in foundation work do show your ability as a florist and should be available to see if required. They can be on show in a side window, if you have one. In this way you can often use 'waste' material to your advantage for an extra day or so.

The packing of your flowers is most important and can make all the difference. It is a good way of advertising, and should be attended to very carefully. Cheap paper is neither good for the flowers nor your reputation! Something really smart that spells out the name of your shop, yet is strong, will do the trick. One sheet of good tissue takes the place of three or four poor quality sheets, so in the end the better quality is often cheaper. There is nothing smarter than having your name on your own boxes, if you can run to it. Again, proper wire-edged ribbon will make a bow that far outshines the water repellent material from the market.

I believe it is right to aim high, and work on the principle that if it is worth doing, it is worth doing properly! There are still people, and always will be those, who want a good job done and are prepared to pay for it.

Remember always to place the cards so that they are clearly visible in the flowers, and to deliver the flowers as soon as you can after packing. Many a bunch has arrived spoilt because of too lengthy a time in transit.

Fancy wrappings can make all the difference to the pretty bunches for Valentine's and Mother's Day. Go back in time and create something of the charm of the Victorian era — it will so enhance your flowers. A lace posy frill and a few strands of velvet ribbon will make such a difference and put the whole effect in a different class.

Always try to keep a happy staff — a busy staff is a happy staff; so organise the work as far as you can to see that it is evenly spaced out. Get your staff into a routine way of working so that certain jobs become a habit; for instance, regular cleaning of buckets in the

Figure 16.3: Presentation bouquet in cellophane. Note that address card and greetings card clearly show

coldstore, and filling up the buckets with fresh water last thing at night ready to receive flowers from the market in the early morning. Then, if someone fails to turn up or is late, those left have a little less to do to cover the extra work.

In slack periods, if you have nothing that the staff can do, send one off early to make up for those late periods worked at other times. What you must do is to treat all alike. Never have staff hanging around with nothing to do — they only start talking about you, and that is fatal!

The Flower Decorator's Work Box

Always take with you the equipment you need to do the job. This should be kept up to date so that everything is to hand, and no time need be wasted when out on a job popping in to here or there to find materials to finish it.

You will need a good stout box with handles that can act as an extra seat in the van if necessary, with a cushion for the top (remembering long journeys of old!). You will also need:

1 pair secateurs
1 pair scissors (each decorator should have his/her own)
1 pair wire cutters
2 reels wire — thick and thin
Wire netting — a few yards rolled up

Dust sheet(s)
Dustpan and brush
Small watering can
Meat hooks
Small length of chain
Tubes (cones)
Sticks
Oasis tape or coloured masking tape ('God's
    Blessing')
String
Hammer
Nails (small selection)
Oasis blocks
A couple of oasis trays
Cloth for wiping up
Duster
First Aid Box
Black plastic rubbish bags
Trowel
Small length of hose with universal tap fitting for use
    when only a wash basin tap is available
Folding stepladder

If you are going to a really remote place, with no residents on the premises, it may be wise to take a flask and some food.

It is important to be businesslike in your approach and to appear efficient and enthusiastic. Get on with the job immediately you arrive on the site, and leave as soon as you have finished, having kept everything clean and tidy.

I remember so well Mrs Spry saying that one should always leave a job seeing that the area around is cleaner and tidier than when you started — some people, if they heard that said of their home, might take exception to the remark, but we knew what she meant, and it still stands today.

It is a great mistake to have too many people on a job. Two or three really working all the time should be ideal, not a gang who are talking and arguing all the time as to who will do this or that, etc. One person should take charge and quickly allocate the work — in fact, in most cases having been to see the job and estimate beforehand, all this will have been worked out, and the whole plan organised before leaving base. Work as a happy team and switch the jobs around from time to time. Each vase should be numbered, with its contents listed, so that they are ready to marry up with numbered buckets.

I often think back on some of the wonderful jobs with which I have been involved, and the beautiful things I have been privileged to see. I do less travelling now because today there are so many more people trained in flowers and able to do the work covering the whole of Great Britain, but there are numerous amusing incidents that I could relate.

For instance, one would hardly believe that work could be stopped by the tide coming in! This was a job which lasted over two days involving church, house and marquee flowers, and wedding bouquets which came down from London on the following day. I shall never forget it; it was my birthday, and one of the hottest summer days on record. Four of us drove down with all the flowers, vases, etc. in the van to the little town of Bosham, near Chichester. On arriving in the early afternoon, we found our road completely submerged by the tide, so after popping into the local for a bite of lunch and to watch the swans float by at window level, we found ourselves in the churchyard for the afternoon stripping Lime to go with the Paeonies and Lilies in the decorations.

Once the water was down, we made a quick dash to the home on the island where we were to carry out all the other decorating. It was on this occasion, and the only one that I can remember, that we had a small disaster. Over the tiny altar in the Lady Chapel was a window set back with a ledge in front. It had been decided that a long vase should stand there — the most difficult of spots to reach. Three of us took up the job — one on the steps, one passing up the flowers, and the other at the back of the church directing the positioning of the stems because all was done from an angle on the steps. The very position of the vase meant that all the flowers had to be flowing forward, but we did not take into consideration how much heavier it would be at the front once the flowers opened. Well, the disaster occurred during the night, and although the lady responsible for the church cleaning said, 'It's that damned cat, he comes through that window often', we knew that it was no fault of the most friendly of cats, and that we had not weighted down the vase enough at the base to balance the group. Water was everywhere and the Altar frontal marked. We had a very big clearing-up job to complete in a short time instead of just topping up the water and checking the groups, and again a tide with which to contend!

We changed the cloth and runners, wiped down the brass and returned a somewhat smaller vase to its former position, as well as arranging a cash deal with the local laundry. Why I tell you this is to stress the importance of balancing your vase correctly. Allow for movement and the change of weight when your flowers open, and always weight down the base of your vase. Lead is excellent, and being so heavy a small flat piece takes up little room. Gravel or wet sand in the base of the vase and, of course, a block of wet oasis or bundle of stub wires tied to the back of the vase will all help.

Estimating For A Job

You should note the following points when going to see a job and when submitting an estimate.

1 DATE and TIME of party.
2 Purpose of the function.
3 COLOUR SCHEME — home, hall or marquee.
4 What CONTAINERS belonging to the clients can be used, and how many will be necessary for you to bring.
5 LIGHTING — Time of year, day, etc., and how many spot lights will be necessary. The final result depends on good lighting, but remember not to subject flowers to too much heat from light.
6 POSITION OF VASES — Any movement of the room setting as it normally stands. Will you have to supply plinths?
7 WATER SUPPLY — Very important to note. Can you get vases under the taps or will a special small hose be needed?
8 FLOWERS/FOLIAGES — Always supply your own.
9 May add a few if available from the garden, but so much will depend on the function. Is the garden to be on show itself?
10 Any authority necessary if rooms are hired to place flowers in certain positions (fire hazard)?
11 Will it be necessary to have to go and clear, or will the client be able to do this and return the vases to you in the very near future.
12 Always take black plastic bags for the rubbish, and a box or two in which to lay good material.

Points To Note And Remember When Decorating

Do not cut or buy too many flowers. Work out the flowers used to the correct costing. Have just one or two of each for reserve to allow for accidents.

Take all vases ready wired and with tubes if necessary — this saves time and van space.

Do not use a lot of fussy flowers — they spoil the shape and are not attractive. Three to five main stems of flowers such as Longi Lily at the centre really attract the eye, and bring everything together; in floristry the term 'cleaning it up' is used.

Have your flowers going up into the top foliage — all long greens with a centre of short flowers does not give the correct effect. You may have to use tubes to get some false height to a few flowers at the centre.

Do not spot small groups about all over the place. Two to three good groups will cost roughly the same, and look much more impressive.

Flowers should be up fairly high for parties where all the guests will be standing. Low bowls will soon be lost. The mantel shelf is the ideal place for one large group — it is the focal point of the room.

Never move clocks, furniture, etc. without permission, and it is always better to ask the owners to do it for you.

Do not try to hide things by covering them — it makes them stand out more. If not able to be moved, make them look an insignificant part of the room.

Decorating large houses
Decorating in large stately and country homes has become somewhat of a vogue, and is something which a florist may well be asked to consider. Up until now some of these homes have been the centre for area exhibitions of the National Association of Flower Arrangement Societies (NAFAS), and finding that it is a way of drawing in the crowds, the owners have looked farther afield and either attract sponsors with a charity in mind who can share in the takings, or they run it with their own staff hoping to be able to raise well in excess of the florist's fee for doing the job. The weather will have a big bearing on the outcome.

Let me give you a few tips which may help should you be required to consider a job of this sort. It is great fun, very hard work, and extremely tiring because these homes were not designed for easy moving around. You will have covered miles at the end of the day unless you have a team of helpers to put the small arrangements around from a central decorating area.

First, I would suggest you pay a visit to the house in question and, armed with a notebook and pencil, follow the route the visitors will take. Look at each room carefully, spot any special feature, take particular note of the colours, and the aspect of the room. If in any doubt, tone down with greens and white rather than trying to achieve a difficult colour and missing the boat. Do not over-decorate — remember Constance Spry's words 'simplicity and suitability'.

One or two arrangements per room will be all that is normally necessary. Remember, if you suggest too many, the cost will be higher than necessary, and the work force will have to be increased, or you will be working all night to get finished. And that brings me to another point — you may well have to be finished by a certain time because of security and the locking up of the premises. Even more worrying is the fact that many old homes not lived in now have very poor lighting, and you may have to take round portable lamp standards with which to work.

Take a note of where the flowers are to be placed. Make a list of containers and flower stands that you may need. It may be that the house in question has vases and pedestals which you can use, and this helps a lot with transport problems. Also they look more at home and often much better and more in keeping than the ones you could produce.

Water supplies are often a problem, and a small piece of hose with a fitting which tightens up on any tap will be most useful. Taps over basins are in many instances too low to allow a bucket under them. You cannot afford to be slowed up when working.

A place in the cool to stand the buckets ready and marked for each arrangement will be most helpful. A large table on which to work, and a place to stand small vases when finished, so that the helpers can carry them to their respective places, are desirable.

Many old vases already *in situ* will not hold water, so linings, or small plastic buckets, may well be a great help. Line the vases first with paper. It is important to try and use these containers because the guide books may well show them in position as a feature of the room.

When discussing times, remember that arranged flowers will only last, especially in the summer, for two to three days in tip-top condition, and it will be no recommendation for you and a disappointment for the visitors if they do not look really good.

You may have to travel a good distance to do a job of this kind, and it takes time to get it all organised and transported. Many of the flowers may well travel already sorted or picked out into their relevant buckets. Surplus foliages and some of the flowers can be boxed. Have your plinths, vases, dust sheets, etc. on the base of the van — the boxed materials then travel on top of these.

Sometimes there will be people on the house staff who are prepared to keep the vases topped up, and carefully cut out any flowers past their best. Normally one person would stay in the vicinity after doing the job, just to go in the first morning and check through each vase while the rest of the staff return after the full day's work. *Remember* food, travelling and overtime for staff when working out your charges.

Remember also that if you have done the job well and your name is publicised in the brochure, it will be good advertising for you.

It is more than likely that you will have to supply all your own foliages and flowers. The gardens of these large homes are on show, and little will be available for cutting.

Remember also the clearing — this is another day's work and must be done well if you are to be asked back! Try to make it coincide with a day when the house is shut to the public — often a Monday.

Finally, I would suggest you submit your estimate in great detail. List each room in order, colours to be used and maybe special flowers such as Lilies, if available, and a price for each vase. Then add the expenses at the end for travelling, overnight accommodation, food for staff, etc. In addition there may be a charge for hire of vases and/or plinths, and lastly do not forget VAT. Working it out like this allows for pruning and discussion rather than a straight refusal.

All florists love these jobs because you are working in such interesting surroundings, and the flowers always seem to look so good.

Packing

First impressions go a long way, and good presentation makes all the difference. A really smart box, possibly printed with the trade name and with an elegant bow, is something one remembers receiving for a very long time. However, it does all add considerably to the cost, and sometimes this extra is just not forthcoming, so improvisation will be necessary — something often called for from the young florist.

You can waste a lot if you do not improvise. We always cut up all the spare market boxes into shield-shaped boards to back our wraps of flowers; these stiff boards go between the backing paper, which carries

Figure 16.4: Cut flowers (Roses) in cellophane box. Double-ended pack tied with ribbon

Figure 16.5: Orchid presentation. Spray in a cellophane box, tied with ribbon

the firm's name, and the wetwrap on which the cut flower stems are carefully laid. Tissue paper separates the layers of stems and helps to act as a cushion on which the flower heads are laid. Once placed out and tied firmly, this backing card gives support and prevents that broken-back effect in a presentation pack, where the top of the flowers bends backwards from the weight of the flower heads. Remember to add your care card, and also any message which should go with the flowers. Attach it so that it may be seen easily. So often these are thrown out with the wrapping paper, and a telephone call follows to find the name of sender and message.

All good market boxes, preferably in white card, should be kept, and then these can be covered with your own paper for packing large orders of cut flowers or wedding bouquets. If extra height is needed for bouquets, secure wood dowling supports in each corner, so that there is no fear of the flowers getting crushed.

For travelling long distances, I would line the box with a sheet of cellophane or thin polythene because this helps to hold the moisture in or, perhaps more important, stops the box from becoming damp and losing its strength.

Place wedding bouquets on a cushion of tissue to support the flower stems. Fill the loops of the bows with plugs of tissue paper, and place any ribbons out flat on pads of paper. Tie into the box by going over the handle and the main spine of the bouquet with loops of packing string attached to a packing needle.

Tie underneath the box with string bows for easy release. Support a few of the main flowers with little cushions of tissue. Spray well and cover with a thin layer of cellulose wool or a sheet of tissue, again damped lightly. The box top must be well above any of the flowers.

It is essential that bouquets are properly tied in, and — what is more — that instructions are enclosed to say how to release the bouquets. I can picture the excited bride tugging at the bouquet and almost stripping the mounted flowers off the wires as it is pulled through the securing string loops!

It is always wise to advise that all the flowers are left in the coldest place, in the boxes, and not touched until needed on the day — a garage floor or cellar is often ideal for storing. If the flowers have to be separated for different addresses, remember to keep them apart when packing. Some may have to be delivered to the church. Planning and organisation must go into this work, and there can be no mistakes. Label well, and mark clearly 'This way up', 'Top', etc.

Neat gummed labels look so much better than written notes, and can be obtained readily. The days of packing for rail and travelling long distances seem to have gone but, whatever the distance, the flowers have to be boxed. First impressions go a long way, and presentation means a lot.

If you are sending a wreath a long distance, or packing for travelling in your customer's car, again I would cover and line the box. (You can cut a market flower box lid in half and staple it together.) Line it with polythene and wetwrap. Tie the frame in three places with the packing needle and string (ties on the underneath). Spray well to cover the cellulose and damp tissue and then cover the box with cellophane, so that the contents can be seen clearly and the box kept the correct way up. Instructions for unpacking will be necessary, as before.

Advertising

I am not prepared to go into much detail on this subject; there are many people to help in this field and various ideas on the subject. Let me say straightaway that much money can be spent on advertising and, if not carefully handled, can easily be wasted.

The best advertising you can do is to provide good service. As I have already mentioned, it takes a long time to get a good name; equally so, you can make a bad name for yourself very quickly and then it takes a long time to lose it. Always try to give value for money. If you are too cheap, many people will be frightened away and if too expensive they will only call once, and then they may not purchase anything!

Always see that your staff are polite and helpful. At the same time they can be firm; if a customer is making a bad choice, for example trying to purchase a plant which needs full light when in fact they are wanting it for a dark corner, the staff should feel free to say so. Helpful advice is often appreciated if tactfully given.

Have smart wrapping paper, neat cards and give a good finish to all your wrapping. This will show all the time. Nearly everyone sees Harrods and Marks & Spencer bags being carried around. Spend that extra on having your name printed on everything; it is much better than putting an advert in the local paper once you are established.

Figure 16.6: Presentation box with bow. Note name of florist for advertising

You will be inundated with requests for flower donations by charities. Set aside a certain sum of money and do what you can. Keep your own record — once you have given, your name will be recorded by others. Be firm about this. Good customers may well be worth supporting, but if you are giving make it worthwhile as an advertisement because your name will go with the flowers. Don't give some awful sample away because you have been unable to sell it — this is no advertisement to you!

Brochures, etc.
These should be well printed on good paper. They should describe in a nutshell the full service which you can offer, but do display your own work, and do not produce something from a film library.

The nicest handout that we ever had is illustrated in Figure 16.7 because it really gave, to my way of

thinking, the right ideas. You can spend a lot of money on something very grand which still will not produce results. Prices should always be printed on a separate sheet, because these will have to be up-dated all the time and nothing looks worse than details which have been crossed out and altered by hand.

Figure 16.7: Design for a wedding flowers brochure

You will, of course, have to order in fair numbers to get a reasonable costing on the job and they will last some time, so store them in clean and tidy conditions. Remember two very important words in the florist's vocabulary — 'if' and 'from'. Always say 'if' available and then if substitutes have to go in you are covered. Prices should be 'from' a certain figure giving a little leeway if suddenly the market prices harden. At the same time, when you can let your customer know that you have been unable to obtain a certain flower but will be using a substitute it does soften the blow. How many times have you heard an irate person saying they will not pay for something because it is not what they ordered?

When established, a well drawn up advertisement from time to time just suggesting flowers for say Easter, Mother's Day, Christmas presents, etc. is well worthwhile. But really money spent on window dressing often pays off better. Be forward thinking and advertise forthcoming events through your display. Show just what you can do in a *wide* range of samples for set occasions. People will get to know that you do this and will come time and time again to see window displays. Try to have a full range of prices and somehow put over that you will make different colour ranges to special order.

Sell sundries, encourage people to do their own flowers and get them keen to purchase all their requirements through your business. Offer discounts to good accounts — it is amazing the number of people today who look for 5–10 per cent off.

Try to work up trade with other concerns, such as the local restaurants or shops, with a fresh window display. Local antique dealers are an ideal situation for flowers. Use one of their vases or some antique on which you can display flowers — it will help to sell both. And, of course, approach the local funeral directors. A vase of beautiful flowers in their office each week may well be a 'sprat to catch a mackerel' or, of course, they may take a fee for all orders placed by them for funeral flowers. It is unfortunate to have to think on these lines, but I am afraid today you cannot afford not to be businesslike and you have to go out looking for all aspects which will turn over flowers and produce some money.

'Who you know' rather than 'what you know' plays a big part in the flower world and one satisfied customer on your side can do a great amount of good for you. Put your best work forward all the time and build up a good reputation. Once you have one, keep it by looking after your staff and encouraging good work from all of them. You cannot afford to have slackness in any department — all must work as a team to get really good results. Efficiency and smartness in the shop and workroom will help a great deal. People enjoy going into a really nice shop where they are treated properly. Again, try to remember names — we are all snobs at heart and do appreciate being recognised!!

A Career In Floristry

Try to join a first-class flower business where you will be offered some tuition, or do a School training to learn the basic techniques under good supervision.

Follow this up by further training in all aspects of the subject with evening classes or day release classes. Simple botany and general decorative horticulture will also be helpful and widen your knowledge of the plant work, so making the reasons for care and handling of flowers and plants more realistic. Simple book-keeping and typing will also help with the office routine work which is so important today in the successful business.

Learning window display and paper sculpture will help you in your shop layout and the way you stage your plants. Everyone today has to be able to tackle everything in a small business.

Try to attend meetings of your trade association and keep up to date with modern trends. You may not always see eye to eye with their ideas but with modifications they may open up new areas for you. The Society of Floristry is all the time aiming for higher standards in the floristry trade and this must be encouraged.*

You will go on learning all the time. Any knowledge you can obtain will make you better able to cope with customers and so you will in turn improve your position within the firm. A good all rounder is what is required in the flower business today.

Be prepared to tackle anything, starting at the bottom and be willing to take advice from others who have been in the business longer than yourself. Many young people today feel that they know it all and cannot be taught anything more — this is the wrong attitude and in the long run it will spoil their chance of promotion.

The manuals of floristry training which have been drawn up by Interflora are excellent and full of useful detail. I would recommend them to everyone who is eligible to see them and suggest that they study them in detail.

What qualifications does the trade look for when taking on young people? I would suggest:

An ability to work hard both with head and hands.

An ability to think quickly and be able to sum up a situation straightaway.

A good general education — the better one is educated the better one is able to cope with the general public.

An ability to add up quickly, handle money and give the correct change, not only in sterling, but be able to cope with other currencies, e.g. dollars and Travellers Cheques.

Being able to drive a vehicle is certainly an advantage. I would say everyone should get a driving licence as soon as they can.

Florists should also be well turned out with a neat, clean and tidy appearance. Very 'way out' hair styles, etc. will not really help when trying to obtain a position in a flower shop.

An understanding and tactful personality.

*Secretary (Council and Examinations Board): Mr. Stanley Coleman, A.S.F., Old Schoolhouse, Payford, Redmarley, Glos., GL19 3HY. Tel: 0531-820809.

GLOSSARY OF MATERIALS

Bun moss and carpet moss Can be laid on the wire netting of a container with bunches of flowers placed in between the moss. It also helps to hide a pin holder on a shallow dish. It is also used as a foundation for funeral designs.

Candlecups Originally made in glass, these are now available in aluminium or other metal. They fit into the candlestick and hold water and flowers around the candle base.

Candle holders to go in oasis These are small green plastic tube-like structures to press into oasis, soil or bark to hold a candle.

Candles Sometimes used in a container with flowers, especially for a table centre. Candles are used in many Christmas arrangements. They are available in many sizes. It is always best to keep them upright in the vase and away from any inflammable materials. Be prepared for them to be lighted — if *you* don't, someone else will think that they are helping you.

Cork bark This comes into this country from Portugal and Spain. It is the bark of the Cork Oak and can be used to make interesting shaped containers for holding plants. It is very light in weight and is useful in plate gardens, taking the place of stone which makes them very heavy to transport.

Cork bark is also ideal for using as a base for dried and Christmas decorations.

Dried and preserved materials These are treated in various ways: glycerined, pressed, etc. They are used when flowers and foliages are in short supply.

Dried seed heads Useful for using in autumn and winter when flowers are expensive. Seed heads can be dried naturally.

Driftwood Natural pieces of wood which have been weathered in the sea or river. These can be found in interesting shapes. Fixed to bases or used in conjunction with a vase they can be most useful on occasions.

Flower picks Used mostly when moss is not available. These are made from strong wood and are of two sizes and types. They are not used in Britain, but are popular in the USA and other countries. There are two designs of picks. The first has a sharp point at each end: one goes into the flower stem, the other end being sharply pointed goes into the base. The other design of pick has a fine black wire on the blunt end. This is wound round the stem of the flower to hold it firmly, then stabbed into the base. Flower picks are available in lengths of 2in (5cm) and 4in (10cm).

Flower tubes or cones These used to be made of metal but now appear only in green plastic. They are used to build up an arrangement where short-stemmed flowers are to be used. The cones are bound tightly onto sticks, ideally from 12–24in (30–60cm) in length (preferably square wood because this bites better in the netting than round bamboo cane). These go in to make a framework in which to arrange a few flowers. You will never achieve flowing lines to a group if you are using only short-stemmed materials, but for an extra special 'bit of colour' you can insert a tube into the group and arrange the flowers in it. Always keep it filled with water — use a little netting in each. Hide carefully in the foliage and never use too many: five to seven should be plenty.

Frog	A heavy base with five or six pins to hold oasis.
Glass/plastic tubes	These are saved from the stems of Orchids coming mostly from abroad. Always save them and use when packing large stems of flowers or introducing cut flowers to a planted garden or bowl of growing plants.

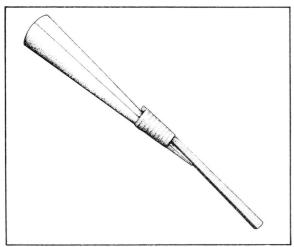

Figure 17.1: Flower cone (or tube) mounted correctly on a square stick

Oasis	A water-retaining substance usually bought in round and brick form and used in conjunction with special holders. The oasis needs to be soaked before using. The flowers are pushed into the oasis to hold them in the correct position. Try a small piece plus wire netting.
Oasis sec	A form of oasis which is hard and used dry — good for Christmas decorations, silk and dried flowers.
Oasis — spring time	Softer and more suitable for spring flower stems.
Oasis tape	This adhesive tape is excellent for securing oasis and wire netting. It is available in rolls of two widths and in green or white colouring. The great secret of its success is to use it on a dry clean surface. If used carefully it can be hidden from view when the arrangement is finished. If not available, clear waterproof tape may be used.
Pebbles/ gravel	Used to hide a pinholder on a shallow dish.

Pin holders	Spikes on a solid base of lead, sometimes on a lighter base, e.g. plastic. They are bought in various shapes, round, oblong and crescent. They are used in shallow containers under wire netting or on their own in a shallow dish.
Plastic covered netting	Used in valuable vases so that the surface of the vase does not get scratched. Used in the same way as wire netting but you do not need as much — the plastic covering makes the netting a thicker gauge. It usually needs tying into the vase because it tends to slip around.
Polystyrene	Non-absorbent material used for dried and artificial material, especially in the cone and ball form. Polystyrene disintegrates when sprayed with aerosol paint sprays.
Reel wire	Used for tying wire netting into a container.
Shadow leaves	Sprayed up and used with dried materials. Or they may be used with flowers instead of foliage when foliage is scarce. Must be kept dry — they go limp when damp.
Wire netting	48mm mesh and 20–22 gauge (.90–.71mm) chicken wire. To use it, roll it from one corner to the opposite corner or crumple it up to form the shape of the container so that you have four or five layers. It is placed into a container to hold the stems of the flowers and foliage.

GLOSSARY OF TERMS

There are certain words which keep cropping up in Flower Arranging and Floristry and florists should understand their meaning.

Arrangement Something made by arranging parts or things together; flowers, foliages and any plant material put together artistically to make a picture. It will include the container and in some cases the base, if used, and any background material.

Balance Stability produced by even distribution of 'weight' on each side of the vertical axis. This may be a visual weight and it has to be correct for the arrangement to look right. It is also actual weight and when incorrect, the vase will fall over. The visual weight may be seen in both asymmetrical and symmetrical arrangements.

Bloom This is a term used to describe a single flower. A good example would be a large individual Chrysanthemum. It is a term also used in connection with fruit. Top quality grapes when arranged should not be handled because this will damage the 'bloom' on the fruits.

Blossom This is a collective name for a number of small blooms on certain plants; for example, apple tree flowers collectively go to make blossom.

Bouquet A word used in various ways; from the flower point of view it is given as flowers picked and fastened together in a bunch. Florists should remember that the French speak of an arrangement as a bouquet. Bouquets may be of two types: formal and informal. Formal are usually wired and may contain rather important materials; these are held together in certain shapes such as a crescent bouquet for a bridesmaid. Informal means really a rather simple bunch just tied together.

Colour harmony This is a subject in its own right and an understanding of it is important. You could not do better than to read Eric Roberts' book on *Flower Arrangement* (Chapter 3). It is in the 'Teach Yourself' books series and well worth reading. In fact, don't just read this chapter — read the whole book and study the beautifully drawn illustrations.

Condition This is an important factor when judging flowers — if their condition is not good, the arrangement will be down pointed. Flowers that are properly 'conditioned' will last a lot longer. The quicker that this is done after picking or purchasing the better they will be. Freedom from pest and diseases, damage and physiological disorders all add to better condition.

Container This is the term we give to any receptacle which we use to hold the flowers. See Chapter 3 for details of suitable shapes and sizes and the different materials from which many are made.

Design This word crops up in many schedules and rule books when showing, and it can stand for a number of things. Really I like to think of it as a decorative pattern conceived and planned in the mind. In designing an arrangement you will have to consider such things as colour, proportion and balance. These may become automatic once you have got going with your flowerwork and it will be your own ideas that will show through. This is where 'rules' so often spoil individuality.

In some countries the term Flower Designer crops up with many jobs and all workroom staff seem to be classed as designers.

Distinction A word that I hate, but it comes up in marking schedules when a points system is used. Something that stands out in quality or has a distinguishing mark about it. An arrangement that has a difference may well be classed as having distinction.

Drapes These are pieces of material hanging or lying in such a way as to enhance the background or base on which the flowers are displayed.

I prefer to see the beauty in the flowers and so often the addition of drapes can distract rather than enhance the arrangement. Must be used with care, well displayed and be in perfect condition.

Driftwood This is wood drifted or floated by water, according to the dictionary, and strictly we do not mean that. Florists use the term for any pieces of wood of interesting shape, colour and texture which can be combined with flowers and foliage. The washed roots of trees found around the Scottish lochs are an excellent form of driftwood, and so are woodland areas where dead branches have fallen and become covered with moss and fungi.

Focal point We hear this term a lot in flower arranging and many times it can be overdone. It is really the point to which the eye is drawn in an arrangement — the centre from which all the stems should radiate.

Fruits When we talk of fruit in flower arranging we really think of grapes, apples, pears, melon, pineapple which can be used in a large group of flowers and foliage. The colour of the fruits should match that of the vase contents.

Really it is a loose term. It is the ripened ovary of a seed plant with its contents and may be in the form of a berry, or seed pod.

Harmony When thinking of harmony with flowers, bear in mind pleasing colour, shape, proportion, line and freedom from any jarring notes. It really is the key to a good arrangement.

Line This word crops up in flower arranging more than floristry, but it does apply to both. It really means the use of a few flowers in which their position is of great importance, as opposed to a mass arrangement where many flowers are used. Line arrangements look good in certain places, for example in modern vases and room settings, rather than in the cottage sitting room.

Miniature An arrangement which is kept strictly to within a set size. 3in (7.5cm) overall is the usual limit but schedules do vary. Some very clever miniature arrangements may be seen at flower shows but they are seldom used in the home.

Proportion A harmonious relation of parts to each other. Again, I believe that this is something that one cannot really teach. You will develop a sense of proportion and balance as you progress with your arranging. Set measurements spoil the individual style and so much depends on the materials being used in each arrangement.

INDEX

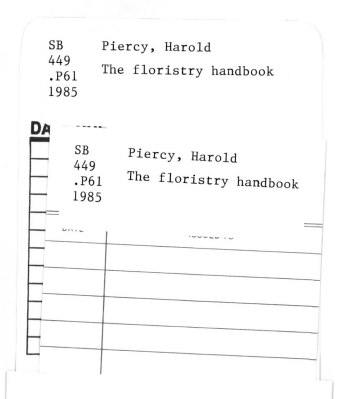

SB
449
.P61
1985

Piercy, Harold

The floristry handbook

DA

SB
449
.P61
1985

Piercy, Harold

The floristry handbook

DATE

ISSUED TO